Unemployment under Capitalism

By the same author

Young Workers (with D. Field), Hutchinson, London (1976)

Unemployment under Capitalism

The Sociology of British and American Labour Markets

David N. Ashton

Contributions in Economics and
Economic History, Number 65

Greenwood Press
Westport, Connecticut

Published in the United States and Canada by
Greenwood Press, a division of Congressional
Information Service, Inc., Westport, Connecticut

English language edition, except the United States and Canada,
published by Wheatsheaf Books Limited

Library of Congress Cataloging in Publication Data:
Ashton, D. N.
    Unemployment under capitalism.

    (Contributions in economics and economic history,
ISSN 0084-9235; no. 65)
    Bibliography: p.
    Includes index.
    1. Unemployment—Great Britain. 2. Unemployment—
United States. 3. Industrial sociology—Great Britain.
4. Industrial sociology—United States. I. Title.
II. Series.
HD5765.A6A84 1986 331.13′7941. 85-21874
ISBN 0-313-25201-7

First published 1986

Library of Congress Catalog Card Number: 85-21874
ISBN: 0-313-25201-7

Printed in Great Britain

This book is dedicated to my parents Sylvia and the late Stanley Ashton, who experienced what we thought was the last Great Depression, and to my children Wendy, Heidi and Kate, who are growing up under the shadow of yet another.

Contents

List of Tables and Figures

Acknowledgements

The problem with writing the acknowledgements last is that I find myself pushing hard against the publisher's word limit. For that reasons they have to be brief but this does not detract from their sincerity. First and foremost I thank Maureen Ashton for her faith in the fact that the book would one day be finished, for cheerfully accepting the disruption in the domestic division of labour, for ensuring the worst abuses of the English language were eliminated from the text, and that the arguments were presented clearly. Without her support it would not have been completed.

The approach adopted here owes a great deal to my former teachers, Ilya Neustadt, who taught me how to formulate sociological problems, and Norbert Elias who taught me how to set about resolving them. Many of the ideas contained in this book were developed through research I have been engaged in with my colleagues in the Labour Market Studies Group at Leicester. In particular I am indebted to Malcolm Maguire for his critical comments on earlier drafts, his help in making me clarify ideas and his invaluable contribution to our research programme.

A number of people have read individual chapters and made constructive comments for which I have been very grateful. My long-standing friend and colleague, David Field, read and re-read drafts of Chapters 1, 5 and 6, and their final form owes a lot to his critical comments. Jill Turbin, Steven Wood, Chris Dandeker and Martin Hoskins have all provided useful suggestions, many of which have subsequently been incorporated into the text. Many others have contributed indirectly through inumerable discussions, not least Peter Brannen and his colleagues in the Social Science Branch of the Department of Employment, who maintain a healthy scepticism about the potential of segmentation theory. They also include other colleagues in the Department of Sociology at Leicester, and many of the graduate students there. To them also I am very grateful.

To Edward Elgar of Wheatsheaf Books I owe a special vote of thanks for refusing to let me use the extra work and disruption suffered as a result of the university cuts as an excuse for failure to deliver the manuscript. Last but by no means least, I record my thanks to Betty Jennings, an excellent secretary who is capable of imposing order in the midst of chaos and whose mastery of a user-unfriendly word processing package made the task of producing this particular piece of work that much easier.

Introduction

The main aim of this book is to show how the level and types of unemployment that occur in contemporary advanced capitalist societies are a result of the intended and unintended consequences of human action. It argues that unemployment is a predictable consequence of the ways in which employment is organised within and between societies. It attacks the views held by political leaders, the mass media and some academics that unemployment is either the result of impersonal market forces over which human beings have no control, or the result of the personal characteristics of the unemployed individual or group. Neither of these positions provides an adequate basis for a sociological understanding of the problem. Market forces are not beyond the control of human beings, for they are no more than the consequences of innumerable human actions, while at the other extreme, personal characteristics do have a part to play in explaining why one person rather than another is unemployed but they cannot help us explain differences in the levels of unemployment within and between societies.

In attempting to provide a more adequate approach to the problem, we have utilised theoretical approaches which are by no means universally accepted. The analysis of the labour market uses theories of labour market segmentation which are relatively recent in origin, but which offer the promise of a more adequate sociological understanding than earlier approaches. In this respect our aim has not been to provide an equal treatment of all available theories. The first priority has been to ask the right questions, that is, to define the sociological problem and then to utilise those theories which offer the greatest step forward in our understanding of that problem. Our aim is, therefore, to produce an intellectual framework for the analysis of unemployment. Such a framework provides a series of questions for use in evaluating new empirical work in the area as it becomes available. In some areas, new work will raise questions about the adequacy of the

framework we have sought to present, and if the reader is
encouraged to question and modify aspects of this framework
the book will have achieved one aim.

We have chosen to ask certain fundamental questions about
the causes and consequences of unemployment, questions
which have their origins in the works of Comte, Marx, Weber,
Durkheim and Meade among others. To answer these
questions means that we have to step back from an immediate
concern with the social problems unemployment generates and
examine the relationship between the state and the labour
market, for it is only through the operation of the labour
market that we can understand the experience of unemployment. This means that we address issues about the institutional
structure of the state and the economy which at first sight may
appear unrelated to the problem of unemployment and which
would not be raised in a conventional approach to the
problem. It also means that we examine areas where our
knowledge is thin and that we cross disciplinary boundaries
when necessary.

Each chapter is an attempt to answer a number of specific
questions. As the experience of unemployment is closely linked
to the way in which the labour market is organised, we ask in
Chapter 1 why the British and American labour markets are
organised in different ways. To answer this we have to examine
the ways in which long-term changes in the international
division of labour affect the internal organisation of the labour
market and seek to explain why the institutional regulation and
functions of the labour market are different in the two
societies.

In Chapter 2 we look at how unemployment came to be
defined as a social problem and how the perception of it by
ruling élites has changed over time. We ask what current
theoretical approaches tell us about the main processes that
prompt some capitalist societies periodically to throw large
numbers of people out of work.

Chapters 3 and 4 deal with questions about the distribution
of unemployment within societies. Chapter 3 seeks to explain
the distribution of unemployment between various labour
markets and why some groups carry a disproportionate risk of
unemployment. In Chapter 4 we examine how the composition

of the unemployed has changed over time; why is it that the long-term unemployed have formed a much larger proportion of the unemployed in Britain than in the USA, and why youths have recently emerged as one of the main groups at risk. We seek the answers to these questions in an understanding of the dynamics of the labour market and the form of its institutional regulation in Britain and the USA.

In Chapters 5 and 6 we examine the experiential aspect of unemployment. Chapter 5 is addressed to the simple question, how do people experience unemployment? The answer is, of course, rather complex. We argue that much depends on the person's previous experience of work and we examine the main ways in which work is experienced in the two societies. This provides the basis from which to examine the distinctive ways in which different groups experience unemployment and the problems they encounter. Once this has been done we ask what, if anything, is common about the experience.

Since Chapter 5 shows that unemployment hurts, Chapter 6 examines the main costs and how they affect the people concerned. We consider the ways in which the main economic and health costs are carried by the unemployed and the rest of society, and then ask under what circumstances the unemployed participate in action designed to alleviate their deprivation.

In Chapter 7 we move on to examine the response of the state to the problem of unemployment and look at the main ways in which the response of the British and American states have been different. Since we identify a low rate of job-creation as the major cause of unemployment, we conclude with a discussion of strategies that have been used successfully by governments to generate enough jobs to ensure full employment.

Throughout the book a number of themes recur. One is the importance of changes in the international division of labour for our understanding of the changes which take place within the labour markets of individual societies. A second is the importance of the relationships between the institutions of state, capital and labour in influencing the way in which changes at the international level affect the labour market. A third is the importance of labour-market segmentation in determining the distribution of unemployment between the various groups in the labour market as well as the ways in which individuals experience the problem. Yet another is the significance of the labour market in the allocation of resources within society. These are not the only themes but we stress them here because they represent aspects of the problem which are often overlooked by those analyses which focus on the immediate social manifestations of the problem. They are all aspects of the problem which the framework offered here serves to highlight.

1. The Historical, Political, Economic and Cultural Context of the Labour Market

Unemployment is a product of market relationships and under capitalism is inextricably linked with the way in which employment is organised within and between societies. For this reason we start historically by exploring the way in which market relationships have transformed societies over time and created an international division of labour. We then examine the part market relationships play in determining the allocation of resources. In the USA the market plays a more all-pervasive role with the result that a person's life chances are almost exclusively determined by his/her position in the labour market. In Britain the provision of a number of significant services such as housing and health care, is through the state, with the result that the influence of the market on life-chances is more restricted. This means that the consequences of job loss in terms of access to income, housing and health care are more serious in the USA than in Britain. To understand the reasons for this we analyse the relationship between the major institutions of the state, economy and culture which determine the structure of the labour market and the function it performs in society.

Unemployment and Market Relationships

The initial impact of market relationships

In order to clarify the impact of the market on relationships we start with a brief discussion of pre-capitalist relations in eighteenth-century Britain. As long as the majority of the population outside the towns were involved in forms of subsistence agriculture, they were largely responsible for generating their own resources of food, clothing and shelter. Paid or waged labour was common, but it was frequently used only to supplement family labour and when hired, often received payment in kind. It remained a personal relationship

1

with the farmer providing his labourers with food and shelter
as part of the hiring agreement. Those without land or
employment were obliged to exist as vagrants, but such groups
were seen as part of the 'natural order' of things.

Capitalist industrialisation transformed these relationships.[1] Agriculture ceased to provide the means of subsistence
for the majority of the population as the growth of
manufacturing and later the service industries came to provide
the main means of employment. Cottagers or labourers could
no longer look to their land or their master to provide them
with food and shelter. When they entered new relationships as
workers in the textile and iron industries, they became entirely
dependent on the money income they received from the sale of
their labour to provide for all their wants: housing, food,
clothing, transport. In the event of a reduction in the demand
for labour, thousands faced the possibility of losing their
income, and with it, their ability to acquire the basic necessities
of life: they were now dependent on the cash nexus, the
impersonal workings of the market.[2] For the vast majority of
the population, the labour market became the only means
through which they could acquire the necessities of life.

The new relationships of production, distribution and
exchange, transformed relationships in other ways. Previously,
members of agricultural communities had enjoyed a relatively
high degree of self-sufficiency, albeit at a low level of existence.
Members of the same community were dependent upon each
other to ensure that the village as a whole produced sufficient
food and shelter for them all. As their economic wants were
limited they required little from outside. Industrial production
changed this and by intensifying the division of labour it
created new occupational groups.[3] Production was no longer
contained in the household, and production and distribution
became separate activities. The manufacture of clothes came to
involve large numbers of specialist tasks such as carding,
spinning, weaving and sewing while their distribution involved
factors, hauliers and shopkeepers. Individual capitalists now
controlled different aspects of the process of production with
their activities being coordinated by the market mechanism;
thus the price at which they could sell their product or service
acted as a signal influencing their level of investment and the

amount of labour they hired. It was such decisions taken by large numbers of capitalists which constituted the 'invisible hand' of the market.

These new relationships pervaded large areas of society undermining the self-sufficiency of communities as their members became involved in specialised tasks. With this increase in the division of labour came an enhanced interdependence as people came to rely on others not only to supply the products and services to meet their family needs but also to supply the materials to ensure the continuity of their employment. Anything which disturbed such exchange relationships, whether it was a change in commodity prices, political uncertainties or strikes, had repercussions throughout society. Previously natural disasters, such as disease and bad harvests, had largely been responsible for creating destitution and starvation, but now it was the impersonal workings of the commodity market. A fall in the price of a basic item such as iron could threaten large sections of the working population with the immediate possibility of hunger and starvation. The closure of iron furnaces affected ironworkers, miners, hauliers, sailors, all of whom could be denied access to the means of subsistence.

The extension of market relationships
While these new relationships were initially confined to Britain, they spread rapidly to other societies and in that process important changes took place in the ways in which production was organised. Britain was replaced first by Germany and later by the USA as the major producer of industrial goods. In the twentieth century the rapid spread of industrialisation further diversified the location of manufacturing capacity. Britain, France, Germany and the USA were joined as major producers by most of the Western European nations. In the Far East, Japan emerged as one of the most efficient centres of manufacturing and has rapidly been followed by South Korea, Taiwan and the city states of Hong Kong and Singapore. In addition, Latin American societies developed their capacity to produce manufactured goods, while many of the socialist societies also established themselves as major industrial producers (Ballance and Sinclair, 1983).

Manufacturing is no longer confined to a few 'advanced' societies.

One consequence of this change is that the bonds of interdependence formed by the industrial division of labour now extend beyond the confines of any single society. Thus, whereas in the nineteenth century goods bought in Britain or the USA were almost entirely manufactured within the same country, by the second half of the twentieth century the manufacture of goods frequently involved the activities of capitalists and workers in a number of societies. For example, the manufacture of the Apple 11E computer involves power supplies from Taiwan, chips from California, Texas and Japan, a circuitboard from Singapore and keyboards from Ireland, where they are all assembled into a German metal box to form the finished computer.[4]

Associated with the extension of market relationships have been corresponding changes in the control and coordination of the process of production and distribution. The individual entrepreneur, who controlled one aspect of the process of production or distribution has been replaced by the giant corporation which integrates within one organisation all the various aspects, namely the acquisition of raw materials, the process of manufacture and the distribution of the final product (Chandler, 1977). The stimulus for the growth of this form of organisation comes from a combination of the development of continuous-process and mass-production techniques and the emergence of the mass market. These first occurred in the USA in the late nineteenth century. For example, the 1880s saw the development of continuous-process techniques of production in the manufacture of soap. With the introduction of these machines, what had started as a by-product of the meat-packing industry for regional markets now required a national market to satisfy the level of output produced by the new technology. This meant that firms such as Proctor & Gamble had to advertise to create the market and organise a national system of distribution. The next step for this and other firms was to integrate all aspects of production within one organisation. The smaller traditional manufacturers and the agents through which they distributed their products were no match in terms of profitability and efficiency for these new corporations. The result was the displacement of them by the corporations which came, within the space of three decades, to dominate their markets. As markets extended across national boundaries, the giant corporations such as Proctor & Gamble, Ford and ICI became the multinational corporations of the late twentieth century.

The growth of the multinationals has gone hand-in-hand with the decline of the 'invisible hand' of the market as the main mechanism for allocating resources within and between national economies. So long as markets remained small and regional in character, then the coordination of activities could be achieved by the numerous decisions of small manufacturers, agents, retailers and financiers. With the advent of the giant corporation, decisions about the allocation of resources necessary for the coordination of large flows of materials through the processes of manufacture and distribution were made by highly-trained managers. The result was a major change in the efficiency with which land, capital and labour were combined in the process of production, and the 'visible hand of management' took over from the invisible hand of the market (Chandler, 1977). Not all industries were equally affected by these processes; the manufacture of clothes and shoes was not transformed by new technology, and much building remained geared to local markets. However, in industries such as food, engineering and chemical products, multinationals dominated world markets (Hannah, 1983).

Unemployment and the international division of labour

Since production is now organised on an international basis, we can no longer seek to understand labour markets and unemployment just by reference to the internal workings of an economy or society. This basic premise has a number of implications. First, the extension of the links of interdependence beyond national boundaries has made millions of people, and not just the populations of Britain and America, dependent on the 'market' for delivering the income necessary to purchase the necessities of life. It has meant that the problem of unemployment has become a common experience in other parts of the western world. Secondly, if we are to understand the origins of major recessions such as that of 1979–82 we need to start our analysis, as many economists do, at the international level and not focus exclusively on the workings of the national economy. It also follows from this that part of the solution to the problem must be sought at the international level through the various financial and other institutions which function to regulate world trade.

We must also refer to the international level if we are to understand the process whereby jobs are created and destroyed in local labour markets. In many areas of the economy decisions about the allocation of investment are no longer made by small-scale family capitalists operating from a local town in response to the 'invisible hand', but are made by managements of multinational corporations with headquarters in other countries. Thus, decisions about the creation or destruction of car workers' jobs in various parts of Britain are increasingly made in Europe, the USA or Japan. The situation in the USA is slightly different because the American economy is less dependent on international trade, and many of the largest multinationals have their headquarters in the USA. However, the same processes are at work in both societies. For political leaders in countries such as Britain and the USA committed to the doctrine of free trade, many of the major decisions about the level of demand are made by groups over which they have little jurisdiction or influence.

While these changes affect all capitalist industrial societies this does not mean that individual nation-states are merely passive recipients and that the level of unemployment within them responds automatically to international pressures. Such pressures are mediated through and responded to by each nation in terms of its own distinctive political, economic and cultural institutions. The result is that not only do unemployment levels vary widely between societies, but so does their impact on the individuals concerned.

Table 1.1. illustrates the wide variation in the rate of unemployment experienced by some capitalist societies in the most recent recession. In many respects they reflect the capacity of the national institutional structures to respond. In the USA and particularly in Great Britain where the political institutions do not facilitate the intervention of the state in the allocation of resources within the economy, the rates were relatively high. In both societies the response was ostensibly to let 'market forces' operate more effectively in the economy in order to improve international competitiveness, although in the USA the effects were modified by state expenditure on arms. The level of unemployment was seen by the political leaders in both countries to be something beyond their control, in the short run at least. This is not the only possible response. In Japan, the state plays a more active role in influencing the industries in which investment is allocated. Rather than leaving market forces to signal where firms can profitably compete, the political, business and financial leaders decide where investment should take place. Together they have been successful in maintaining Japan's position in world trade and achieving a low level of unemployment.

The Role of the Labour Market in British and American Society

Within capitalist societies the impact of unemployment on the individual also shows considerable variation depending on how much importance is attached to a free market in labour as the mechanism for allocating the resources necessary to acquire food, clothing and shelter. In contemporary capitalist society there are three main ways of acquiring the financial resources necessary to purchase such goods and services: (i) through returns from the investment of capital, (ii) the sale of labour and from (iii) direct allocation through the state administrative machinery. In the USA reliance is placed on the first two, which for the vast majority of the population means that in practice they are dependent on their participation in the labour market to ensure access to resources. For those who cannot sell their labour and who subsequently became part of the long-term unemployed their access to goods and services is severely curtailed. In Britain the balance of provision is different. Although investments remain an important source of income, for the vast majority reliance on the market mechanism has been partially restricted, as the alternative of allocating resources through the state administrative machinery has been more extensively developed. Allocation may be

Table 1.1: International Comparison of Unemployment Rates

	United States	Canada	Australia	Japan	France	Germany	Great Britain	Italy	Netherlands	Sweden
	Unemployment rate (%) Approximating US concepts									
1965	4.4	3.6	1.3	1.2	1.4	0.3	2.0	3.0	(2)	1.2
1966	3.7	3.3	1.5	1.4	1.7	0.3	2.1	3.2	(2)	1.5
1967	3.7	3.8	1.8	1.3	1.8	1.3	3.2	2.9	(2)	2.1
1968	3.5	4.4	1.8	1.2	2.3	1.1	3.2	3.0	(2)	2.2
1969	3.4	4.4	1.8	1.1	2.2	0.6	3.0	3.0	(2)	1.9
1970	4.8	5.6	1.6	1.2	2.4	0.5	3.1	2.8	(2)	1.5
1971	5.8	6.1	1.9	1.2	2.6	0.6	3.8	2.8	(2)	2.5
1972	5.5	6.2	2.6	1.4	2.7	0.7	4.2	3.3	(2)	2.7
1973	4.8	5.5	2.3	1.3	2.6	0.7	3.1	3.2	3.1	2.4
1974	5.5	5.3	2.6	1.4	2.8	1.6	3.1	2.7	3.7	2.0

1975	8.3	6.9	4.8	1.9	4.1	3.3	4.5	3.0	5.1	1.6
1976	7.6	7.1	4.7	2.0	4.5	3.4	5.9	3.4	5.2	1.6
1977	6.9	8.0	5.6	2.0	4.8	3.4	6.2	3.5	5.0	1.8
1978	6.0	8.3	6.2	2.3	5.2	3.3	6.1	3.6	5.1	2.2
1979	5.8	7.4	6.2	2.1	6.0	2.9	5.5	3.8	5.2	2.0
1980	7.0	7.4	6.0	2.0	6.3	2.8	6.9	3.8	5.9	2.0
1981	7.5	7.5	5.7	2.2	7.5	4.0	10.4	4.2	8.8	2.5
1982	9.5	10.9	7.1	2.4	8.5	5.8	12.0	4.7	12.0	3.1
1983	9.6	11.8	9.9	2.7	8.6	7.2	13.2	5.1	17.1	3.4

Source: US Bureau of Labor Statistics.
Note: A discussion of the problems involved in making international comparisons is contained in the Appendix.

made, through family allowances, pensions, the health service, unemployment benefits, student grants and housing benefits. This alternative method of allocating income and distributing resources does not in any sense replace the market as the main means for acquiring the monetary resources necessary for the effective participation in society. However, the existence of a welfare state does restrict the significance of the market in the determination of life chances. In important areas such as health, access to services is not dependent on 'the ability to pay'.[5] For those unable to participate in the labour market, such as the long-term unemployed, this network of provision has provided an alternative. Thus, to understand the impact of unemployment on people in the two societies we need first to seek an explanation of why they place such a different emphasis on the labour market as the means for allocating resources.

The precise balance which emerges at any one point in time between the use of the labour market as opposed to the administrative apparatus of the state for the allocation of resources reflects the overall distribution of power in the society. There are three main resources which determine this balance: control over the legitimate use of physical force and taxation (the state); capital and labour (the economy); and values (cultural). Here it should be stressed that these are analytical distinctions. In reality they interact to produce the differences described above, and nowhere can they be observed as acting independently. All we are doing here is to treat them separately in order to tease out their relative contributions in explaining differences in the role of the labour market.

The State

The state is defined here as those institutions capable of sustaining an effective monopoly of the means of force and taxation over a given territory. In Britain these correspond to the institutions of the armed forces and central and local government and are relatively easily identifiable and observable, precisely because they are highly centralised in their operation. In the USA this definition may at first seem more problematic precisely because the institutions through which political power is exercised are more diverse. Local, state and federal governments each have their own distinctive powers and responsibilities, and the boundaries between them are not always clear cut or agreed upon. Each individual state has its own laws covering education, welfare, local services and control over its own police and armed forces (militia). The independence of each of the constituent states is enshrined in the constitution and guaranteed in material terms by its right to levy taxes to finance these activities. Yet while states differ in the use they make of their powers, and struggle with the federal government over the extent of their jurisdication, they sustain an effective monopoly over the use of force and taxation in the USA.

The fact that the USA is a federal system of formerly autonomous states is not the only important difference between Britain and America. The USA is much bigger in both area and population. This difference in size means that the administrative problems posed for the federal government are that much greater than is the case in Britain. Thus when the political leaders in Britain were faced with the problem of youth unemployment they were able to respond rapidly by establishing the Youth Opportunities Programme, a centrally-directed scheme which was implemented at the local level outside the control of the local authorities. In the USA the size of the country and the existence of relatively autonomous states makes such a response more difficult. In practice the federal government when implementing similar schemes usually operates through the states.

In order to develop this comparison a distinction must be made between two main dimensions of centralisation: the first is the extent to which the highest level of state authority (in Britain the Parliament and in the USA the federal government) has achieved control over lower levels of administration (Cawson, 1982, pp.70–4); the second refers to the extent to which forms taken by political parties and constitutional arrangements facilitate control over the administrative machinery of state.

With regard to the first dimension, we have already noted the greater decentralisation of power in the USA. In Britain the Crown in Parliament has effectively centralised power over most areas of state administration. The reasons for these differences lay in the previous development of the two societies. In Europe the early establishment of an effective monopoly over the use of physical force was essential if the monarch was to maintain his independence of others and secure control over his own territory. In Britain the Crown's dependence on its control of the sea for security led to the early development of the Navy. The development of a sophisticated army structure was more periodic, as Parliament tended to disband a standing army when it could. Eventually an effective monopoly of force was established by the Crown in Parliament. This continued rather than resolved the distrust which existed between the Crown and Parliament. This distrust was also evident in the struggle between the two over the local administrative powers exercised by the aristocracy and gentry. Thus the forms of local government which developed in the nineteenth century had a tradition of local autonomy to build on but found their powers increasingly curtailed in the twentieth century by an ever-more powerful central state. The growth of the British Empire and the country's intensive involvement in two world wars led to the extension of the power of the central administration over the local authorities (Burgess, 1980), which are now subservient to the Westminster authorities in a number of ways. First, their administrative powers are tightly controlled by the central authorities. While local authorities provide local services such as public housing, refuse collection, road maintenance, recreational facilities and educational provision, these are regulated by policy guidelines laid down by central government. Secondly, while the property rating system is a form of local taxation and provides the authorities with an independent income, it is not sufficient to finance all their activities and so they remain dependent on central government for a large part of their income. This gives the central government considerable influence over the activities of local authorities. Given these central powers it is relatively easy for the national government to impose uniform social and economic policy either through the local authorities, as it does in the case of education, or independently of them, as it does in the case of manpower policy, through the Manpower Services Commission.

This is in marked contrast to the experience of the USA. The lack of a feudal past and the fact that the USA was sheltered from participating in international conflict and competition until the later nineteenth century meant that it faced relatively few pressures for the early establishment of strong, centralised administrative structures. The conflict with the American Indians did not pose a major threat to the existence of the state and could be handled without recourse to the development of a large standing army. This conflict did not undermine the historical distrust of professional armies. In addition the creation of a federal system by previously autonomous states restricted the powers of the central body. Thus the federal government, with limited powers and few external pressures to enhance them, developed only a very weak form of central control. In that sense the constituent states are not merely agents of central government but rather separate and independent political entities (Badie and Birnbaum, 1983, p.128). Thus it is often at the level of the constituent states and not at the federal level that important decisions about social policy, welfare benefits and occupational licensing are made. In the case of the administration of unemployment benefit, while in Britain there is a single system, administered centrally, with the same rules concerning entitlement throughout the society, in the USA the federal government decided to administer the system through the states which enables them to vary the rules concerning entitlements.

The two political systems also differ in the ways in which control is exercised over the central administrative apparatus. The struggle between the King and Parliament that characterised the formative period of the modern state in Britain finally resulted in the supremacy of the House of Commons as the law-making body, with decision-making powers in the hands of the Cabinet. While legislation still has to pass through the House of Lords, and has to receive the Royal Assent, the powers of the Lords or the monarch to withhold consent to legislation that has passed through the Commons are now very limited. In practice this means that whichever political party controls the Commons has few checks on the legislation it can pass.

The constitution of the USA was designed to prevent any

such concentration of decision-making powers. The three separate institutions, Presidency, Senate and House of Representatives, were orginally formulated in order to safeguard against the concentration of power that occurred under the absolutist monarchs in Europe. They still serve to fragment the decision-making process, apart, that is, from foreign affairs. In practice this means that no law can be passed without the consent of the three bodies, and each can act as a check on the power of the other. Moreover, all laws are further subject to the jurisdiction of the Supreme Court, which has the power to nullify them if they violate the rights enshrined in the Constitution.

The differences between Britain and America in this respect are also reflected in the structure of the political parties. In America, unlike most industrial societies, political representation was granted to the mass of the population before industrialisation. The new class of industrial workers did not have to struggle for political rights as was the case in Europe; in the USA they were merely incorporated into the existing system of parties. This had two major consequences. It meant that there was no separate political struggle in which the American working class could forge a distinct political identity and that working-class aspirations were catered for by the existing parties and organisations, which themselves were no more than loose coalitions of interests. In Britain, as in a large part of Europe, the situation was very different. There, the working class was excluded from membership of the political community and had to struggle for political, economic and civil rights. This struggle helped the working class to forge a strong sense of identity and to form its own political party through which to pursue collective interests. Thus, by the mid-twentieth century the political struggle in Great Britain was between two class-based, ideologically-opposed parties, each of which had developed strong, centralised party organisations.

What this necessarily brief comparison of the two main dimensions of the institutional structures of the state reveals is that Great Britain has a smaller but more powerful central state through which intervention in the economic and cultural spheres can take place. The independent central administrative apparatus has the authority to act at all levels. In the USA the central administration is more susceptible to political and business pressures and has more circumscribed powers of intervention *vis-à-vis* the individual states. The institutional control of the central administrative apparatus exacerbates these differences in the centralisation of power. In Britain the decision-making machinery is centralised. A party with a majority in the Commons can initiate legislation which because of the centralised administrative apparatus can be enacted with considerable speed. In this way the institutional structures of the state facilitate radical change. The combination of institutional elements works in the other direction in the USA. The separation of powers leaves control over the administrative apparatus in three institutions and makes it a slow and difficult business to get legislation through, especially when the political parties are also fragmented. The result is that legislative change is less radical and more piecemeal in the USA.

Capital and Labour

As noted earlier, the total dependence of the worker on the income from the sale of labour to purchase the necessities of life gave the employer a very powerful sanction with which to control the behaviour of workers.[6] As industry has developed, groups of workers in all capitalist societies have sought to limit the effects of their dependence on waged labour in the determination of their life chances. Sometimes they have developed their own insurance schemes or put pressure on employers to provide them, but in Britain and Western Europe the most powerful advances have derived from political action which has taken the provision of certain services, such as housing and welfare rights, out of the market altogether. In the USA, capital has been particularly successful in maintaining the centrality of the market principle. In this section we seek an explanation for this difference.

The historical development of capitalism in Britain created a number of unique features in the relationship between capital and labour. Since Britain was the first society to industrialise, its manufacturers faced relatively little competition as they entered new markets (Hobsbawn, 1968). This meant that British manufacturing industry became diversified. It also meant that the organisation of industry was characterised by relatively small-scale family-owned units of production, operating on a rule-of-thumb basis. This in turn meant that control over the economy and the labour market was decentralised and in the hands of a large number of families scattered throughout the country. The shelter provided by empire markets enabled these characteristics to be maintained well into the twentieth century when the typical form of manufacturing units in the USA and other industrial societies had long since changed (Channon, 1973, Ch 3; Chandler, 1976, pp 24–8).

A second unique feature of British development was the subordinate position of the early manufacturers (Scott, 1982). While they were leading the world in the process of industrialisation they were in a subordinate position to the aristocracy in their own society both socially and politically. They were excluded from access to positions of political power, and although the Reform Bill 1833 gave them the right to vote it was not until almost 150 years later, in the more recent parliaments, that their representatives formed a majority in the Cabinet (Guttsman, 1968).[7]

Their exclusion from political power limited the extent to which they could use the state's monopoly of physical force (troops) in their attempts to control labour. During the early nineteenth century the aristocracy were suspicious of the manufacturers' ability to control the large concentrations of labour their factories had created. These suspicions were enhanced by what they saw as the manufacturers' refusal to accept responsibility for the welfare of the poor they employed (Bendix, 1963, Ch. 2). As a result the sanction of prison for workers who disobeyed their masters and the availability of troops to quash workers' protests were withdrawn from use.[8] Once this happened the employers had to resort to the use of non-violent tactics in their struggles with workers and their organisations, a situation which led many of them to recognise unions.[9] Compared with American manufacturers the British were far more constrained in the extent to which they could utilise the repressive apparatus of the state.[10]

The persistence throughout the nineteenth century of small-scale family-owned units of production, also influenced the development of unions, by making it easier for unions to establish themselves. The existence of large numbers of employers made it difficult for them to organise and counter unions, while from the unions' point of view the existence of large numbers of employers, scattered across the country, made it easier for them to play one employer off against another. By the second half of the ninteenth century strong, nationally organised trade unions had been established in a number of industries, such as cotton and engineering (Turner, 1962). Against a strong, nationally organised trade union there was relatively little that any one employer could achieve. Indeed the later emergence of employers' organisations was largely a response to the gains made by the unions (Phelps Brown, 1965). Thus throughout the nineteenth and early twentieth centuries the British manufacturers were decentralised, controlling small units with each responsible for only one aspect of the production process. On the other hand, the working class, after an initial influx of Irish immigrants, rapidly became self-recruiting and, because it was concentrated in a few urban centres connected by the new rail networks, soon mastered the rudimentary techniques of worker organisation. By the early twentieth century the newly-emergent business class faced a relatively cohesive and powerful working class.

As the manufacturers joined the landed aristocracy and commercial interests to form the business class, aristocratic values remained important and, in the first half of the twentieth century at least, subordinated the interests of the manufacturers. An appreciation of this is particularly important for understanding the growth of welfare services in Britain. From the Elizabethan period onwards the acceptance on the part of the upper classes of responsibility for the poor had been embodied in the provision of the Poor Law. Although the law was amended in 1834 in order to make the poor more 'self-reliant', that responsibility was never denied altogether. Against this background, the concessions made by the Liberal governments (1906–15) to the working classes, in the form of pensions and, after the first world war, housing provision, could be seen as an extension of that tradition. Similarly, the concern with the effects of unregulated competition on the well-being of the poor led the same Liberal leadership, under Lloyd George and Churchill, to modify the working of the labour market through the introduction of wages councils and labour exchanges.

This concern with the welfare of the poor was given a further stimulus, from a very different direction and tradition, during and after the first and second world wars. The continued growth of trade unions, this time among the semi-skilled and unskilled at the turn of the century, was accompanied by the spread of socialism and a commitment to socialist principles by the Labour Party. In exchange for working-class cooperation during the second world war the Labour Party was able to obtain the introduction of what was then a fairly comprehensive set of welfare measures. These were consolidated immediately after the war when the Labour Party was returned with a large majority. In effect, measures such as The Education Act 1944, and The National Health Service Act 1946, together with other developments in the field of public housing, took the delivery of health care, education and a substantial part of housing out of the market. In addition, welfare rights were extended to include free meals for school children, pensions and social security which aimed to provide a minimum income at all times not necessarily related to earning power (Bruce, 1968). The ensuing balance in the provision of goods and services between the state and the market formed the basis of the post-war political consensus.

With regard to the position of capital, the movement towards oligopoly and monopoly based on the new centralised forms of business organisation that we noted above, did not proceed as rapidly in Britain as it had done in America (Chandler, 1976; Hannah, 1983). While new and more innovative techniques of production and business organisation were being developed in the USA in the late nineteenth century, the growth of cartels and holding companies in Britain kept manufacturing capital fragmented and the size of the enterprise units small. More recently the loss of Imperial and Commonwealth markets, together with increased competition from American and later European and Japanese manufacturers, has changed this situation. In an attempt to compete in international markets British capital has had to consolidate into larger oligopolistic units subject to effective central control. This has meant that the emergence of centralised control over a large part of the production process took place much later in Britain than in the USA.

At the political level this increasing concentration of capital and of control over production was associated with the emergence of representatives of the financial and manufacturing interests as the dominant group within the Conservative Party. In the Conservative government of 1979 and 1983 the aristocratic tradition of concern for the welfare of the poor of Disraeli's 'one nation' was subordinated to the interests of business. The post-war consensus was broken and attempts made to reintroduce market principles into the distribution of resources previously undertaken by the state. For example, the public housing programme was reduced and some of the housing stock sold, inroads were made into the principle of free health care by the introduction of greatly increased payments for dental care and medical prescriptions and cuts made in social security benefits. While this has by no means eradicated the provision of resources through the state, it has modified it. It illustrates how much the balance achieved at any one point in time between provision through the state administration or the market, represents the outcome of a political struggle.

In the USA the more powerful position of the manufacturing class has enabled them to maintain the allocation of resources through the market. One reason for this lay in the absence of any effective opposition, either from above, in the form of an aristocratic heritage, or from below in the form of worker organisation. Unlike the situation in Britain where the manufacturing class had been subordinated to that of the landed aristocracy, the manufacturing class in the USA rapidly freed itself from such domination (Barrington-Moore, 1967, Ch. 3). Freedom from British rule, and thus from subordination to imperial interests, came as a result of the struggle for independence. The victory of the North in the Civil War witnessed the final triumph of the manufacturing interest over the only other group that could subordinate it, the southern aristocracy. Following the Civil War the bourgeoisie were then free to use the machinery of the federal state to facilitate the growth of industry (Schneider, 1971, Ch. 4). This was done in a number of ways: by erecting tariff barriers to protect certain industries, by expelling the Indians, so making land widely available, and by encouraging immigration from Europe to ensure an adequate supply of labour. The industrial interests were given constitutional protection from state or federal legislatures which might be dominated by anti-business forces through a clause in the fourteenth amendment, which forbade any legislative body in the USA to deprive a person of 'life, liberty or property' without due process of law. Since a corporation was defined as a person, the Supreme Court could invalidate legislation which sought to impose special restrictions on corporations. Indeed, in the early years neither the federal nor state governments attempted to exert much control.

These distinctive circumstances also affected the development of labour. In the absence of restraints imposed by an aristocratic ruling class on the use of the courts, federal troops or state militia, the full resources of the state apparatus could be mobilised against early forms of worker organisation. In 1892 both militia and federal troops were used to break the first national strike of railroad workers. Similar tactics were used on a number of other occasions. In addition the federal and state courts regularly broke strikes with anti-union injunctions (Greenstone, 1970, p.20).

Partly because of this ability to use the resources of the state in an unhindered manner the process of industrialisation took place far more rapidly in the USA. Although it started later than in Britain, the process of change, especially in the organisation of industry, soon outstripped the British experience. Whereas the smaller traditional manufacturers, with their rule-of-thumb methods of organisation dominated the market in Britain throughout the nineteenth century, in the USA they rapidly gave way to the large corporations, with their emphasis on exploiting advances in science and in techniques of managament. Within the space of three decades the new corporations came to dominate their markets. By the second decade of the twentieth century large sectors of the US economy were controlled by a small number of major corporations (Chandler, 1976). In a country that was politically decentralised this centralisation of economic power gave the captains of industry considerable power in relation to other groups.

On the political front, as the USA became more actively involved in international conflicts during and after the second world war, so the resources controlled by the federal state and its administrative apparatus grew. Industrialists were drawn into a closer alliance with the political leaders to ensure the smooth functioning of the economy. The consequences of this growing centralisation of power on the relationship between the political and economic élites has been the subject of a number of studies (Mills, 1956; Baron and Sweezy, 1966; Galbraith, 1967; Rose, 1967). These have documented the unprecedented concentration of control over resources which these changes have created. However, as the discussion of the international division of labour has shown, the more successful of the new corporations, the multinationals, have extended their power well beyond the confines of the US economy.

When viewed alongside this rapid accumulation of power by capital, the subordinate groups in the USA have been very slow to organise. Initially the pattern of union development was similar to that which had occurred in the British working class, with the skilled workers being the first to organise. However, the development of industrial unions took place under very different conditions in the USA (Elbaum and Wilkinson, 1979). The emergence of a unified national market and the early growth of the large corporations at the beginning of the twentieth century meant that a relatively few manufacturers had established control over product and labour markets well before the unionisation of unskilled and semi-skilled workers took place. When the unionisation drives got under way in the 1930s they did so in a labour market that was shaped by the power of the large corporation supported by that of the state. Under these circumstances union organisation was and is more difficult, as companies can play off one group of workers against another by transferring production from unionised to non-unionised regions of the country—a tactic which was not available to the same degree in Britain.[11] From the unions' point of view the sheer size of the country made worker organisation on a national basis difficult in the USA. In addition the different organisational forms developed by the skilled and semi-skilled workers resulted in separate national federations of labour organisations; the AFL (skilled workers) and CIO (semi-skilled), which perpetuated divisions within the working class. They did not merge until 1955 to provide one voice for labour.[12] Moreover, unlike the situation in Britain, the American unions have not been very effective in extending membership among white-collar workers and the growing number of female clerical and professional workers in financial services and retailing. As a result they are left with a narrow industrial and occupational base and, compared with Britain, a relatively limited political influence.[13]

As a result of this narrow union base and limited political influence there has not been the same pressure as there was in Britain to have the provision of health care and welfare services taken out of the market. In the 1950s and 1960s labour, together with old people's organisations and welfare organisations was responsible for securing federal medical provision for the old and poor through the Medicare and Medicaid Bills. However, the combined opposition of the American Medical Association, the U.S. Chambers of Commerce and the insurance companies, together with the problems of pushing radical legislation through a decentralised decision making process, combined to limit the effectiveness of even that reform (Rose, 1967, pp. 400–65). The result was that twenty years after Britain had established a comprehensive and uniform system, labour in the US secured a very partial and fragmented form of provision. The market remains the main means of allocating health care resources.

Values
Differences in values are also important in determining the role of the labour market in the allocation of resources. In both societies the centrality of market relationships (in the form of private enterprise and the sale of labour) as the means for distributing resources is explained and justified by reference to the values of individualism and hard work. There the similarity ends, for even a brief acquaintance with British and American societies reveals considerable differences in the meanings given to these values and the degree of consensus they command.

In Britain, notions of individualism, and especially individual liberty, had their origins among the aristocracy and gentry. In their struggle to prevent monarchical abuse of power they argued that individual liberty was synonymous with property rights. Those without property rights were excluded from the political process and it was seen as the duty of the aristocracy to rule and look after the welfare of such groups, especially the poor. In return they expected the poor to offer unqualified obedience (Bendix, 1959, Ch. 2). For the manufacturing class, the idea of liberty was broadened to include a greater emphasis on self-reliance. It was the manufacturers who, through their entrepreneurial activities, had built up the new industries. They had 'proved' through their own actions the value of self-help and personal responsibility which their creed espoused. Through their ideological spokesmen, such as Samuel Smiles, they used these values to attack what they saw as the unwarranted privileges of the aristocracy on the one hand and the indolence of the poor on the other (Perkins, 1969, pp. 221–30).

With the gradual assimilation of the manufacturing middle class and the aristocracy that took place in the late nineteenth and early twentieth centuries, the values of self-reliance and individual achievement were more widely accepted by the upper class. Within the upper sections of the working class, Methodism and other nonconformist religions also helped broaden the social appeal of the ideas. However, the relatively slow rate of growth of the economy did not create the opportunities for mobility that were necessary for the widespread adoption of the creed. It was not until the 1950s and 1960s that economic expansion and the growth of white collar occupations provided the opportunity of upward mobility for large sections of the middle and working classes. This provided the basis for a more widespread adoption of the belief in hard work, self improvement and career advancement as a reward for individual effort. Indeed, it was not until the advent of the 1979 government that the Conservative Party adopted individualism as the central focus of its ideology. However, in spite of these recent changes, substantial numbers of the population still do not share in the main tenets of this belief. Elements of the old aristocracy still maintain more traditional beliefs although the main opposition comes from the manual workers' unions. Their members' past experience has taught them to look to their collective strength as a source of protection against the insecurity of the market. As self-improvement was not a realistic option for the majority, their only source of improvement was through collective action. Thus collectivism, as embodied in the ideologies of the trade union movement and the Labour Party represents a viable alternative belief, which has shaped the part played by the labour market in the allocation of resources.

In the USA the more widespread adherence to the value of individualism, a belief in self-reliance, responsibility for one's own actions and well-being, and individual self-determination was a product of the society's early history. The settlers and their offspring had to rely on their own initiative and resources to cope with the problems of taming and organising their new world. Unlike the Western European societies which were dominated by powerful ruling groups and their administrative apparatus, the early Americans (apart from the Indians and blacks) developed a tradition of making their own decisions. Having established new communities and run their own affairs, their belief in the power of the individual to determine his/her own future merely reflected their past achievements.

As the process of industrialisation transformed this commercial agrarian society, a vast new range of jobs were created in the manufacturing and tertiary sectors. Moreover, the speed at which the process took place meant that a substantial proportion of the population experienced rapid social advancement. The almost insatiable demand of an expanding economy for labour created a continuous stream of employment opportunities for each new wave of immigrants. Their arrival resulted in those already established vacating the menial jobs and moving up the status hierarchy. At the same time, the belief in individualism took on the additional meaning of working hard and improving one's standard and style of living, and one's position in the labour market, without the help of the state or any other collective agency.[14] Henderson (1896), an ideological spokesman of the new industrial élite, encapsulated some of the main ideas of this new belief:

competitive commercial life is not a flowery bed of ease, but a battlefield where the 'struggle for existence' is defining the industrially 'fittest to survive'. In this country the great prizes are not found in Congress, in literature, in law, in medicine, but in industry. The successful man is praised and honoured for his success. The social rewards of business property, in power, in praise, and luxury, are so great as to entice men of the great intellectual faculties. Men of splendid abilities find in the career of manufacturer or merchant an opportunity for the most intense energy. (Quoted in Bendix, 1963, p. 256).

By the middle of the twentieth century the greater wealth available to all sections of the society and the domination of the economy by the large corporations wrought modifications to this belief. The 'struggle for existence' between entrepreneurs had been replaced by competition between college graduates for access to careers. Success was still seen to be a product of hard work, but now it was also a reward for time invested in training, with the most able receiving the highest rewards because of their importance to society.[15]

Henderson also alludes to the difference between the two countries in the value attached to free enterprise. Following the American Civil War, with few checks on the power of the manufacturing class, the values of industrial capitalism reigned supreme. A belief in private entreprise was enshrined in the legal system and, throughout society, became almost synonymous with the American way of life. Business leaders were the celebrities of American society and in the educational system the business schools of MIT and Harvard were regarded as among the most prestigious learning establishments.

In Britain, the belief in private enterprise and work in industry and commerce has been tempered by the aristocratic heritage. While the aristocracy encouraged the growth of private enterprise they never fully accepted the values of those engaged in it, and initially sought to exclude them. The education that was deemed suitable for the sons of the establishment class was concerned to produce Christian gentlemen capable of running the Church, Army and Civil Service, but little or no prominence was given to the acquisition of the skills necessary for success in industry (Scott, 1982, Ch. 5). Indeed the needs of industry were totally subordinated within the educational system to those of the landed aristocracy, the professions and public service. Even in contemporary Britain the curriculum of state educational systems, shaped as it is by the entrance requirements of the Oxbridge colleges, perpetuates this dominance by the professions. Industry is still regarded by many who are academically successful as an undesirable option. So deeply rooted is this antipathy to industry in the educational system that only in the last two decades has there been a serious attempt to develop business studies as an important part of the curriculum at university level.[16]

We have sought to demonstrate some of the reasons why the labour market should play such different roles in the allocation of resources within the two societies. As we stated earlier we have treated the state, capital and labour and values as analytically separate sources of power, whereas in reality they interrelate. Thus we cannot explain the more extensive system of health and welfare benefits in Britain just by reference to the greater organisational strength of the labour movement. Without a centralised state administration and governmental decision-making process it would not have been possible to put through radical health care and social security legislation. Moreover, the tradition of aristocratic concern for the poor laid the foundations for such a system and together with the widespread belief in socialism facilitated the acceptance of such restrictions on the operations of the market. In the USA the various elements worked in the opposite direction, a weak labour movement and powerful capitalist class meant that there was little impetus for extensive state provision as an alternative to the market. The decentralised political system created further obstacles to the introduction of the necessary legislation while the widespread adherence to the values of individual responsibility militated against public support for such a system.

2. The Problem of Unemployment: perceptions and causes

This chapter considers how perceptions and understanding of the problem of unemployment have changed over time. The first part examines how unemployment came to be defined as a social problem and why it took over 100 years of industrial capitalism for this to occur. The second section traces the changes which have taken place in the way in which the problem has subsequently been defined by ruling élites, and seeks an explanation of those changes in international relations and in the internal balance of power between the classes. As the definition of the problem and its solution reflect the immediate interests of the ruling élites[1], the longer-term structural changes which influence the level of unemployment tend to be ignored. For this reason the third section appraises some alternative theories, which seek to explain why some capitalist societies periodically have high levels of unemployment.

The Emergence of Unemployment as a Social Problem

Unemployment, in the general sense of being without work, has been with us for much of human history[2]. Garraty refers to Acts of Pericles in Athens authorising the erection of vast buildings so that the undisciplined multitude 'should not go without their share of public salaries and yet should not have them given them for sitting still and doing nothing' (Garraty, 1978, p.13). In medieval society vagrants and beggars constituted the unemployed. Not until the medieval peasant and wage labourer had been transformed into what we recognise as the working class did unemployment in the modern sense emerge. The earliest use of terms to refer to the social condition we recognise as unemployment was among trade unionists in the 1820s (Williams, 1976).

However, it was not until the turn of this century that the term 'unemployment' was widely used, and only in the 1920s in

27

Britain and the 1940s in the USA did governments consider the problem sufficiently serious to warrant the regular collection of statistics. Yet in spite of this late recognition of the problem, it is clear that throughout the nineteenth century British workers were being thrown out of work because of fluctuations in the business-cycle.

Part of the reason for the lack of recognition of unemployment as a problem in the nineteenth century lay in the length of time it took for market relationships to permeate not just the sale of labour but also the provision of goods and services. Another reason was the kind of explanations offered for 'the want of employment' as it was known. The dominant explanations were those offered by representatives of the aristocracy to explain what they saw as the poverty and idleness of the lower orders. In predominately agrarian societies the pattern of work was largely controlled by the elements: the seasonal variations in temperature, rainfall and daylight. From the point of view of the aristocracy, the work of the lower orders took the form of bursts of activity interspersed with periods of 'idleness'. From the labourers' point of view they worked in order to procure the bare essentials, there being no virtue in work for its own sake. Even craftsmen lived on a day-to-day basis with limited time horizons and little incentive for steady labour. This pattern of time-allocation was endorsed by the Church and State through the provision of 50 to 60 religious holidays in addition to weekly days of rest.

Industrialisation changed all this. Entrepreneurs had very different requirements for labour and placed a different value on work. In their attempts to extend market relationships they had to subordinate the lower orders to the requirements of industrial production (Pollard, 1965). In practice this meant that the new 'workers' had to turn up for work regularly and work consistently for long hours. Public holidays were reduced and the lot of that section of the poor drawn into factory work became one of unremitting toil. In the face of resistance by the lower orders to submit themselves voluntarily to this discipline, employers sought to make the conditions of those who refused as harsh as possible. Existing provision for the poor, which stemmed from the obligation felt by the aristocracy for the lower orders, had to go. The 1834 Poor Law in Britain partially accomplished this, making relief to the destitute only available to the able-bodied and their families in workhouses, in conditions which made all relief less attractive than 'independent poverty'. In practice the institution of the workhouse with its prison-like structure and conditions created an additional fear to the dread of poverty that haunted the emergent working class.

For the new manufacturing class, some of whom had risen from a relatively humble background, idleness was the 'obvious' cause of poverty. Hard work, industry and thrift were virtues which enabled the individual to climb out of it. As the carriers of a new social order, they never doubted the ability of the economy to generate work for all those who needed it. Hence, idleness or the 'want of employment' had to be a result of the individual's moral failure, a character defect.

The view of unemployment as being caused by the moral failure of the individual was challenged at the end of the nineteenth century. Marx had already demonstrated the relationship between changes in the business-cycle and the level of unemployment. For him it was a result of the need for a reserve army to keep wages low relative to profits (Marx, 1887, vol. 1, p.633). In addition, early social inquiries produced evidence for the existence of large-scale 'involuntary' unemployment during troughs of the business-cycle. However, such was the power of prevailing beliefs that Booth, who in the mid-1880s carried out one of the first exhaustive surveys of the conditions of the poor in London, was still able to conclude that 'the unemployed are, as a class, a selection of the unfit' (Booth, 1902, vol. 1, pp.149–52). Nevertheless, the more widespread use of the term 'unemployment' implied a subtle shift in perspective, which was developed in the work of Beveridge (1909). In the USA the leading citizens of Boston, at a meeting in December 1893 about the soaring number of destitute people seeking relief, reflected this shift:

The problem was of a different sort from that which was normally dealt with by the charitable agencies of the city, for the existing distress was . . . due chiefly to non-employment, and not to the ordinary causes of poverty. (Garraty, 1978, p.121)

Unemployment was being seen as a social problem. After 150 years of industrial capitalism the ruling élites had come to regard unemployment as a product of market forces and the business-cycle. It was something over which a person as an individual had little control.

This acknowledgement on the part of the ruling élites of the social character of unemployment, was not just a result of advances in social and economic research. It was primarily a consequence of a substantial shift which had taken place in the balance of power between the classes. The increasing interdependence of all groups produced by the advancing division of labour had increased the dependence of ruling élites on the cooperation of the working class. In addition the working class in both Britain and the USA were becoming effectively organised. As a result ruling élites were obliged to adopt a definition of the problem which was no longer at total variance with the experience of the working class.

Changes in the Definition of the Problem

Like any social problem the public definition of the problem of unemployment, that utilised by the government and media, has changed over time. It is possible to identify three main phases in which the perception of unemployment was informed by a different economic theory. From 1910 to 1940 the neo-classical theory produced a view of unemployment as an inevitable product of the business-cycle. From 1940 to the late 1970s this was replaced by the Keynesian view of it as a product of aggregate demand and therefore subject to manipulation and control by the activities of the state. In the late 1970s this view was subsequently replaced by monetarism which again. sees it as a product of market forces over which the state has no direct control. From a sociological perspective the problem is to explain these shifts in the definition of the problem by ruling élites. It will be argued that two main sets of relationships are important in this, one being the changes taking place in international relations and the division of labour, the other being the changing balance of power between the classes within the society.

The Beveridge view of unemployment as an inevitable consequence of market forces provided the parameters for public discussion on both sides of the Atlantic throughout the 1920s and 1930s. Given that it was a product of the business-cycle, there was little that governments could or should do about it. He saw some unemployment (about 2 per cent in the skilled trades) as necessary for economic growth. If it persisted at high levels, as it did in Britain in the 1920s, and in both societies in the 1930s (see Table 2.1), it was because unions, monopolistic employers and government legislation were interfering with the free workings of the market. All that social policy could do was to 'reduce the pain' it caused to the unemployed. It could do this in two ways: by increasing the efficiency with which employers and workers contacted each other, through the government provision of labour exchanges; and by easing the financial hardships of short-term unemployment through insurance schemes. The solution could only stem from the operation of market forces for there was an assumption in neoclassical economics which amounted to an act of faith, that left to its own devices, the economy would move towards an equilibrium at the level of full employment: an act of faith which as Table 2.1 indicates has not been borne out in practice (Labour Studies Group, 1983).

This view of the problem was held throughout the Great Depression when whole industries were devastated. In Britain unemployment was heavily concentrated in certain regions, thus unemployment rates varied from 13 per cent in the South East to 38 per cent in Wales. In individual communities, particularly those dependent on the traditional industries of coal, shipbuilding and textiles, rates were much higher, reaching between 60–70 per cent in some towns (Stevenson and Cook, 1979). In fact, faced with problems of this magnitude, with national rates of unemployment of 22.5 per cent in Britain in 1932 and 24.9 per cent in the USA in 1933, the governments were not totally inactive.

In practice both governments had been obliged to 'interfere' with the workings of the economy. In Britain a combination of import controls, a ban on the export of capital, and low interest rates helped revive the economy before mobilisation for war finally 'cured' the problem of unemployment (Eatwell, 1982).

Table 2.1: Unemployment Rates; Britain and the USA, 1920–84

		1920	1921	1922	1923	1924	1925	1926	1927	1928	1929	1930	1931	1932	1933	1934	1935	1936	1937	1938	1939[1]
USA	unadjusted a	5.2	11.7	6.7	2.3	5.0	3.2	1.8	3.3	4.2	3.2	8.7	15.9	23.6	24.9	21.7	20.1	16.9	14.3	19.0	17.2
	adjusted c	3.9	11.4	7.2	3.0	5.3	3.8	1.9	3.9	4.3	3.1	8.7	15.2	22.3	20.5	15.9	14.2	9.8	9.1	12.4	—
GB	unadjusted b	—	—	11.6	10.9	11.2	12.7	10.6	11.2	10.0	14.6	21.5	22.5	21.3	17.7	16.4	14.3	11.3	13.3	11.7	—
	adjusted c	1.9	11.0	9.6	8.0	7.1	7.7	8.6	6.7	7.4	7.2	11.1	14.8	15.3	13.9	11.7	10.8	9.2	7.7	9.2	—

		1940	1941	1942	1943	1944	1945	1946	1947[2]	1948	1949	1950	1951	1952	1953	1954	1955	1956	1957	1958	1959
USA	unadjusted	14.6	9.9	4.7	1.9	1.2	1.9	3.9	3.9	3.8	5.9	5.3	3.3	3.0	2.9	5.5	4.4	4.1	4.3	6.8	5.5
GB	unadjusted	6.0	2.2	0.8	0.6	0.5	1.3	2.5	3.1	1.5	1.5	1.5	1.2	2.0	1.6	1.3	1.1	1.2	1.4	2.1	2.2

		1960[3]	1961	1962	1963	1964	1965	1966	1967	1968	1969	1970	1971	1972	1973	1974	1975	1976	1977	1978	1979
USA	unadjusted	5.5	6.7	5.5	5.7	5.2	4.5	3.8	3.8	3.6	3.5	4.9	5.9	5.6	4.9	5.6	8.5	7.7	7.1	6.1	5.8
GB	unadjusted	1.6	1.5	2.0	2.5	1.6	1.4	1.4	2.3	2.5	2.5	2.6	3.5	3.8	2.7	2.6	4.2	5.6	6.0	6.0	5.6
	adjusted d	2.2	2.0	2.8	3.4	2.5	2.2	2.3	3.4	3.3	3.0	3.1	3.7	4.7	2.9	2.9	4.1	5.5	6.2	6.1	5.8

		1980	1981	1982	1983	1984
USA	unadjusted	7.1	7.6	9.5	9.5	7.5
GB	unadjusted	7.3	10.2	11.9	12.7	13.2
	adjusted	7.3	10.4	12.0	13.2	13.6

Sources:

a USA statistics from *Historical Statistics of the US, Part 1*, US Dept of Commerce, Bureau of the Census (1975), Series D. 85–6.

b UK/GB statistics from B. R. Mitchell, *European Historical Statistics 1750–1975*, Macmillan, London (1981), Table C2 Unemployment Figures for 1975–84 are from the *Employment Gazette*.

c A. Maddison, *Phases of Capitalist Development*, Oxford University Press, Oxford (1982), Appendix C.

d C. Sorrentino, 'Unemployment in International Perspective', in B. Showler and A. Sinfield, *The Workless State*, Martin Robertson, Oxford (1981). The figures 1980–84 are from the Bureau of Labor Statistics.

Notes:

1, 2, 4. Unadjusted figures refer to the official figures produced by the Bureau of Labor Statistics in the USA, and the Department of Employment in Great Britain. The adjusted figures are derived from the official estimates which are then adjusted to improve international comparability. In the British figures this represents a change in the categories of people included in the count. Because of these changes the series are, strictly speaking, not comparable.

3 USA figure includes Alaska and Hawaii.

In the US Roosevelt's 'New Deal', involving massive schemes of federal relief and public works, provided a more dramatic example of the way in which action by the state could alleviate unemployment. During this time, Keynes' ideas were gaining greater acceptance, although it is important to note that only at the end of the recession when the problem had been cured was his help enlisted to provide an explanation. The involvement of the state in regulating all aspects of the economy during the war, and in the reconstruction of Western European economies that took place afterwards, appeared to confirm the validity of the idea of the state being responsible for actively managing the economy. This, together with a commitment by the British and American governments to full employment as a policy objective, and the achievement of very low rates of unemployment in the 1950s and 1960s, led to the widespread belief that unemployment had been overcome.

The achievement of Keynes was to re-cast the debate on the nature of unemployment. He established that it was no longer an inevitable consequence of the business-cycle but part of the normal functioning of the economy. He argued that unemployment is caused by deficiencies in the level of aggregate demand, with the level of demand being the product of the level of investment and consumption. While consumption may be fairly stable in the short run, investment fluctuates erratically. In a cyclical downturn business confidence recedes and, as business expectations about future profits become depressed, less investment takes place. In this way business expectations are self-fulfilling, causing investment markets to jam at high levels of unemployment. Keynes saw no reason why, when employment levels fell in a recession, this should be followed by a fall in wages which would inevitably create a demand for more labour. In this respect he questioned the laws of supply and demand as applied to the labour market and refuted any notion of an automatic tendency to full employment. At a time of falling employment levels he considered it vitally important to maintain or increase the level of investment, as this would increase the demand for labour. This analysis made sense of the situation which persisted throughout the 1930s (see Table 2.1). The 'cure' for unemployment was state intervention, which could operate in two ways to achieve a stable relationship between savings and investment at the level of full employment. It could stimulate investment through either manipulation of interest rates, or direct investment in public works. This would increase the level of aggregate demand in the economy and hence the level of employment. With careful management by the state, high levels of unemployment could be a thing of the past[3]. Widespread adoption of his ideas meant that unemployment was no longer seen as a product of market forces over which governments had no control.

In order to explain why successive governments on both sides of the Atlantic adopted Keynesian ideas and committed themselves to pursue policies of full employment, a number of factors have to be considered. The second world war was of fundamental importance. While both governments had taken measures to reduce unemployment before the war, the need for enhanced output and the reduction of the labour force occasioned by the needs of the armed forces rapidly created a situation of full employment. It also demonstrated the possibility of running the economy effectively with almost zero rates of unemployment. The other effect of the war was that it enhanced the dependence of ruling élites on the active cooperation of the population. The need to avoid the disruptive effects of disloyalty and of production stoppages on the success of the war effort created additional pressures to make concessions to the working population. In both societies this pushed political leaders towards an acceptance of full employment as a policy goal.

In Britain, where the dependence of the ruling élites on the working class was exacerbated by the country's more prolonged involvement in the war, a number of other concessions were gained. Positions of political power were given to working-class leaders and legislation was introduced which consolidated and extended welfare provisions. In the USA, although the concessions were less extensive, the Full Employment Act was passed in 1946, and the labour movement did obtain some legal protection in the field of collective bargaining through the Taft–Hartley Act. Once the commitment to full employment was implemented this created conditions which tilted the balance of power further towards labour, although still leaving labour in a subordinate position.

Indeed, the increasing power of the organised working class has been seen as one of the factors contributing to the inflationary pressures of the post-war period (Goldthorpe, 1978; Crouch, 1978).

Governments were also able to sustain their commitment to full employment through the growth of international trade. Following the second world war trade was given stability and organised either directly or through international agencies by the USA. Fuelled by a massive outflow of American investment funds, world trade grew rapidly. The average rate of real growth per capita in advanced industrial societies was 3.8 per cent—three times the average for the previous 130 years. Even though the efficiency of manufacturing industry in both Britain and the USA was deteriorating relative to their competitors, the overall expansion of trade permitted both countries to sustain high levels of employment (Maddison, 1982; Rostow, 1983).

By the 1970s circumstances had changed substantially. The poor performance of the two economies relative to those of other advanced industrial societies continued and their share of world trade fell. The growth of the automobile and consumer goods industries which had contributed to the post-war boom was slowing down (Rostow, 1983). Changes in the location of capital associated with the growth of new industrial nations meant that the pattern of international trade had changed substantially since the war, and with it, the stability which the financial institutions based on American dominance had created. Against this background of international financial instability generated by the changing pattern of international trade, and a shortage of raw materials, the dramatic increase in oil prices which started in 1974 triggered off a rapid increase in inflation. The material and institutional basis of the post-war boom was being undermined. As British, American and other Western governments followed a policy of deflation, unemployment started to rise (Maddison, 1982). These changes weakened the position of labour and tilted the balance of power back in the direction of capital.

The fear of unemployment acts as a brake on the power of organised labour on the shopfloor and on workers' wage demands. For management it may be an opportunity to restore managerial prerogatives and impose greater 'discipline' on the workers[4]. Substantial changes in the level of unemployment do not, in any direct sense, cause these changes, but they do create conditions which are likely to favour one interest rather than another. Thus, with 3 to 4 million unemployed in Britain, workers are less likely to offer resistance to managerial attempts to tighten discipline or to introduce new labour-saving technology. Under these circumstances the economic and social consequences of job loss are much more severe for the individual than in times of full employment when other jobs are readily available.

This combination of rising inflation and rising unemployment led to the questioning of some of Keynes' basic ideas. One of his most important ideas was that of a stable relationship between unemployment levels and inflation levels. Previously it was believed that higher unemployment meant lower inflation (and lower unemployment meant higher inflation). It was argued that as unemployment decreased there was an increase in the bargaining power of unions, which were then in a stronger position to obtain increased wages. In a buoyant market employers could easily pass on these increased costs as higher prices. In this way it was possible to trade off inflation against unemployment. As a way of managing the economy this trade-off was useful as long as the relationship was stable. However, changes at the national and international level had created instability in this relationship. Inflation accelerated independently of the very factor (i.e. the level of unemployment) which was previously thought to determine it. Control of this accelerating rate of inflation became the major policy priority of a number of western governments.

Keynesian techniques of demand management were increasingly criticised and one answer to the problem was sought through monetarism, whose adherents predicted that if unemployment was persistently held below its 'natural' rate this would result in continuously accelerating inflation[5]. Put simply, the monetarists argue first, that the quantity of output and level of employment is determined by non-monetary factors in the economy; and secondly, that if the money supply is increased then inflation will follow as more money is chasing the same number of goods and services. The cure for inflation is thus to reduce the money supply, which in practical terms means reducing state expenditure. While this may cause unemployment in the short run, eventually employment will gravitate to its 'natural level'. If the market is left to operate freely, with a minimum of interference by unions or the state, this 'natural level' will be at the level of full employment. There will still be some unemployment due to people changing jobs and industries growing and declining, but the 'natural rate' of unemployment will have been achieved. If unemployment is above the natural rate, this is because of an imbalance in supply and demand, with the supply of labour exceeding demand. The cause of the imbalance is usually attributed to wage rates being too high, largely as a consequence of union power.

Thus, unemployment is seen as a consequence of inflationary pressures. In addition it is argued that where the level of state benefits is above that provided by the lower paid jobs, then benefits will act as a disincentive to work. As people can get more from the state they will not offer themselves for work and as a consequence wage levels will rise above their 'natural' level. In both instances the 'cure' is to restore the operation of a free market, where workers will bid down the level of wages for which they are prepared to work, and because labour is cheaper, demand for it will increase and full employment will be restored. In terms of the public definition of the problem, unemployment was once again seen as a product of impersonal market forces over which governments have no control.

In the same way that Keynesian policies, by helping establish full employment, created conditions which helped shift the balance of power between capital and labour in favour of labour, so monetarist policies have the reverse effect. In both societies their implementation has been associated with cuts in state expenditure on social welfare payments. In Britain, attempts have been made to curb 'the power of trade unions' by curtailing the closed shop and outlawing 'union labour-only' clauses in subcontracts. Even where state expenditure has been allowed to increase, as in the case of the various youth employment schemes, there has been a conscious attempt to lower the level of youth wages. The result of these policies has been to reduce the proportion of resources allocated for welfare through the state administrative machinery, and to increase dependence on the market mechanisms as the means of distributing the resources necessary for survival. This tilts the balance of power further in favour of capital. In the USA it has taken the form of welfare cuts, roll-back agreements on wages and a decline of union membership. The difference between the two countries' use of monetarism is that in Britain it has resulted in cuts in most areas of state expenditure, while in the USA it was initially used to justify cuts in welfare expenditure but then fairly rapidly abandoned as expenditure on defence increased. All this is not to deny the importance of controlling state expenditure in relation to changes in national output. It merely illustrates how monetarism has been used by conservative élites to justify changes in the internal balance of power and how this has involved a return to earlier views of unemployment as a product of impersonal market forces over which governments are seen to have little control. It suggests that their ideological commitment to the restoration of a 'free-market' obscured their perception of the forms of action available to governments to reduce the problem. In this respect it is clear that the ideological commitment of the British Thatcher administration to monetarism is much stronger than that of the Reagan administration which abandoned the doctrine when it conflicted with the requirements of the defence budget and the pressures of international relations.

The Causes of Unemployment: current theoretical approaches

Cyclical theories
The neo-classical, Keynesian and monetarist theories are all cyclical theories—for all three see unemployment as a product of the business-cycle. It has long been noted by economists that business activity proceeds in cycles. Several years of expansion in both production and employment are followed by a period of slower growth or contraction. For example, in the USA unemployment rose from 4.9 per cent in 1973 to 8.5 per cent in 1975 before falling again in 1976 (see Table 2.1). These fluctuations occur throughout the economy and are not confined to any one industry. Yet while they are recurrent they

are not periodic in that the time intervals involved vary from more than two years to as long as ten to twelve years (Moore, 1983).

The reasons for these fluctuations are not fully understood, hence the emergence of conflicting theories.

Structural theories
Outside the field of conventional economic theory writers have addressed the problem of unemployment from a different perspective. They have argued that recent unemployment levels can be seen as a consequence of broader structural changes in society.

Two recent theories are the Marxist analysis provided by Jordan (1982) and a non-Marxist 'technological' explanation provided by Jones (1982). To Jordan the root of the crisis lies in the process of capital accumulation. Like many contemporary writers (see the long-wave theorists) he traces the specific origins of the present problem to the period 1965–75. During this time employment in the industrial manufacturing sectors of the advanced societies began to decline, and the growth of industrial output in Britain and USA started to slow down, reflecting a gradual fall in the rate of profit. He regards this relationship between the long-term decline in industrial employment and the growth of unemployment as clear-cut, although the explanation of the relationship is more complex.

It is insufficient, Jordan argues, to attribute the increase in unemployment to the effects of new technologies, for after all, new technology has constantly been introduced throughout the process of industrialisation, without necessarily causing unemployment. In the past, output and employment continued to expand in parts of the industrial sector so that when recovery got underway the displaced workers could find alternative employment. Thus, although automation (defined as the use of new technology to increase worker productivity more rapidly than output) occurred in the 1920s and 1930s, some industries such as vehicles, gas, water and electricity, chemicals and electrical engineering still continued to witness a growth in both employment and output. This is not the case in the 1980s as employment in all sectors has contracted. Capital accumulation is no longer occurring in advanced societies through the employment of additional labour because there are no major areas left where investment will create new jobs. This means that the fall in the rate of profit has to be rectified, within the context of these societies, by a reduction of labour costs through using new technology to displace labour. The only other way in which the rate of profit can be improved is by exporting capital to countries with lower wages and higher rates of profit. It was for this reason that investment in new jobs in the more labour-intensive industries took place in industrialising countries such as Spain, Portugal, Brazil, Taiwan and South Korea. The effects of this process in increasing the level of unemployment were particularly acute in countries such as Britain and America which were in a weak position internationally because of their falling share in world trade. The outlook, especially for Britain, is of higher levels of unemployment.

For Jones, the high rates of unemployment witnessed in the late 1970s and 1980s are a symptom of one of the most radical changes that have ever affected human societies; a post-industrial revolution, whose impact is equivalent to that of the first industrial revolution. The basis of this new revolution is information technology, which facilitates a 'vast increase in transactions based on the collection, manipulation and dissemination of information by computerised technologies.' Jones conceptualises the development of human societies as proceeding by a series of discontinuous stages caused by technological change, which increases productivity in specific areas (for example, agriculture, manufacturing) and in the medium term 'releases' people who can work in other areas. The first stage was the industrial revolution, in which agriculture ceased to provide the dominant form of employment. In the next phase manufacturing and directly related industries dominated the labour market. As industrial employment started to decline (for Britain in 1951 and the USA in 1950—Jones, 1982, p.1) they entered the third phase, in which employment in the service sector dominated the labour market. This phase is of short duration, as technological development in the information processing industry will significantly reduce employment there. The microelectronic revolution of the 1980s has overturned this basic relationship between employment and output and threatens devastating effects on employment levels. This is because microelectronics permit an exponential rise in output, together with an exponential fall in input such as energy, capital and labour. We have thus reached a stage where output can be increased with a continual reduction of input, especially of labour. While microelectronics does affect industries in the manufacturing sector, its most dramatic effects are expected by Jones to occur in the service sector. There, elaborate computing systems and word processors will significantly reduce or eliminate repetitive service employment. The effect of this quantum leap in productivity will be to reduce the amount of work available and this will usher in the post-service society. A choice would then have to be made between either a 'golden age of leisure' for all, which would require a conscious reorganisation of work, or an unprecedented decline in the numbers in work in the manufacturing and service sectors and a subsequent rise in unemployment. The outcome depends on how we respond to the impact of the new technology[6].

Long-wave theories

Long-wave theories view the most recent increase in unemployment as part of a longer-term process of change integral to the development of capitalism and not as a consequence of either the short-term business-cycle or a unique set of structural changes. It proposes that underlying the short-term fluctuations of the business-cycle are longer periods of booms and slumps. This idea was originally made popular by Kondratiev, a Russian economist[7]. His ideas have been developed in a number of different directions. The general theme is that the process of capital formation (accumulation) proceeds in a discontinuous fashion. Long periods in which there is a high rate of profit are followed by long periods in which the rate of profit stagnates or declines. These long waves are associated with corresponding rates of high and low unemployment[8]. Each wave lasts for a period of approximately 50 years. The discontinuities are caused by the need for capital to exploit new areas of growth when the rate of profit falls. As new areas of high profitability are found, there develops an incompatibility between the institutional forms (the forms of worker control and the organisation of labour markets) which developed around the previous growth industries and the new forms required to exploit the new areas of growth. The result is considerable social disruption as new social forms come into being.

While a number of authorities agree that there is sufficient evidence to warrant the idea of long waves being taken seriously, there is considerable debate over what causes new areas of growth to emerge. Some argue that they are a result of changes which take place within society, such as technological, social or demographic changes. Others point to the importance of external factors such as wars and international monetary arrangements. If these external factors are of decisive importance then it may be that the idea of long waves or swings will give way to what Maddison (1982) calls 'phases'. This term highlights the fact that they have no fixed periodicity precisely because each phase is produced by a unique combination of events such as the second world war which triggered the boom of the 1950s and 1960s.

One variant of the general thesis has been proposed by Freeman *et al.* (1982) who emphasise the part played by technical change as the engine of this process. Freeman's approach was based on the ideas of Schumpeter. For Schumpeter, technological innovations such as railways and electric power create new opportunities for profit. Once established in the market, these innovations then attract a swarm of investment attempting to exploit new opportunities for profit and to improve on the original innovation. This creates the boom conditions of the upswing. However, the ensuing competition between producers reduces profits, and when this happens investment falls as lower returns are expected, unemployment increases and the economy moves into recession. To test these ideas Freeman *et al.* studied the plastics and electronics industries which were important in generating the fourth and latest of the long waves. Their analysis illustrates the swarming of investment which accompanied major innovations and which helped generate the boom conditions of full employment in the 1950s and 1960s. This was caused by employers investing in new capacity to increase their market share and so creating new jobs. As the new industries mature, the economies of scale are exploited and the pressure shifts to produce cost-saving innovations in process technologies. These are capital-intensive and their introduction either slows or stops employment growth. While their main focus is on technical change they are aware of the part played by other factors. Thus, another reason they give for the fall in employment is that boom conditions strengthen the bargaining power of labour, which in turn helps further erode the rate of profit and reduce business confidence.

While focusing on technical change as the motor for generating the process and changing the level of profitability, Freeman *et al.*, like Schumpeter, do not offer a form of crude technological determinism. They are aware of the importance of other changes both on a national and international level in determining the course and outcome of these long waves. Thus war and international conflict played an important part in stimulating the development of radar and computers, two of the major innovations in the electronics industry. In addition, they see leadership in the field of technological innovation passing from one society to another as a result of international competition. For example, this passed from the UK in the first of the long waves, to the USA and Germany in the later waves, while both are now seen to be challenged by Japan.

Gershuny and Miles (1983) also draw on the insights of long-wave theory, to argue that in contemporary society information technology provides the potential basis for a new upswing but such a development would require a major investment in a telecommunications infrastructure. In much the same way that the development of the road network provided the basis for the growth of the motor industry, so the possible development of a telecommunications infrastructure will determine the prospects for future industrial and service innovations and the associated growth of jobs. Gordon *et al.* (1982), in their more recent writing have also utilised this approach. They stress the importance of institutional factors such as stable, national and international financial institutions and cooperative collective bargaining as essential for encouraging investment and the realisation of profits. They see instability in these institutions as leading to a reduction in investment, stagnation and high unemployment.

An evaluation of the theories

Do these theories help to explain why, periodically, large numbers of people become unemployed in capitalist societies? Any answer to this question requires some knowledge of the work of economists, but our main concern is with the part played by social, political and institutional factors in this process.

The first point to be made is that not all advanced capitalist societies are equally affected. Unemployment rates in Japan and Sweden have so far remained below 3 and 4 per cent respectively (Table 1.1). The USA and especially Britain have had much higher rates, and while the US economy recovered rapidly in 1983/84, reducing the level of unemployment, the British economy failed to do so. Thus, explanations are sought at two levels. First, what is it about the structure of these societies that produces long-term changes in the level of unemployment? Secondly, why are some societies more vulnerable than others? For instance why are Britain and the USA more vulnerable than Japan and Sweden, and why should Britain be more vulnerable than the USA? While we cannot provide definitive answers, we can point to some of the most important factors involved.

With regard to the first problem, the cyclical theories make only a limited contribution. They focus attention only on the short-term fluctuations in the level of unemployment. Yet, if we examine the data in Table 2.1 it is evident that at the trough of each business-cycle since the mid-sixties, there has been a tendency for the level of unemployment to increase progressively. This underlying increase has been particularly noticeable in Britain where between 1966 and 1984 falls in the level of unemployment were only recorded in four of these years, with a dramatic increase taking place between 1979–83. Such a trend suggests longer-term, more deep-seated changes are occurring which transcend the business-cycle. They may help us explain movements in the rates from one year to the next, but tell us little about the direction of the longer-term changes.

Another problem with cyclical theories is that by focusing on conventional economic factors, they direct attention away from the broader, political and socioeconomic changes which have been taking place in inter-state relations and the international division of labour. For example, the emergence of new centres of industrial production, and the new ways of organising industrial investment and production as pioneered in Japan, all have an impact on employment levels.

All three cyclical theories have been used by governments to justify the action which their political interests and the constraints of office lead them to pursue. Therefore, it is important to distinguish between their technical merits and the contribution they make in furthering the interests of specific groups. Keynesian theory has been used by governments anxious to accommodate the interests of the working class. It pointed to ways in which governments were able to manage economies at high levels of employment for 20 years[9]. It has shown how governments can help regulate the level of unemployment. Indeed, the American recovery of 1983/84 was partly caused by the traditional Keynesian technique of a budget deficit increasing aggregate demand and so reducing unemployment. In this respect the insights to be derived from it still represent a significant advance in our knowledge of the cause of unemployment. However, as we noted earlier, in recent years it has encountered problems in explaining the existence of high levels of inflation and high levels of unemployment.

Monetarism has been used by governments more anxious to further the interests of sections of business. In Britain it has played an important part in reducing the level of inflation from 9 per cent when the Conservative government took office in 1979, to 4.5 per cent in 1984. However, the cost in terms of reduced state expenditure and investment was to increase the level of unemployment. In America it was fairly rapidly abandoned by the Reagan administration. It is essentially a backward-looking doctrine which in part explains its attraction to traditional élites (Mannheim, 1953). The idea, that left to themselves markets will clear and solve the problem, stems from the wishful thinking of eighteenth and nineteenth-century theorists. It seeks to restore the economy to a largely fictitious past, where the invisible hand of the market ruled supreme, and before the 'imperfections' created by modern forms of business organisation and unions were introduced. Although the theory may be logically consistent, its basic assumptions are empirically unproven.

The structural theories of Jordan and Jones both seek to provide an explanation of the exceptionally high levels of unemployment that occurred in the early 1980s. These point to important factors which have been at work and over which politicians have less direct control. Such theories provide academic justification for more popular beliefs about the current situation. Jones provides an answer for those who regard technological change as being responsible for unemployment by producing a permanent fall in the demand for labour and thereby necessitating radical adaptations in the organisation of work and leisure. Jordan speaks for those on the Left who see a massive programme of public ownership and central planning as the solution to high rates of unemployment.

On an academic level both these theories raise serious questions about the causes of the latest recession. There is a growing body of evidence to substantiate Jordan's claim that the latest recession is different in important respects from that of the 1930s. In the case of Britain, job losses in the 1930s were heavily concentrated in a limited number of traditional industries while employment continued to grow in other areas of manufacturing. In the period 1979/83 net job losses were recorded in all manufacturing industries (Aldcroft, 1984). This suggests that we may be witnessing a major structural shift in social and economic development. Evidence is also starting to appear which supports Jones' argument that micro-electronic information technology is capable of producing unprecedented increases in productivity which are transforming the traditional relationship between employment and output (Gershuny and Miles, 1983; Rostow, 1983; Rajan, 1984). Both theories raise the possibility that we are undergoing a major structural transformation in the pattern of sectoral location creating a new phase in the development of capitalist societies.

The stress which structuralist theories place on the once-and-for-all change in the relationship between output and employment, while being a major strength in forcing us to re-evaluate our assumptions, can also be seen as a source of weakness, especially in comparison with the long-wave theories. For the structuralist theories tend to ignore the possibilities raised by the long-wave theories, namely that new products and product markets, together with new sets of institutional arrangements, could be created, thereby generating new opportunities for profit, output and employment. In Jordan's terms this would mean that capital accumulation would once again occur through the employment of additional labour. In relation to Jones' argument, it would mean the development of new products and services which were labour-intensive and not subject to the impact of the micro-electronics revolution.

The theories of the long swings provide one of the most fruitful means of explaining the fluctuations in the level of unemployment depicted in Table 2.1. However, before proceeding to a discussion of these theories it is important to note that the statistical evidence on which they are based is by no means universally accepted as proof of their existence. There have only been four such waves and the statistical data relating to the early ones are of necessity somewhat thin (Freeman *et al.*, 1982, Ch. 2; Maddison, 1982, Ch. 4). Nevertheless, what evidence there is points in the direction of long-term changes in the level of economic activity and employment, as reflected in Table 2.1. However, while acknowledging that this approach is still in its infancy, it does offer the promise of identifying some of the factors responsible for long-term changes in the level of unemployment.

One of the valuable features of the long-wave theories in this respect is their focus on inter-societal relations. As noted in Chapter 1, changes in the international division of labour are increasing the interdependence of societies and making it more difficult to understand changes merely by reference to factors 'internal' to the society. Moreover, they point to the fact that leadership in the area of economic growth and social development moves from one society to another. Thus, Japan, which is now moving into a position of leadership, has come through the latest recession with one of the lowest rates of unemployment.

The policy implications of the long-wave theories are also of a different order. If at present we are in either a long downswing, or alternatively the start of a new phase, there may be little of immediate practical significance that governments can do about the magnitude of the problem. At best their actions may only make marginal improvements in the short term. The eradication of high levels of unemployment may depend upon the development of new social institutions to handle the conflict between capital and labour within the society and/or new international institutions to increase financial stability. If Freeman *et al.* and Gershuny and Miles are correct in their diagnosis for Britain, it would require a radical alteration in the economic and social relationship between the state and industry for sufficient resources to be allocated to achieve the level of technological and social innovation necessary to establish new growth industries.

On a conceptual level the structural and long-wave theories represent a break with the traditional approach to explaining unemployment. They dispense with the idea of the economy as a self-correcting system with a tendency towards equilibrium, in which extraneous events such as wars, changes in the international balance of power or international competition are seen as chance intrusions. Instead, these factors become important, if not central, constraints on social and economic development. In view of this, social development is better seen as a process involving the reallocation of resources between industries and groups, which leads to structural change because of the impact on existing institutional arrangements, thus creating crises of adjustment. These are subsequently resolved through a series of struggles between groups out of which a new accommodation emerges. It is in moving towards such a view of social change that work in a number of social science disciplines is starting to converge.

From this perspective unemployment is one consequence of these broader structural changes which can be managed with a battery of policy measures in the same way that other social problems are managed. Whether that management takes the form of the policy of containment and enhanced social control or measures designed to create jobs and reduce unemployment levels will depend in a large part on the priorities of those in positions of political power.

3. The Distribution of Unemployment and Labour Market Shelters

The extent to which unemployment is disproportionately borne by certain social groups is documented in Tables 3.1 and 3.2. Like all social statistics, care should be taken in interpreting unemployment rates. For a discussion of the problems see the Appendix. In Britain, males who are particularly at risk are unskilled manual workers and semi-skilled/personal service workers who are all greatly over-represented among the unemployed. The groups who are under-represented are the professionals, employers and managers. The tables show that for males in Britain, the higher the status, the less the chance of experiencing unemployment. For females the situation is slightly different in that the groups particularly at risk are semi-skilled/personal service workers and not unskilled manual workers. In the USA the pattern is similar to that found in Britain. Those groups with the highest rate of unemployment are the non-farm labourers, and especially the construction labourers whose unemployment rate was eight times that of professional workers. Craft workers had a lower rate, but those groups least at risk were clearly white-collar workers and especially professional, technical and managerial workers. For blacks the rate is roughly twice that of whites in both societies.

Conceptualisation of the Labour Market

Until recently these differences in the distribution of unemployment among the various occupational groups would have been explained in terms of the personal characteristics of the workers. The high rate of unemployment among the unskilled was seen to be a result of the workers' ill-health, poor employment records and especially their failure to invest in education and lack of qualifications. As a result their labour has a relatively low productivity for the employer. Given that employers hire on the basis of rational criteria then those who are hired are the ones with higher productivity (Norris, 1978a).

Table 3.1: Unemployment by Socioeconomic Group and Sex, Great Britain, 1982

Socioeconomic group	Males		Females	
	% working population	% unemployed population	% working population	% unemployed population
Professional	6	2	1	0
Employers/ managers	18	6	6	5
Intermediate non-manual	9	4	18	6
Junior non-manual	8	5	37	32
Skilled manual	41	43	7	7
Semi-skilled/ personal service	15	26	23	42
Unskilled manual	3	15	8	7
n =	6287	777	4437	394

Source: Amended from *General Household Survey,* London, HMSO (1982), tables 6.33 and 6.34.

In this context it is tempting to see the labour market merely as a set of allocating mechanisms by which the supply and demand for labour are matched. On the one hand, there are employers with a variety of job vacancies searching for labour to fill them, or with the need to contract and deciding which workers to fire. On the other, there is a range of people with different social and demographic characteristics who offer themselves for work, or who wish to keep those jobs they already have. The pricing mechanism then ensures an adequate match. The situation is very different in reality.

Table 3.2: Unemployment by Occupation, Sex and Race, USA, 1982

	Males	Females
White-collar workers	4.1	6.3
Professional & technical	3.4	3.9
Managers & administrators	3.2	4.7
Sales workers	4.9	7.1
Clerical workers	7.2	7.5
Blue-collar workers	13.7	16.8
Craft & kindred	9.7	7.2
Operatives	19.2	19.4
Transport workers	10.5	9.7
Non-farm labourers	18.4	16.7
Construction labourers	27.2	*
Other labourers	16.1	15.4
Service workers	10.9	10.5
Farm workers	4.7	10.3
Whites	8.6	8.0
Blacks & others	18.2	16.0

*insufficient numbers
Source: US Bureau of Labor Statistics, *Employment and Earnings Monthly* (November 1982).

To conceptualise the labour market as a simple matching process is inadequate. Taken in isolation, the hiring or firing decision may appear as a straightforward attempt to fill jobs with the best people. Yet the criteria used to establish the suitability of the candidates, and often the very existence of the job itself, are the outcome of a number of struggles between management and worker over the price of labour, the control over the labour process, and job security (Keil *et al.*, 1984). In this sense the labour market is more adequately seen as an arena in which a series of issues are constantly fought over, rather than a simple matching process. From management's point of view the criteria to be adopted will depend on a number of factors, such as the location of the job in the production process, whether or not they wish to recruit union members or whether they feel any sense of loyalty towards their current workforce. The criteria may have little to do with the workers' potential productivity. From the point of view of professional bodies or trade unions it may be important that people without credentials are prevented from competing for certain jobs, even though they may be perfectly capable of performing them.[1] The use of such criteria means that even at the level of semi-skilled work a number of categories of people will have been excluded before any matching takes place: some because they were either union members or not union members; some because their credentials were inadequate; others simply because they were of the wrong sex or colour; and yet others because they did not have personal contacts with employees in the firm and did not hear of the vacancy (Manwaring, 1984).

If we conceptualise the labour market in this alternative manner then the analysis of unemployment involves asking two separate questions. First, why are some people more often put at risk of unemployment than others by losing their job? To explain this we need to examine the factors which operate to provide job security. Job security is enhanced in two ways: by workers obtaining some protection from arbitrary dismissal by their employers, and by protecting jobs from being lost as a result of fluctuations in the demand for labour. The mechanisms which are used to obtain this security we refer to as labour market shelters.[2] The way in which they operate to protect workers and the reasons some groups are able to establish more effective shelters than others are discussed in the first part of the chapter. Thus, the differential distribution of labour market shelters explains why some groups are more at risk of unemployment than others. Recent research by Schervish in the USA has shown that positions endowed with power in the relations of authority (e.g. self-employed and managerial positions) are most capable of shielding their incumbents from unemployment. A second group who are slightly more at risk of unemployment but relatively 'safe' when compared with the working class are those in the higher professions, where the application of professional standards and membership of a prestigious profession reduce the risk of unemployment. His findings also show the working-class positions to be most vulnerable to unemployment. Analysing national survey data for males in the period 1969–78 he has shown that factors such as social class, economic sector and business-cycle make a significant contribution to the distribution of workers in unemployment—a contribution over and above that produced by factors such as race, age and education (Schervish, 1983).

The second question we need to ask is, why is it that some types of worker rather than others are able to obtain access to jobs which provide shelters? The answer is to be found partly in the way in which people are prepared for the labour market by the educational system and partly in the recruitment policies of employers and the professional bodies which control access to jobs. Together, these factors combine to give members of some groups access to secure and highly paid jobs and to make the labour of other groups marginal. This is discussed in the second part of the chapter.

The origins of this alternative explanation lay in the work of segmentation theorists.[3] Segmentation theory points to the existence of a number of institutional barriers which restrict movement in the labour market and conceptualises the labour market in terms of a number of different segments. These are sets of jobs within which labour mobility is confined. They sometimes stretch across a whole range of industries, as in the case of secretarial or clerical work where the same skills are required in both the manufacturing and service sectors. In other instances they may consist of similar jobs in different firms within the same industry, such as a toolmaker or miller in the engineering industry. In some segments movement is largely confined to jobs within the same firm; for example, the telephone engineer in British Telecom. Even at the level of semi-skilled and unskilled work there are a number of factors such as sex and race discrimination by both employers and workers which act as barriers to movement and which mean that some semi-skilled and unskilled jobs are closed to males or females; for example, few women become labourers in the construction industry, and few males become sewing machinists.

Labour market shelters are analytically distinct from segments but are empirically-related features of the labour market. They take a number of forms ranging from employment in the civil service, state licensing of occupational activities to either employer- or worker-imposed internal markets (Freidson, 1982).

Segments and shelters are sometimes empirically indistinguishable; for example, professional medical jobs form a labour market segment, for once people qualify they usually only change jobs within medicine as they pursue their career; they rarely move outside. At the same time their professional organisation provides them with one of the most secure forms of shelter; they are rarely made redundant or unemployed. At the lowest levels, the labour market is highly segmented, but such segments do not necessarily provide shelters from the risks of unemployment. Because of this, it is important to retain the analytical distinction between segments and shelters.

The forms of labour market shelter which have been most extensively discussed in the literature are internal labour markets (Doeringer and Piore, 1971). These consist of formal rules or customs which determine issues such as who has access to which jobs, how people are promoted, the nature of pay differentials, the price paid for labour and the circumstances under which workers can be sacked or laid off. They take two main forms: firm internal labour markets and occupational internal labour markets (Althauser and Kalleberg, 1981). Firm internal labour markets, as the name implies, are found within companies. In the larger, bureaucratically organised companies these consist of formal, written administrative rules and procedures. They determine the ways in which jobs are graded into a series of categories, often in accordance with the level of skill and responsibility involved. The imposition of such rules can mean that all entrants to the firm have to start on the bottom grade and by training, experience and length of service they can move up the hierarchy. In this sense they generate careers. Movement up the hierarchy is regulated by rules which specify the training and qualifications required before a person can be considered for promotion, and the criteria to be used in the selection of candidates. Written agreements specify the circumstances under which workers will be fired or laid off and so provide security against the arbitrary use of power by management.

Occupational internal labour markets are found in occupations which transcend particular establishments. Movement between the jobs involved is determined by rules and procedures specific to the occupational group and not by the individual employing establishment. The higher professions such as medicine provide a clear example of this. Recruitment and training is controlled by a professional body which lays down a set of procedures to be followed in order to secure promotion. Such rules and regulations also govern the movement of personnel between organisations. In the higher professions membership is a virtual guarantee of life-time employment and dismissals or withdrawal of membership of the profession only takes place under specified circumstances. This type of internal market is not confined to the professions, elements of it are also found among certain groups of manual workers, such as some of the licensed craftsmen in the USA (Strinchcombe, 1959), and to a lesser extent craft workers in Britain.

The need for market shelters stems partly from the fact that the labour market is always in a state of flux or movement. Some firms grow in size, others decline as their markets shrink, yet others are liquidated. As new products are created such as aeroplanes, whole new industries emerge, while older products become obsolete and employment in those industries falls. The result is the expansion of some occupations and the decline of others. For example, in New England, Bluestone and Harrison (1980) estimate that the turnover of jobs in the 1970s, was in the region of 2 million, of which half were lost and half created.

Decisions which lead to these changes in the turnover of jobs are made by those in control of capital. At present there is a tendency to think of all such decisions as being motivated by a desire to maximise profit yet this is not what we always observe. In some instances considerations of national security and defence are important in determining the level and location of investment, in other instances as in some of the nationalised industries in Britain, decisions about the level of investment have taken account of the interests and job security of the workers, for example in extending the period over which rationalisation was phased in the railways.

In order to understand the impact of these non-economic factors on investment, it is necessary to distinguish between those decisions made by people in control of private capital and those made by people responsible for capital controlled by the state. The former decisions are primarily determined by the expected rate of return on the capital invested. Such decisions about the creation of jobs come from corporations and individual capitalists investing in new products or expanding investment in existing products and services. Decisions about the loss of jobs take a number of forms. Some result from the desire to move capital out of declining industries into expanding ones. Thus in Great Britain in 1980 ICI withdrew capital from textiles and closed two of its fibre plants. Others stem from the relocation of capital from one society to another, for example, closing down a manufacturing plant in Britain or America and investing in a new plant in South Korea where labour costs are lower (Frobel, Heinricht and Kreye, 1979). Others take the form of what McKersie and Sengenberger (1983) call internal restructuring, that is, re-investment within existing firms in new products, technology or in improving human resources.

Decisions made by agencies of the state which involve the creation and destruction of jobs are subject to other, usually political influences. These decisions are of two main types, those which relate to what Offe terms the allocative function of the state, and those which relate to its productive functions.[4] Allocative decisions are those which determine how the resources controlled by the state are distributed. Examples of this are the transfer of income from taxes to welfare payments or defence expenditure and the decisions about the use of state subsidies. These are clearly political decisions, influenced by the ideology of the ruling party and its attitude towards the role of the state in society. Decisions about the state's productive functions are less overtly political. In Britain they determine the level of investment in coal, steel and railways, as well as the National Health Service. In the USA, although nationalisation or public control of industry is less extensive, the federal state still plays an important part in determining the level of investment in space research, construction, public transport networks and weaponry. While considerations about the expected return on capital invested influence these decisions, they do not determine the outcome as they do in the private sector.

In both countries, but especially in Britain, these political influences can be of a very different ideological character from one period of office to another, depending on which party is in power. The Conservative Party tends to place emphasis on business criteria, while the Labour Party claims broader social and political objectives. Another important political influence is the state of international relations. In the late 1930s it was the decision to arm in preparation for war that helped to create jobs and reduce unemployment in both countries. More recently President Reagan's decision to increase arms expenditure played a significant part in creating jobs and boosting the recovery from the recession of the early 1980s. Thus, while we tend to think of the loss and creation of jobs as a product of 'market forces', in reality they are a result of decisions made in very different areas of society which are subject to different sets of political and economic influences.

Sources of Labour Market Shelters

There are three distinct spheres of action which account for the emergence of shelters; action by those in control of the state, by those in control of private capital and by workers in their attempt to control the supply of labour.

The state
Figure 3.1 depicts the different ways in which the state influences labour market shelters. By guaranteeing the sanctity of private property and defining the contract of employment as a legally-binding agreement between two equal parties, it determines the framework within which the labour market operates. Basically this is one in which the contract of employment takes place between parties with unequal bargaining strengths producing what Kreckel (1980) refers to as a primary or fundamental asymmetry in the relationship between capital and labour. This is largely created by the fact that when labour is not employed it creates an immediate crisis of personal income for workers and their families, whereas when capital is not employed it can 'wait' or be transferred to alternative uses or to consumption. It means that in struggles between employers and workers over pay, internal restruc-

turing and job security, the scales are tipped in favour of the employer. Over time, certain limitations have been placed on the 'freedom' of capital to utilise labour, such as health and safety legislation which in both countries restricts the type of labour that can be bought. However, these restrictions have never been sufficient to alter fundamentally the asymmetrical character of the relationship between the two parties.

State
resources; primarily its monopoly of the legitimate
use of physical force and taxation

Indirect influence on the formation of shelters		Direct influence as an employer		
Guarantees legal frame work and hence the primary asymmetry	Determines legitimate tactics to be used by employers and workers to resolve conflicts	Licenses certain occupational activities	Through allocative function, e.g. in the administration of tax	Through productive function, e.g. in Post Office and nationalised industries

Figure 3.1: The Influence of the State on the Formation of Labour Market Shelters and Segments

The state has the power to determine the tactics which management and worker can legitimately use in their struggles over the distribution of resources and job security. One of the most important of these is the right of trade unions to have legal recognition. Without legal recognition it is much more difficult for semi-skilled and unskilled manual workers and white-collar workers to establish effective unions. Skilled workers use their control over the knowledge and techniques of production as a basis from which to control the supply of labour and bargain with employers independently of the state's recognising their activities as legitimate. By contrast the organisational techniques necessary for the unionisation of semi-skilled, unskilled and white-collar workers depends on the union having strong centralised control over finance and administration. Such an organisation is difficult to sustain without legal recognition as the recent experience of workers in Brazil has shown (Humphrey, 1980).

The success of unions in influencing wage levels, working conditions and job security is also dependent on the kind of tactics the state permits them to use. As the attempts by most groups of workers to erect shelters and influence the behaviour of employers is through their control of labour, then any action by the state which either hinders or helps them achieve that objective, is very important in determining the outcome of the struggle. For example, workers have never been permitted the use of violence. In the UK for a period in the early nineteenth century even strike action was illegal and still is (in both countries) for certain categories of state employee. In the USA the Taft–Hartley Act currently defines the weapons that unions cannot use in their struggles (Hanson, 1982). Specifically, they are prevented from using the secondary boycott, which serves to limit the effectiveness of industrial action in their bargaining with individual employers, and the pre-entry closed shop (Mayhew, 1983, Chs. 3 and 4). In Britain similar restrictions were imposed on the use of secondary picketing and the closed shop in the Employment Acts of 1980 and 1982 and on the use of strikes in the Trade Union Act 1984. Such restrictions limit the power of workers and their unions to influence the price of labour and its supply to any particular establishment and hence to impose seniority rights or similar restrictions on management's authority. The task of achieving the security which seniority rights provide, through the policy of last-in, first-out, is much more difficult. In their absence, employers have greater freedom to substitute the labour of the non-unionised unemployed for that of existing employees, that is, to hire and fire at will.

A third and potentially powerful instrument in influencing labour-market behaviour is the state's licensing activities. In the case of many of the professions in both Britain and the USA, and to a lesser extent the craft workers in the USA, these activities of the state play an important role in erecting market shelters, especially occupational internal labour markets. Licensing can take a number of forms, such as granting a local board the right to license practitioners in certain trades, as in the case of craft work in some states in the USA (Freedman, 1976). For the professions it can involve granting the professional body the right to control the training and certification of practitioners, as is the case of the medical profession. When this form of licensing occurs in conjunction with a powerful, centralised occupational association, as it does in the case of the medical professions, then this creates one of the most effective forms of shelter (Larson, 1977). In these circumstances, the ability of the professional body to control access to the occupation by limiting competition is sanctioned by the state's monopoly of physical force. Where the professional bodies and occupational associations have not been successful in securing the right to license occupational activities, the state may nevertheless license and supervise the accreditation body. In Britain it does this with the nursing and teaching professions. This gives the state control over recruitment, which means it can rapidly increase or decrease the supply of labour. However, in all these cases the state, by excluding the non-qualified or providing the sanctions to ensure their exclusion, thereby improves the market capacity of certified practitioners which increases their relative earnings and job security (Freedman, 1976).

The state can operate more directly as a source of shelter through its activities as an employer. The level of job security it provides depends on whether the job is performed in the context of the state's allocative or productive function. With regard to its allocative function the state as an employer has a certain autonomy in relation to the ebbs and flows of the business-cycle. The administration of its activities continues independently of the business fluctuations, at least in the short run. At times of severe recession when the national income falls there are pressures on the state to reduce its level of spending and hence its activities. But there may also be other pressures which run counter to this; for example, a severe recession increases the number of unemployed and hence demand for social security benefits. In the short run it may indeed be possible for the level of expenditure on the state's allocative functions to remain constant or even increase because of the possibility of deficit funding.[5] For these reasons employment within the civil service can provide greater employment security than that found in manufacturing. Indeed, Schervish has shown that the proportion of male unemployment in the state sectors was lower than in other sectors of the economy.[6] Such employers are not immune to job loss. Both the Reagan and Thatcher administrations, in their attempts to confront the economic problems of the late 1970s and early 1980s have sought to reduce the number of civil servants. However, because these are also political decisions they are subject to leverage from a political constituency (Cawson, 1982), a process which tends to modify the speed at which they can be implemented. Thus, in Britain, reductions were achieved through natural wastage and voluntary redundancies, rather than through the mass firings and compulsory redundancies which occurred in the private sector.

Employment in the state's productive function offers less shelter, although it may still be more than can be achieved in the private sector. In organisations such as the Post Office and railways, and in Britain, the coal, steel, and aircraft industries, the financial resources of the state have enabled internal restructuring to take place over a longer time-span. Thus, employment in the railways in the UK fell from 477,000 in 1963 to 230,000 in 1973 and is still falling. In the USA it fell from over 1 million in the 1940s to 500,000 in the late 1970s (McKersie and Sengenberger, 1983). This gradual process of internal restructuring is not an inevitable consequence of public ownership. The pressures on the government to take action in radically restructuring an industry may be strong enough to ensure that reductions are accomplished in a short period of time, or the government itself may decide not to use its resources to shelter the industry and leave its restructuring to market forces. The steel industry in Britain provides an example, for between 1974 and 1981 intensified international competition, overcapacity and technological change led to massive job losses in the region of 100,000. With the change of government in 1979 this process was intensified as the Conservative administration sought to speed up the process by withdrawing state support, a tactic it later used in relation to the coal-mining industry. However, whether or not they are used in particular instances, the important point to note is that the state can use its resources to shelter certain industries.

Private capital

As we noted in Chapter 1, historically employers have played an important part through the legislative process in placing limitations on the tactics workers have been able to use in their struggles to obtain job security and higher wages. This may suggest that there is little or no incentive for them to provide market shelters. In fact there are a number of pressures operating on some employers which encourage them to provide relatively well-paid and/or secure employment for some, if not all, of their employees: these are depicted in Figure 3.2.

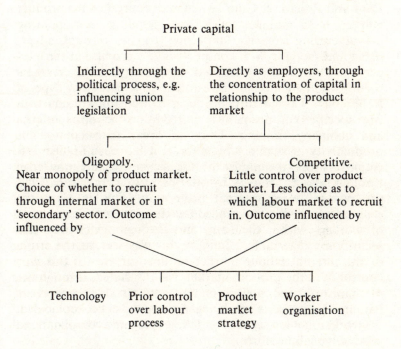

Figure 3.2: The Influence of Private Capital on the Formation of Labour Market Shelters

The distinction between oligopolistic firms with some control over the product market and those firms operating in competitive product markets where they have little control over the market is seen as of central importance in any attempt to explain the relatively privileged labour market position of some segments of the labour force. It formed the basis of the early formulation of dual labour market theory (Doeringer and Piore, 1973; Piore, 1975). Internal labour markets comprised the primary sector and firms operating in the external market comprised the secondary sector.

In Chapter 1 it was noted that heavy capital investment and large-scale production is often associated with some degree of market control. This was the case with the large corporations which first developed in the USA in the early decades of this century (Chandler, 1977; Hannah, 1983). Such giants as ICI, Ford and Proctor & Gamble achieved control of the product market in a number of ways, including monopolising manufacturing capacity, stabilising demand through advertising and merging with competitors. To produce at the level necessary to satisfy national and international markets requires a high level of investment in a particular type of technology. This in turn produces a need for workers with firm-specific skills normally acquired by on-the-job experience and company training. Thus, in order to maximise the productivity of such a labour force, it has been argued that employers seek to minimise the loss of expertise and knowledge through labour turnover, by offering workers higher pay and the possibility of internal promotion. This involves the elaboration of rules and procedures that govern the movement of workers within the firm, and through which pay and security are determined. Initially this was seen as the origin of the internal labour market outlined above. In this way control over the product market was translated, through the mechanism of the internal market, into a stable demand for labour. The interests of management and workers coincided, the workers got job security and the employers a compliant and productive labour force.

Firms operating in more competitive product markets were seen to have no such control over the demand for their products. They tend to be smaller firms producing goods which are labour-intensive and involve a relatively low level of capital investment, firms such as those in the textiles, footwear, clothing and food industries. These product markets are characterised by large seasonal fluctuations in demand and intense competition. Such a competitive product market and labour-intensive methods of production combine to create pressure on the employers to keep labour costs down. Because the technology is relatively unsophisticated the skills required by the labour force are rudimentary and quickly learnt. Firms cope with fluctuations in demand by hiring and firing workers, and offer low paid and insecure employment, characteristics of the secondary market (Bosanquet and Doeringer, 1973, pp.422–5).

More recent research has shown that the links between the product market and firm internal labour markets are not as deterministic as that suggested by the early formulations of dual labour market theory. More specifically it is becoming clear that employers may decide to introduce or abandon internal markets for reasons that are only loosely related to their position in the product market, and that the same technology is compatible with different labour market strategies. Thus, the work of Edwards *et al.* reveals that the introduction of internal labour markets can result from a definite labour market strategy on the part of employers, which aims not just to introduce labour stability but also to enhance management control over the labour process (Edwards, 1979; Gordon *et al.*, 1982). By introducing an internal labour market, management can encourage workers to identify with the company and forestall the emergence of unions. Where unions already exist, internal markets can weaken their influence over the ways in which labour is used within the plant.

Control over the labour process is a constant source of conflict between management and worker (Baldamus, 1961). The establishment of bureaucratic career structures (internal markets) have been used as one potential weapon in this struggle. Early attempts to control worker behaviour, for example, through the methods advocated by exponents of scientific management, involving the use of direct supervision or piecework schemes, and focusing on only one aspect of worker behaviour, namely physical output, proved of limited value the long run.[7] This was particularly true where the employer required a more general commitment from labour, with a willingness on the part of the employee to apply his/her skills across a range of tasks, the elements of which could not be easily measured. In these circumstances forms of payment by results are inadequate. Yet, by imposing a hierarchically organised internal labour market the employer can offer the prospect of progressive increases in income, status and seniority in return for a more general commitment by the employee to the interests or goals of the organisation. In this way the employer exerts control over a broader range of employees' behaviour. For as long as there are prospects of further promotion or the threat of demotion employees have a powerful material incentive to identify with and accept the demands of the organisation. In return the organisation offers not only a progressive increase in income but security against the threat of unemployment; the material security on the basis of which employees and their families can plan for the future.[8] Thus internal markets, wherever they develop, function to provide labour market shelters. Schervish (1983) found this to be the case in the USA, in what he termed the oligopoly sectors (construction, state and utility), where age-based jobs and benefit ladders coincided with age-based insulation from unemployment, and a low level of firings and quits.

Not all large oligopolistic firms choose to utilise internal labour markets as a means of control. Large companies such as Pye in England, with considerable market power and product leadership, may operate largely in the secondary labour market (Lawson, 1981). Such examples point to the choice firms have in adopting their labour market strategies, and which we illustrate in Figure 3.2. The same employer may recruit in separate markets, as the major utilities in Great Britain do. Gas, electricity and water boards provide extensive internal markets and job security for their skilled manual and some white-collar employees, but also recruit in the secondary market for unskilled manual workers and routine clerical workers. Unskilled workers are not offered the chance of promotion and are expected to remain as labourers, while the clerical workers are often part-time and not subject to the same terms and conditions as the full-time workers (Ashton, Maguire and Garland, 1982).

While most of the research in this area has focused on the large oligopolistic firms, the same point can be made with regard to smaller firms in more competitive product markets. Although the scope for the development of formal bureaucratically organised internal markets is limited, other forms of worker control have been introduced with implications for the job security of workers. Ashton and Maguire (1984) report a number of small firms operating in highly competitive product markets in Great Britain which provide labour market shelters in the form of internal markets based not on formal bureaucratic rules and regulations but on informal custom and practice. In some instances the security they provide extends to the whole of the workforce, in other cases just to a smaller group of 'core' workers.

The relationship between technology and the labour market strategy adopted by employers is also contingent. As Gordon *et al.* (1982) argue, many firms have introduced new forms of technology specifically to undermine the power, status and job security of skilled craftsmen and de-skill the labour process. This has enabled them to lower the costs of production, and recruit low-paid, unskilled labour with little or no job security. Yet as Rubery *et al.* (1984) point out, while the introduction of new technology in the American steel industry had the effect of undermining the craft union and de-skilling the labour force, in Britain, the technology was introduced in such a way as to reinforce the status and pay of skilled workers. There is nothing determinate about technology *per se*.

The fact that employers can and do change their labour market strategy means that the distribution of labour market shelters and segments changes over time. One area where the labour market is currently changing is the retail trade.

Until recently one of the most common forms of organising retail outlets has been the department store. This was usually a locally-based family firm which recruited a large number of full-time sales assistants, some of whom were subsequently trained for junior management. Senior management was usually in the hands of the family. Since the 1960s this form of organisation has been replaced by the chain-store. These nationally-based organisations represent a much greater concentration of capital, and because of their size and organisational structure, have been able to intensify price competition. As a result they have progressively replaced the department store, and because their use of labour is different, they have also changed the structure of the labour market in retail distribution (Bluestone and Stevenson, 1981).

They have done this in two main ways. First, the concentration of capital has created the need for professional management to replace the old owner/manager and his family. The national basis of their organisation and its bureaucratic character has produced the basis for an extended career for managers and administrators. Secondly, the changing techniques of selling and the introduction of modern computer-based technology in the form of electronic point-of-sale equipment have transformed the sales labour force. The use of national advertising to sell the product, and of pre-packaging during manufacture to prepare the product for sale, has completed the process whereby the job of selling has been de-skilled. Employers can now recruit unskilled labour without any previous sales experience. At the same time, electronic point-of-sale equipment establishes at what time of the day sales peak, so times at which labour is required can be located more precisely. The result has been the progressive replacement of full-time workers by part-time workers, whose job is simply to staff the tills or re-stock shelves at times of peak demand. For the remainder of the day, the tills are staffed either by a small group of full-time workers or by professional staff. Labour costs have been reduced, sales turnover increased and the use of labour made more flexible. In the labour market, full-time jobs which offered some degree of security and the occasional chance of promotion, have been replaced by lower-paid, part-time casual jobs (Ashton, Maguire and Garland, 1982). Eventually, as more firms adopt this strategy of cutting labour costs by reorganising their internal markets, the competitive advantage it produces will be lost and so pressures will be created for new innovations which may further transform the character of this particular segment of the labour market.

When it comes to deciding which strategy to use, oligopolistic firms—especially the multinationals—have more options from which to choose. For example, a large multinational footwear manufacturer can choose to produce in Britain using modern factory-based technology and a unionised workforce, or in Italy using domestic labour and a putting-out system. For small firms based on factory technology and obliged to recruit in the local markets such options do not exist, and consequently the constraints of technology and worker organisation are more powerful determinants of their own labour market strategies than they are for the multinationals (see Figure 3.2).

As Rubery *et al.* (1984) have pointed out in their refinement of segmentation theory, there are a number of factors which influence the labour market strategy of the firm. Changes in a firm's international competitiveness may affect its control over the product market and hence its ability to maintain an internal market. Competition between large employers aimed at increasing their market share may lead to firms switching from offering an internal market to recruiting in the secondary market. Even where workers do have the protection of internal markets in the private sector these are always contingent.

Labour

Whether or not employers seek to create internal markets, they cannot be certain of the outcome of their labour market strategies because of the influence of worker organisations (Rubery, 1978). These also attempt to exert control over the labour process and labour market. By exerting control over the labour process, restricting the allocation of labour between jobs, and specifying the conditions under which it can be fired, unions and professions can enhance job security. They can also enhance job security by strategies of social closure, that is by controlling the supply of labour and restricting employers' access to alternative sources (Parkin, 1974, 1979; Krekel, 1980; and Freidson, 1982). This can involve labour in struggles with the state over licensing rights or union recognition, with employers over pay and security, and with other workers or the unemployed who may undermine their privileged position by offering to work for less (see Figure 3.3).

The kind of power which the organisation of labour can create is best illustrated by the established professions of law and medicine; they have forged the most effective forms of occupational internal labour market (Larson, 1977). In Great Britain and the USA both the medical and legal professions

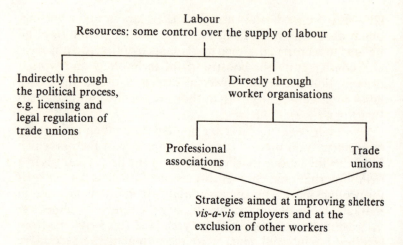

Figure 3.3: The Influence of Labour on the Formation of Labour Market Shelters

obtained control over licensing, entry and training before the expansion of industry and the apparatus of the modern stàte took place. This enabled their professional bodies to maintain control over the development of the occupation and to maintain a high level of self-employment among members.

Those professions which have formed in the wake of the modern state or the development of modern industry have been less successful in controlling the supply of labour and creating such effective occupational internal markets. The expansion of public education and welfare, together with philanthropic provision in these fields, created the basis for the contemporary teaching and social work professions, while the growth of large-scale bureaucratic capitalist enterprises created the demand for engineers, accountants and scientists (Johnson, 1972). In most of these occupations it is thus a combination of some form of licensing, with the bureaucratic structure of the career, as embodied either in the state apparatus (teachers) or the modern capitalist enterprise (managers, accountants), which created the main basis for the labour market shelter. In Britain the teachers have neither a unified professional body nor control over licensing and hence are more vulnerable to control from the state. In both societies managers are a 'profession' without a unified professional body, but in their case they are sheltered by their position within the system of production (Schervish, 1983).[9]

While the professions have tended to look to the state to provide them with protection, the unions have experienced more hostility from that direction and have channelled most of their energies towards the struggle with employers and in some instances, other workers. Like the professional workers, the strategies they can adopt in securing shelters are related to, but not determined by, the kind of skills they bring to the market and their success in controlling the supply of labour. The most powerful groups have been the craftsmen or skilled workers. In Britain a great deal of the country's early industrial prosperity was founded on the labour of skilled workers in the engineering, building, iron, textiles and mining industries. This left a legacy of relatively strongly organised local groups with some control, through the apprenticeship system, over the entry and training of recruits. This was usually sufficient to enable them to raise the price of their labour substantially above that of the unskilled labourers. In addition, they developed early forms of insurance against unemployment and sickness and sought to defend the trade interests of their members, not just against the power of the employer, but also against the attempt by less-skilled workers to poach 'their' work. Their strategies have been exclusionist, as they sought to prohibit other workers from access to their trades (Phelps Brown, 1983).

In both Britain and America these unions still have considerable success in influencing pay levels, and job security, and have been able to establish rudimentary occupational internal labour markets. In the USA, craft organisations have been able to secure licensing agreements with a number of states (Freedman, 1976). Other unions in the construction industry have maintained effective control over the supply of labour in their trades (Doeringer and Piore, 1971). In the manufacturing sector, for reasons discussed earlier, they have been less successful than the British craft unions. In Britain the earlier establishment of skilled workers' unions provided the base for stronger opposition to attempts by employers to impose control over the process of production, whether in the forms of scientific management, new technology, or internal markets (Littler, 1982). Thus the skilled workers' unions have prevented or delayed the introduction of uniform firm internal markets.[10] Similarly, groups such as printers have been successful in maintaining their skilled status when the technology in relation to which their skills were originally exercised had since disappeared. Indeed, some observers have argued that the ability of a group to define its labour as skilled owes as much to its ability to control the supply of labour as it does to the skills actually required to perform the tasks (Turner, 1962; Lee, 1981). Certainly, the skills required to perform the task are only one factor in determining the ability of groups to maintain their position in the labour market (Littler, 1982, Ch. 2; Manwaring and Wood, 1984).

In both countries, white-collar unions have been less effective in creating market shelters. This is partly because the bureaucratisation of white-collar work already provides the opportunity for career advancement and for market shelters, which are absent from a great deal of manual work. It is also because white-collar unions are dependent on state and employer recognition to facilitate their growth (Bain, 1970). In Britain this has encouraged the growth of white-collar unions, while in the USA the need for a majority of employees to vote in favour of a union before recognition is given, together with the more hostile attitudes of employers, has inhibited the growth of such unions (Mayhew, 1983, Ch. 3). There, management has been more active in creating alternative forms of shelter. In both countries the main function of white-collar unions remains largely confined to producing improvements in pay and career structures and consolidating shelters which large bureaucracies already provide.

For the semi-skilled and unskilled, the problems facing them in their attempts to erect shelters have been more formidable. Consequently it is among these groups that we find the highest levels of unemployment. Their unions could not depend on control over the supply of skill or training as a basis on which to build occupational internal labour markets. Instead they relied on highly centralised organisations that were more capable of handling a large turnover of members, to procure some control over the supply of labour (Turner, 1962). They organised workers who had no incentive to identify with a trade, who were doing routine, often physically demanding and boring work, workers whose requirements were for higher wages and better conditions. The strategy adopted by such unions varied in accordance with national and local conditions. In the USA industrial unions have directed all their energies to procuring the best deal they could from individual employers. This has produced lay-off agreements which provide some form of job security as workers laid off retain their seniority rights and are the first to be re-employed once rehiring starts (Schervish, 1983, pp.104–6). Research suggests that between 50 and 88 per cent of those laid off are re-hired.[11] Those without union protection are fired without any such rights.

In Britain the situation is very different. Unions operate more extensively on the political front. Many of their gains in terms of increasing job security and severance payments have been achieved by political action. Their economic actions have been primarily oriented to obtaining better pay and conditions, although the more extensive use of the closed shop has provided them with some protection against insecurity. One of the most significant effects of the closed shop is the potential it gives to workers to impose their own controls over the movement and allocation of labour within the plant. In its more extreme forms this can involve the union or worker representatives taking on the responsibility for the recruitment of labour and for its allocation between tasks.

Like management's labour market strategies, workers' strategies are fluid. Strong labour market shelters imposed on employers by the actions of professions or unions can be undermined by technological advance, changes in international competitiveness and the relocation of capital. Industries can disappear, as was the case with the British motorcycle industry, or be drastically reduced in size, as has been the fate of the iron and steel and shipbuilding industries (Williams, Williams and Thomas, 1982). As these industries decline, so too do the shelters they provide for certain groups of workers. New legislation on what are permissable tactics for unions to use, may either enhance or weaken the ability of unions and professions to protect their members against the threat and experience of unemployment. The shelters and the segmentation they create in the labour market are always contingent. They depend upon the underlying struggle between capital and labour, on the competition between employers in product markets and on the competition between groups of workers for access to jobs.

Access to Labour Market Shelters and Segments

Having examined the source of market shelters and segmentation, the next problem is to explain why some groups rather than others, obtain access to those segments which provide shelter against the threat of unemployment.

As a result of the high level of rewards and job security that accrue to those in the professions, management and better-paid manual occupations, there is always considerable competition for entry to those jobs. This upward pressure is sustained by an ideology which claims that occupational positions are open to competition and filled on the basis of merit. Thus, during times of full employment employees vacate the jobs in the secondary labour market as opportunities in the better-paid, more prestigious occupations open up. In the economic boom of the late 1950s and 1960s in Britain, this created a shortage of labour in the low-paid and less-skilled jobs into which immigrant labour was recruited (Braham, Rhodes and Pearn, 1981, sections 1 and 2).

A number of social mechanisms serve to regulate this competition. One of these is the system of education and certification. This functions to allocate those seeking entry to the labour market for the first time to different labour market segments. A second is the recruitment strategies adopted by employers. These strategies perform a gatekeeping function, determining who is recruited.

Education and certification
The function of the new educational system in allocating people to different parts of the occupational structure is well documented in the literature (Banks, 1975). In both societies the public or state educational system allocates people to the

middle and lower levels, with élite positions being filled by those from private educational establishments. Because of the resources required to purchase education in a private school—or as they are somewhat misleadingly termed in Britain, public schools—the children of the working class and large sections of the middle class are excluded. This ensures that the children of upper and upper-middle-class parents obtain the necessary forms of educational certification, and equally, if not more importantly, the necessary personality attributes (Mills, 1956, pp. 63–8; Scott, 1982, p. 162).

Research in Britain (Guttsman, 1968; Urry and Wakeford, 1973; Stanworth and Giddens, 1974) has established a clearly-defined route for the children of the upper class, through public schools to Oxbridge, with the graduates of these institutions moving into élite positions in politics, the civil service, finance and the larger companies. In the USA there is a similar pattern established by certain private schools and the Ivy League universities (Domhof, 1967). In an 'open' society it would be very difficult to restrict entry entirely to members of the upper class. Indeed, there is mobility into élite positions as new entrepreneurs emerge, and perhaps more commonly, as some of those in adjacent status groups succeed in gaining entry to élite positions later in life. In this respect a comparison of the evidence suggests that the USA is the more open of the two societies.

The ways in which the process of allocation operates at the middle and lower levels has been analysed by Bowles and Gintis (1976) in the USA, and Ashton and Field (1976) in Britain. In both societies it is the process of educational certification which provides the most important mechanism, linking a person's educational performance and adaptation to the educational system to their destination in a specific occupational segment (Gray *et al.*, 1983). As this is also related to their social origins, then the process of certification links a person's social origins to his/her occupational destination. Those from the lower working class encounter problems with the culture of the school and perform worse than those from the middle classes. Hence they either drop out of school or fail to obtain the educational certificates necessary for entry to the jobs in the professions, management or skilled manual work.

As a result they enter the lower occupational segments which, as we have seen, offer few if any shelters. Those from the middle classes adapt better to the culture of the school and obtain the forms of certification necessary for entry into the professions and other more sheltered occupations. The process is not always as determinate as this, for one of the advantages of depending on the process of educational certification is that it also allows for an element of fluidity in the process. Those children from the lower working class who adapt and perform well move up, while those from the middle classes who perform badly tend to move down. Once in the labour market the rate at which mobility occurs will depend to a large extent on the performance of the economy and its ability to generate jobs.[12]

Recruitment strategies

Our knowledge of employers' recruitment strategies is still relatively thin. However, it is clear that they operate in a different manner for those first entering the occupation on leaving school as opposed to those moving jobs with previous work experience. This distinction is not so important in the case of the higher professions, where, because of the extended period of education required in order to obtain the appropriate form of certification, almost all entry is direct from college or university.

With regard to those first entering the labour market, educational qualifications play a particularly important role as employers have few other means by which they can discriminate between candidates for jobs. Thus, for entry to many lower managerial, technical, administrative and other white-collar jobs, educational qualifications are used as a means of screening candidates. In the absence of prior work experience qualifications are also used to ensure that the candidates have the appropriate motivation and commitment to operate effectively in a bureaucratic environment. However, final decisions are usually made by recruitment officers on the basis of personality and attitudinal criteria (Ashton and Maguire, 1980; Maguire and Ashton, 1981; Hunt and Small, 1981). What they are looking for is people who have the 'right' attitude to work, who can show that they will work hard, have an interest in the company, will attend regularly, and be willing to subject themselves to industrial and commercial discipline. In addition they need to be able to 'fit in' with the work group. In the absence of previous work records employers look for indications of such traits or attributes in the appearance and performance of the candidates at interviews. For recruitment into the lower levels of the occupational hierarchy where competition is less intense educational qualifications are not so extensively used.[13] In Britain they play a part in the recruitment of young people into apprenticeships, but in both countries those responsible for recruitment at this level tend to rely almost exclusively on the personal attributes such as attitude and willingness to work as the basis on which to make decisions (Osterman, 1980, p.26; Ashton and Maguire, 1980).

When employers recruit school- or college-leavers they are usually recruiting labour either for its potential for training or for general labouring. When adults are recruited employers can realistically expect the person to have acquired some 'technical' skills and work experience. Consequently 'technical' criteria and the previous work record play a much more important part but personality characteristics associated with work motivation and compliance remain important.[14] In order to defend or protect the shelters of certain groups, employers, with union support, may exclude those without appropriate training, for example, by refusing to employ as a skilled man anyone without an apprenticeship training. In other instances they may exclude certain categories of worker as a means of safeguarding access to their internal markets (Osterman, 1980, pp.69–74). Thus, when employers recruit for jobs involving shift work, the most important criteria are often the attitudes of the worker to industrial discipline, and their acquisition of family responsibilities in the forms of children and financial debts. These personal circumstances ensure that the worker needs to maximise income and hence will attend regularly and perform well. In addition to differentiating the labour force in terms of skill and age employers' recruitment strategies also differentiate on the basis of sex and race. This means that women and blacks are often excluded from these more highly paid manual occupations where competition for entry is most intense.

Marginal groups and access to the 'secondary' sector

In those segments at the bottom of the status hierarchy where shelters are few, employers recruit labour which is cheaper to employ because its costs of social reproduction are lower or because it can be hired and fired at short notice. This usually means youths, women, blacks and older workers; groups which are frequently excluded from access to those segments which provide forms of market shelter. They are then confined to the 'secondary' jobs where the level of skill is low, wages minimal, and labour interchangeable. These are the groups which the very organisation of the labour market renders subject to high rates of unemployment.

Not all youth labour is seen as marginal. Where the job requires extensive training as in the case of many professional, technical and administrative and craft occupations the labour of youths has advantages. It is relatively cheap to employ, the person has not acquired the 'wrong' work habits and so can be easily trained in the ways of the company. In comparison to older workers, youths are seen as more adaptable. At the other extreme, there are some jobs for which employers regard the labour of youths as so marginal that they refuse to recruit them. This is the case in semi-skilled work where the employer looks for previous work experience, or where the employer cannot meet the costs of training young people or regards young people as irresponsible and unreliable, especially where the work may involve shifts or unsocial hours or is part of an internal labour market. Thus it is largely in unskilled work, where labour is virtually interchangeable and where a high labour turnover may be advantageous to the employer as in some retail and manufacturing firms, that the cheap labour of youths can be a distinct advantage (Osterman, 1980; Ashton, Maguire and Garland, 1982).

Not all types of female labour are seen as marginal. Many single women with training, and married women pursuing careers in nursing and teaching, have access to shelters (Dex, 1984). Employers perceive the labour of females are marginal when recruiting for full-time jobs in semi-skilled and unskilled work and for the growing number of part-time jobs. On a theoretical level there is considerable debate as to the sources of this marginality, whether it stems from the organisation of the process of production or from the women's role in the reproductive or domestic system (West, 1982), or from an interlocking of the two systems (Cockburn, 1983, pp.191–209; Westwood, 1984, pp.2–10). Empirically it is rooted in employers' beliefs about the characteristics of female labour as well as from the priority accorded by some women to their domestic commitments (Chaney, 1981). With regard to young females, the beliefs are slightly different, with many employers believing they will not stay in the labour force long enough to make an appreciable return on any investment in their training before leaving to start a family. For this reason young females in Britain are excluded from some career jobs. As for married women, many employers use women's domestic commitments as the reason for excluding them from sheltered jobs. However, when recruiting for boring, low-paid jobs such as those in the textile industry, women are seen to have advantages over men. Not only is their labour cheaper, but they are seen to be better able to cope with boredom and have greater manual dexterity (Ashton and Maguire, 1980a). The result of these pressures stemming from employers' beliefs and the domestic division of labour is the virtual segregation of large parts of the labour market, especially in the manual and service occupations. It has left a large and increasing proportion of them confined to low paid, part-time work (Wainwright, 1978; Gordon *et al.*, 1982, pp.204–6).

The marginality of blacks in both countries is of a different order to that of youths. Membership of the youth category is temporary simply because young people mature into adults. In the case of blacks it is based on a racist belief often shared by both employers and workers, in the inferiority of the group as a whole. In the USA this had its origin in their history as slaves and in the UK to the 'inferiority' of the black races supposedly 'civilised' by white colonial rule. In the USA there are similar beliefs about the inferiority of the various ethnic minorities such as the Poles, but these never became institutionalised to the same extent as do those about blacks. When such racist beliefs do become institutionalised the sources of exclusion involve not just employers through their recruitment policies but also unions and other white employees. In both societies the blacks moved in to fill the least desirable jobs as the white population vacated them.[15] Once in poorly-paid jobs with bad working conditions and insecure income the pressures of institutionalised racism have functioned to keep them there, creating for some a vicious circle of low-paid work, bad social conditions, poor educational performance and entry into 'secondary' employment (Braham, 1981; Gordon *et al.*, 1982, pp.206–10).

Racist beliefs are distinctive in that they also transcend skill differences. Thus, acquiring educational qualifications or technical skills is not sufficient to ensure that blacks have access to those segments for which such criteria are essential (Troyna and Smith, 1983). Neither is it possible for one section of the group to obtain access in order to ensure that other members follow. The battle against racism has to be fought in each separate employing organisation. Because of this ability to transcend other sheltering mechanisms, racist beliefs are one of the most powerful forms of discrimination that are operative in the allocation of labour to the various segments.

The marginality of older workers is also very different from that of the other groups. In some cases, as in those firms in the USA with seniority agreements, older workers are protected against dismissal through the operation of internal markets, lay-offs and dismissals are conducted on a last-in, first-out basis (Schervish, 1983, p.144). In other instances, where unions have not established seniority rights and when large-scale dismissals or redundancies are made, older workers may be particularly vulnerable (Casey and Bruche, 1983, p.1). However, the distinctive feature of the marginality of the older workers lay not in their particular vulnerability to dismissal or their concentration in low-paid, insecure occupations but in their particular difficulties in gaining re-entry to employment once they have lost their job.

Employers discriminate against them for a number of reasons. First and foremost, it is because of the tendency for a workers' productive capacity to decline with age; secondly, they are less able to adapt to new requirements imposed by technological change and thirdly, employers obtain a longer return from their investment in the training of younger workers. As a result of such policies it is estimated that vulnerability starts between the ages of 40 to 45 and considerably worsens between 55 and 65 (Casey and Bruche, 1983, pp. 1–4). For many in the latter group their premature expulsion from the labour market becomes a form of compulsory early retirement. Indeed, social policy and practice has increasingly been directed towards facilitating their exclusion from the labour market and into the socially acceptable role of 'early pensioner'.

This discussion has focused on some of the mechanisms involved in the process of allocation which function to exclude certain categories of labour from sheltered occupations, resulting in a far greater susceptibility to unemployment as part of their experience of the labour market. Thus, the social composition of the unemployed takes on distinctive characteristics, with certain categories such as youths, blacks, the old and the unskilled over-represented (Hawkins, 1984, pp. 37–8; Hill *et al.*, 1973). In this respect the workings of the labour market have exposed the same groups in both Britain and the USA to high levels of unemployment.

4. Changes in the Social Composition of the Unemployed

In this chapter we move on to examine changes in the social composition of the unemployed which take place over time. As unemployment levels rise there are three main changes which take place: the old, sick and unskilled are joined by workers from a wide range of industries and occupations so that the characteristics of the unemployed start to resemble more closely those of the employed; the long-term unemployed increase as a proportion of the total unemployed; and the proportion of youth increases. The decline of the old, sick and unskilled as a high proportion of the total unemployed is largely a product of the dynamics of the labour market; that is, changes in the rate and type of jobs which are created and destroyed. The growth of long-term unemployment is a product of the same forces, but differences in the proportion of the long-term unemployed in total unemployment in Britain and the USA indicate that differences in the institutional organisation of the labour market also play an important part. When it comes to explaining the growth of youth unemployment it is argued that both factors (labour market dynamics and the institutional arrangements) are important.

Labour Market Dynamics and Changes in the Composition of the Unemployed

As we saw in Chapter 3, at times of full employment the more marginal workers, such as the old and those with poor work records, are disproportionately represented among the unemployed. The ability of a society to maintain high levels of employment depends not just on attempts to preserve jobs—that is, to stop people becoming unemployed—but also on the rate at which new jobs are created.[1] We can understand this process by first comparing the record of Britain and the USA and then show by detailed examination the way in which the process of job-creation affects the flow of people into and out of unemployment.

Historically, the growth of jobs has been more rapid in the USA, as witnessed by the speed at which the process of industrialisation got underway. Starting later the USA quickly outstripped Britain in terms of both productive capacity and the speed at which jobs were created. Since the second world war American society has managed to continue creating jobs in sufficient numbers to match the growth in the labour force. As Figure 4.1 shows, during the last decade this process has slowed down but not to the same extent as in Britain. Until the 1970s job-creation in Britain managed to match the slower growth of the labour force. However, in the last decade not only has the rate of job-creation failed to match the rate of growth of the labour force but the number of jobs created has actually declined.

In the USA, Ginzberg (1979) estimates that between 1950 and 1976 the population of working age increased by 47 per cent. In the same period civilian employment expanded from 59 million to 87.5 million, a gain of 48 per cent. From 1973 to 1984 employment continued to expand. The impact of the recession has meant that net gains between 1979 and 1981 were approximately 1.6 million jobs, or 1.5 per cent, with only 1982 recording a fall (of 0.6 million) in the total number of jobs available. However, by 1983/84 employment was expanding again with the upturn in the business-cycle. For most of the recession America continued to produce a net increase in jobs, and at the end of it created sufficient new jobs, especially in the service sector (OECD, 1984a), to reduce unemployment significantly Figure 4.1.[2]

In Britain the situation has been very different. From 1973 to 1979 350,000 new jobs were created but this was less than half the increase in the labour force (see Figure 4.2). The effect of the recession has been to reduce dramatically the number of jobs, with a net loss of almost 2 million jobs or 7.3 per cent between 1979 and 1982. Moreover, in the recovery from the recession in 1983/84 the creation of additional jobs has not been sufficient to offset the increase in the labour force and unemployment continued to rise.

Our understanding of the effects of this failure to create jobs

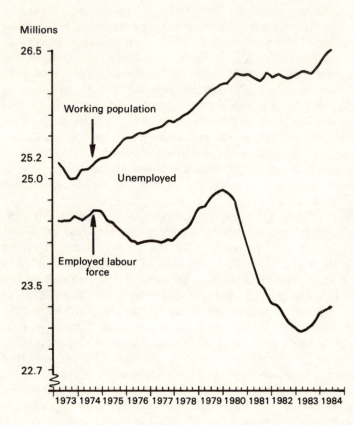

Figure 4.1: Working Population and Employed Labour Force in GB

Source: Employment Gazette vol. 92, no. 10 (October 1984).

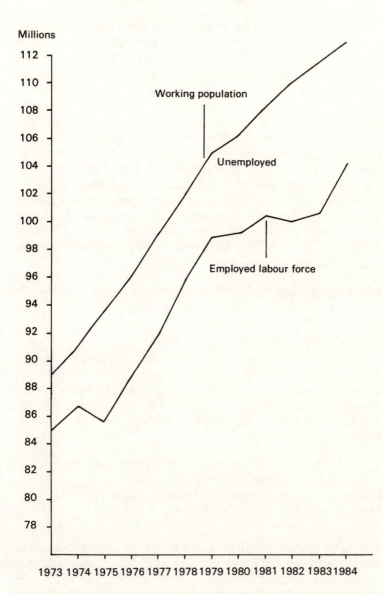

Figure 4.2: Working Population and Employed Labour Force, USA

Source: Statistical Abstract of the USA, US Dept of Commerce, Bureau of the Census, Table 624, *Monthly Labor Review.*

on the problem of unemployment has been furthered by the distinction between the stock of unemployed, the total number who are unemployed at any one point in time, and the flow, the movement of people into and out of unemployment. When this distinction is used to analyse unemployment it becomes clear that the increase in the total numbers unemployed is not necessarily due to an increase in the number of jobs lost. Despite the fact that this is generally seen as the cause of high rates of unemployment, it is only one factor. In both Britain and the USA a substantial part of the increase in the level of unemployment in the last recession is to be explained by the failure of the society to generate new jobs at the rate at which it had done in the past. As a result, those who were unemployed or who became unemployed found it more difficult to get back into work and so the average duration of unemployment increased.

Stocks and flows

Table 4.1: Stocks and Flows, Great Britain

	1973	1976[b]	1979	1982
Average monthly inflow	294000	365000	270000	344500
Average monthly outflow	309000	348000	273250	320000
Number unemployed[a]	486000	1371000	1200700	2984000
Percentage of labour force unemployed	2.1	5.7	5.1	12.5

a December stock figure.
b 1976 figures refer to average of ten months, January to October.
Source: Employment Gazette, various issues.

Table 4.1 shows the flows into and out of unemployment in Britain between 1973 and 1982. In 1973 the average monthly inflow was 294,000 and the average monthly outflow was 309,000 which produced an annual stock of 486,000 or 2.1 per cent of the labour force. In 1979 the average monthly flows were similar—an inflow of 270,000 and outflow of 273,250—yet by that time the total number unemployed had risen to 1,200,700 (or 5.1 per cent of the labour force), more than double the size of the stock in 1973. In the subsequent recession this balance between the inflow and outflow changed, the inflow rose in 1980/81 and the outflows remained relatively constant. The result was a large rise in the stock in 1981/82, after which the flows returned to their previous level. In 1982 with almost 3 million registered unemployed the inflow was less than it was in 1976.

The other change which is closely associated with changes in the size of the stock is the average duration of unemployment. In 1967 when the unemployed stock numbered just under $\frac{1}{2}$ million the average duration of unemployment for males was 7.1 weeks and for females 4.4 weeks. In 1977 when the stock figure was 1.3 million the average duration of spells had risen to 17.1 weeks for males and 11.2 weeks for women (Economic Policy Review, 1978, p.33). By 1983 when the numbers officially recorded as unemployed had risen to 3 million the mean average duration of uncompleted spells was 16 months for adult males and 12 months for females (OECD, 1984).

Rones (1984) has produced a similar analysis of inflows and outflows in the USA showing their significance in explaining the dramatic rise in long-term joblessness between 1979 and 1983. Since 1979 the average increase in the newly-unemployed (i.e. those unemployed less than five weeks) never exceeded 13 per cent in any year. Yet during the same period total unemployment rose by 74 per cent. Again the reason for the dramatic surge was the increase in the duration of unemployment, for the number of those jobless for more than six months more than trebled. The same pattern has occurred throughout the last seven recessions in the USA, although there has not been a comparable rise in inflows to that which took place in Britain between 1980 and 1982.

At the end of each recession Rones points to a lag before the fall in the rate of long-term unemployed takes place. This is because employers first stop laying off people and then recruit either those they have recently laid off, especially in the USA, or the short-term unemployed. This reduces the stock of unemployed but not that of the long-term unemployed. It typically requires a sustained period of recovery for the long-term unemployed to be able to find work. In the USA the recovery of 1983/84 was strong enough to achieve this. In Britain the combination of increases in the inflow between 1980/82 and a weak recovery in 1983/84, during which unemployment continued to rise, produced a continuous rise in the proportion of long-term unemployed.

Changes in the types of job created

Other factors which affect the composition of the unemployed are long-term changes in the occupational structure. There are significant differences between the types of job being lost and those being created. Two major interrelated processes have been at work: (i) the decline of manufacturing industry; and (ii) the growth of the service sector. Table 4.2 illustrates these changes.

The decline of manufacturing industry

As we noted earlier, industrialisation involved the transfer of a large part of the working population from agriculture to manufacturing industry. In recent years this pattern has changed as the proportion of the labour force employed in manufacturing industry fell. In both societies this started in the 1950s although in the USA it became particularly evident after 1967 (Urquhart, 1984).

The causes of this fall are not fully understood. It may be related to the relocation of capital in labour-intensive industries to low labour-cost countries (Jordon, 1982) together with the kind of quantum shifts in productivity to which Jones (1982) refers. Whatever the causes, it is now possible to sustain a high level of output of manufactured goods by employing only a relatively small proportion of the working population.

The growth of the service sector

In occupational terms the increase in jobs has been in the professional, scientific and business services, community services and the leisure industries. This growth has not been uniform throughout the service sector, but has been spread across three broad functional areas: producer services, such as business services and finance; social services, such as health, education and welfare; and distributive services, such as eating, drinking and leisure establishments (Gershuny and Miles,

Table 4.2: Distribution of Employees in Employment, Britain and USA

	1973[a]	1979[a]	1983[a]
USA			
Agriculture	4	4	4
Manufacturing	25	23	20
Mining	1	1	1
Construction	5	5	4
Total industry	31	29	25
Wholesale & retail	21	22	22
Transport & public utilities	6	6	5
Finance, insurance	5	5	6
Government (federal, state, local)	17	17	17
Other services	16	18	21
Total services	65	68	71

	1973[b]	1979[a]	1983[a]
Great Britain			
Agriculture, forestry and fishing	2	2	2
Manufacturing	34	31	26
Coal, oil & gas extraction	2	2	2
Construction	6	5	5
Total industry	42	38	33
Wholesale, retail, hotel, catering & repairs	18	18	20
Transport, postal services, tele-communications, electricity & gas	8	8	8
Banking & finance	5	7	9
Public administration	19	21	22
Other services	6	6	6
Total services	56	60	65

a Annual averages.
b June figures.
Source: Percentages calculated from *National Institute Economic Review,* November 1984, Table 8. 'Some aspects of labour markets in Britain and the United States'.

1983). In both societies the state has played an important part in this process. In Britain the growth of jobs in the health service, educational provision and the social services in the 1960s and 1970s helped offset the jobs lost in manufacturing until the cuts in state expenditure in the mid-1970s. Since 1979 some jobs have been created in retail and distribution as well as in finance and other services.

In the USA the growth of federal, state and local government spending on health, education and welfare created a similar if less dramatic expansion of public sector jobs. In the period 1950–76 Ginzberg (1979) estimated that the employment growth rate of government at all levels was 150 per cent, second only to the other service industries, although the main source of public sector jobs has been at the state and local levels where the numbers trebled between 1950 and 1976. Since 1979 the increase in employment in the USA has been absorbed by private sector services where the biggest increases were in finance and 'other' services (Urquhart, 1984).

This shift from manufacturing to service sector employment is important because it involves the creation of different types of jobs.[3] In both societies it has meant the loss of full-time, higher-paid jobs and the growth of part-time, low-paid jobs. Ginzberg refers to these as 'good' and 'bad' jobs, respectively. Using earnings as an indication of 'good' jobs which have high earnings, opportunities for promotion, regularity of work, etc. he concluded that in the USA

between 1950 and 1976 about two and a half-times as many new jobs were added in industries that provided below average weekly earnings as were added in industries that provided above-average earnings. More than three out of every five new jobs created in the past 26 years have been in the retail trade or services where many jobs are part-time and wages are traditionally low. (Ginzberg, 1977, p.47).

The same process has been happening in Britain, where between 1970 and 1981 a net loss of 1 million jobs was recorded in manufacturing. These were in the traditional manufacturing industries such as engineering, textiles and shipbuilding where the jobs lost were full-time jobs, usually filled by males. In contrast, the new jobs that were created in the service sector, of which there were approximately $1\frac{1}{2}$ million, were primarily part-time jobs filled by married women. Clark (1982) shows that two-thirds of these new jobs were part-time and were concentrated in three industrial orders: miscellaneous services, distributive trades and professional, and scientific services. This points to a process common to a number of advanced industrial societies in which full-time relatively well-paid jobs in manufacturing are declining and are being replaced largely but not exclusively by low-paid, part-time jobs in the service sector.[4] The difference between the two societies is in the balance they have achieved between jobs lost and jobs gained. In Britain the loss of full-time jobs extended over a longer period of time (OECD, 1984).

Consequences for the composition of the unemployed

This change in the character of the jobs being generated does, of course, have implications for the composition of the labour force and the unemployed. Older men are finding it increasingly difficult to sustain their attachment to work. American and British males in their late forties and early fifties are increasingly being ejected from the labour force. On the other hand, there has been a dramatic rise in the proportion of female workers. Female activity rates have increased as women have moved into the labour market to fill the new part-time jobs. Thus, in Britain, female participation has increased from 37.5 per cent in 1961 to 59 per cent in 1980 (OECD, 1984). Similar increases have occurred in the USA. In terms of its consequences for unemployment, it has meant that as manufacturing industry continued to shed jobs in the 1983 'upturn', adding more male workers to the unemployment register, the new jobs in the service sector were continuing to attract women into the labour force. These changes also affect the outflow from long-term unemployment. Thus, White (1983) found that adult females were more likely to leave the ranks of the long-term unemployed than males but to do so they had to accept part-time jobs in the service sector.

The other group to have been drawn into the labour force by the attraction of part-time work have been college students, although as will be shown later, this is primarily an American phenomenon. In the UK in 1975 0.5 per cent of workers under 20 years were part-timers compared with 25.5 per cent in the

USA (OECD, 1983). Nevertheless, in both societies the results of these changes have been to transform the character of paid employment. The USA data for 1982 show that those who worked full-time, all year constituted only 55 per cent of the labour force (Flaim, 1984). It is no longer appropriate to think of paid work as constituting a full-time, all-year job.

These long-term changes in the occupational structure have a number of other consequences for the composition of the unemployed. First, as more women are drawn into the labour market so unemployment among women, especially married women, becomes identified as more of a problem (Sorrentino, 1981). In the USA the same is true of college students. Secondly, during severe recessions these underlying structural changes in the occupational structure tend to be accelerated, and this also affects the composition of the unemployed (Gershuny and Miles, 1983, pp.65–9). For example, in the 1979/82 recession we have seen a major contraction of certain basic manufacturing industries such as steel and textiles. As this occurred, traditional market shelters were destroyed and large groups of prime-age males entered the ranks of the unemployed (Hawkins, 1984).

The effects of these changes have recently been documented in the studies by both White (1983) and Rones (1984). In his analysis of the long-term unemployed in Britain White distinguishes three groups at risk: (i) young people with a history of recurrent unemployment. These tend to have been in unskilled and semi-skilled jobs in the lower occupational segments, frequently having left such jobs because of the boredom or poor pay and then finding it difficult to get other employment in a contracting labour market. Any jobs they do eventually get tend to be short-term in small establishments, often terminated by redundancy. (ii) 'established workers', who fall straight into long-term unemployment from long-lasting jobs. They are generally older workers who have been in white-collar or skilled manual work, who enter the ranks of the unemployed through redundancy or ill-health. Once unemployed there is a strong tendency for those over 55 to give up trying for work, especially if they have an occupational pension. This often represents a psychological reconciliation with long-term unemployment which is less traumatic for those over 55 than for those in their forties. (iii) 'occupationally downgraded', these are the casualties of structural change in the manufacturing industries. They tend to come from those industries in long-term structural decline and, once having moved out of the industry, find it difficult to obtain other skilled work. Their skills are redundant and so the only jobs they can find tend to be unskilled, which are insecure and often lead to unemployment. As White's sample were drawn from the unemployed in 1980 before the increase in unemployment which took place in 1981 we would expect the long-term unemployed in 1984/85 to be even more representative of the working population. Thus, youths with a history of job-hopping would be joined by those with no experience of full-time paid employment, and adults from industries in structural decline would move straight into the ranks of the unemployed directly they were made redundant.

In his study of long-term unemployment Rones has shown quite clearly how changes in the industrial distribution of jobs that occurred in the 1979–83 recession had similar effects on the composition of the long-term unemployed in the USA. As the figures for June 1979 show, (in Table 4.3) there was little difference among industries in the USA in the probability of a worker becoming unemployed for any length of time. As the recession bit, substantial differences emerged in the long-term unemployment situation among industry groups. Those manufacturing industries most susceptible to either long-term structural decline or the fluctuations of the business-cycle shed labour, increasing the incidence of long-term unemployment among the prime-age males who form half of their labour force. The effects of this can be seen in the figures for June 1983. While about 4 per cent of the labour force had been unemployed for at least 15 weeks in June 1983, more than 7 per cent of the construction and durable goods labour force had reached that level. In primary metals, which is largely steel, each worker was nearly 20 times as likely to be jobless for 15 or 27 weeks as four years earlier. In trade and finance which are not as badly affected by recessions, and where males form a smaller proportion of the labour force, the effects on a worker's chances of being subject to long-term unemployment are less severe.

Table 4.3: The Effects of Recession on Long-term Unemployment in the USA

	Unemployed 15 weeks or longer % of labour force		Unemployed 27 weeks or longer % of labour force	
	June 1979	June 1983	June 1979	June 1983
Total	1.0	3.9	0.5	2.5
Construction	1.6	7.0	0.5	4.2
Manufacturing	1.3	6.4	0.6	4.5
durable goods	1.3	7.5	0.6	5.3
primary metals	0.8	14.0	0.5	11.4
autos	1.3	8.4	0.5	6.7
non-durable goods	1.3	4.9	0.5	3.4
Trade	1.0	3.8	0.4	2.1
Finance	0.8	2.4	0.4	1.5

Source: Adapted from Rones, *Monthly Labor Review,* 1984.

One further effect of an increase in the proportion of prime-age workers entering the ranks of the unemployed is to produce a change in the definition of what constitutes a marginal worker. As Sinfield (1981a, pp.140–2) has pointed out, at times of full employment in the 1960s, employers encouraged older workers to stay on, special arrangements were made by firms, including the provision of nursery facilities, to encourage women to return to work, ramps and machines were installed to enable disabled and handicapped workers to participate, language training was provided for foreign workers and probation officers used to recruit those coming out of prison. As unemployment increases, these workers become marginal, as do those who may otherwise be regarded as non-compliant (young people) or unadaptable (older people).

Long-term Unemployment and the Institutional Regulation of the Labour Market

When the rate at which a society creates jobs starts to slow down and unemployment levels rise, the long-term unemployed start to increase as a proportion of all the unemployed. The major factor in explaining the growth of long-term unemployment is the rate at which jobs are created. Yet the comparison of the long-term unemployed in the two societies (Table 4.4) reveals that they always form a larger proportion of the unemployed in Britain than in the USA. For example, those unemployed for 12 months or over formed 13.3 per cent of the total in the USA in 1983 compared with 36.2 per cent in Britain.

Table 4.4: Proportion of Long-term Unemployed (12 months or over) in Total Unemployment

	1973	1975	1977	1979	1980	1981	1982	1983
Great Britain	26.9	13.7	19.8	24.5	19.0	21.6	33.3	36.2
USA	3.3	5.3	7.2	4.2	4.3	6.7	7.7	13.3

Source: Amended from OECD (1983), Table 24; OECD (1984), Table 4, p.107.

Table 4.5: Percentage of Total Unemployed of Less than Five Weeks Duration

	1973	1975	1979	1981	1982	1983	1984
Great Britain	22.2	30.7	14.4	11.7	8.6	9.7	9.6
USA	51.0	37.0	48.1	41.7	36.4	33.3	43.4

Source: Adapted from *National Institute Economic Review*, November, 1984.

Such differences stretch back over at least ten years; in 1973 when the rate was lower in Britain than in the USA, the long-term unemployed still formed a much higher proportion in Britain. At the other end of the spectrum these differences are reflected in the proportion of the short-term unemployed, those with less than five weeks duration (Table 4.5). This remains much higher in the USA, even when the overall level of unemployment rises. Whereas this group represent less than 10 per cent of the unemployed in Britain in 1984, in the USA they formed over 40 per cent. This suggests that a much higher proportion are moving between jobs in the USA.

This interpretation is also consistent with data on job tenure which show that while both countries have a high labour turnover, which coexists with a high degree of relatively permanent job attachment, they differ in the proportion of the labour force with short-term jobs. The USA generates a high turnover in the form of short-term jobs, while in Britain there is a lower probability of the worker leaving in the first few years (OECD, 1984, Ch. 4). It suggests that the proportion of the labour force in Britain with some form of job security is higher than in the USA which has a much larger 'secondary' sector. This interpretation is further supported by data on the proportion of the total labour force who become unemployed. In Britain, the 1976 and 1977 *General Household Surveys* recorded that 10 per cent of men had experienced some unemployment in the previous twelve months, twice the proportion of those unemployed when interviewed. In the USA the proportion with some unemployment experience is between two and three times as large as those unemployed when interviewed (Sinfield, 1981).[5] Unemployment is a more common experience in the USA.

A second difference is in the distribution of unemployment. Chapter 3 showed that it is unevenly distributed in both societies but in Britain it is more heavily concentrated among the lower paid (Smee, 1980).

Research in Britain suggests that those entering unemployment have not spent long in their previous jobs—$2\frac{1}{2}$ years compared with the average of $9\frac{1}{2}$ years for all workers (Stern, 1982; OECD, 1984, p.66). Another study sponsored by the Manpower Services Commission found that of those who had moved back into work within ten months, 62 per cent had lost or changed their initial jobs after a further ten months and 40 per cent had worked in two or more jobs. Moreover those who found jobs within a month of becoming unemployed were just as likely to be out of work again after 20 months as those who took five months to find a job. The reasons for this impermanence are instructive, for they show the unemployed often taking jobs for negative reasons, that is, because it was better than being out of work, or because there was no better work and for this reason they were more likely to accept short term contracts, casual or seasonal work (*Labour Market Quarterly*, February 1983, p.5). Thus, if they were not already in short-term jobs, once they became unemployed they tended to get locked into low-paid, insecure jobs in the lower segments of the labour market. Such workers find it difficult to enter long-term stable jobs.

One possibility these findings suggest is that the institutional regulation of the labour market is more extensive in Britain than the USA. There it would appear a higher proportion of jobs are characterised by a higher turnover of labour and more open access than in Britain, and this would partly account for the lower proportion of long-term unemployed as unemployment is shared out among a larger proportion of the labour force. However, before moving on to explore this possibility we need to exercise some caution in interpreting the statistics because differences in the method of collection may account for some of the variance. During a recession American firms tend to lay off workers who then register as unemployed, but they may be taken on again when demand revives. British firms tend to adopt short-time working which means that the workers in Britain do not appear on the register as part of the short-term unemployed. Secondly, American workers who become discouraged from looking for work are not counted as unemployed whereas in Britain they tend to continue with their registration, a practice which is likely to influence the figures.[6] However, the magnitude of the difference still suggests that the problem of long-term unemployment is far more serious in Britain than in the USA.

The institutional regulation of the labour market
The term institutional regulation refers to the powers of the state, employers, professional organisations and unions to determine the movement of labour within the labour market and the conditions under which it is bought and sold. There are a number of reasons for suggesting that this may produce differences in the pattern of unemployment in the two societies. In Britain we have already seen how the more widespread influence of trade unions, the greater legal regulation of the labour market and the extensive powers of professional

associations produce a more wideranging set of controls. These provide a greater security to those already in work, reducing labour turnover and thereby making it more difficult for those out of work to obtain re-entry. In the USA the area of the labour market where the movement of labour is closely regulated (the primary sector) is much smaller, hence the barriers to re-entry are less extensive permitting easier access to a larger part of the labour market by the unemployed.

One way of measuring the extent of union influence in the labour market is through union density, that is union membership expressed as a percentage of the potential membership (Price and Bain, 1983), or more loosely as a percentage of the labour force. The differences between the two countries can be seen in Table 4.6.

Table 4.6: Union Density in Britain and USA

	1911	1921	1931	1941	1951	1961	1971	1976	1980	1983
Britain	17.7	33.8	24.0	37.5	45.0	44.0	48.7	51.9	53.6	52.0*
USA	9.3	15.5	8.6	19.5	29.6	26.4	25.9	25.3	21.3*	—

*The estimate for the USA is derived from data in the *Statistical Abstract of the United States* (1982/83), Tables 624 and 682; and Bureau of Labor Statistics. For Britain the estimate is derived from data in the *Employment Gazette* (February 1985).
Source: Bain and Price (1980), Tables 2.1 and 2.3; and Price and Bain (1983).

The outstanding feature is that this is twice as high in Britain as in the USA and that these differences persist over time. In both countries union membership fell in the depression of the 1930s and this has also occurred in the latest depression. What is not evident from the table is the fact that the British figure of 53.6 for 1980 represents a fall from the high of 55.4 in 1979.

When the figures are disaggregated they reveal interesting and important differences in the location of union influence within the labour market. In both societies union density is high among manual workers in the private manufacturing sector where in Britain in 1979 it reached a peak of 80.3 per cent. In their study of the closed shop Hanson *et al.* (1982)

identify a number of industries in both societies which are characterised by a high degree of union density—printing, docks, shipping, entertainment, steel, coalmining and construction. Yet, as we have seen, these are in the part of the economy where jobs are being lost. In white-collar work, where jobs are increasing, the experience of the two countries diverge significantly. In Britain white-collar workers have been extensively unionised since the second world war, although union growth has not been as rapid as the overall growth of white-collar jobs. Nevertheless, by 1979 white-collar workers formed 40.3 per cent of total union membership in Britain. The experience of American unions has been very different, for while British unions were making successful recruitment drives among white-collar workers in the early 1970s the American unions were making little headway. Thus, in 1972 when Britain had 27 per cent of white-collar workers in the private sector in trades unions, the comparable figure for America in 1973 was only 9 per cent. Similarly, in the public sector, the British trade unions have had considerable success in organising employees. In 1972 85 per cent were in unions. In the USA the unions were far less successful and by 1973 had organised only 28 per cent (Mayhew, 1983, p.43). However by 1976 about one-half of all states and local government employees were in unions or associations (Hanson 1982, p.181). In the latter part of the 1970s American unions had more success but by 1979 white-collar workers still formed only 18.7 per cent of total union membership in the USA, which is less than half the corresponding figure for Britain.

As well as differences in the extent of union influence the institutional regulation of the labour market is affected by differences in the form of union influence; these affect both the structure of the internal labour market and the range of issues covered by collective bargaining. In the USA this is important in determining the kind of security which access to the job provides. As we have seen union development in Britain led to the creation of a large number of craft unions, although amalgamations in recent years have reduced their numbers. With each union claiming jurisdiction over its own craft the result is many different unions operating across a variety of industries and organisations. Thus, the electricians' union represents its members not just in the electrical engineering industry, but in mechanical engineering firms, car plants, food processing plants and in the health service. It has been estimated (McKersie and Hunter, 1973) that such craft unions represent about 25 per cent of British workers. this means that there are relatively few industries where internal markets can provide for a single career ladder for all manual employees. Indeed attempts to impose uniform internal markets have been a relatively recent development in Britain. Thus ICI, one of the largest employers, only negotiated their introduction into its chemical division in the 1960s. In their absence the various grades of worker, unskilled, semi-skilled and the skilled trades each negotiated their own terms and conditions independently of the other workers (Owen, 1979). As a result the internal market is fragmented and may consist of a number of separate markets for each group of workers.

In the USA the craft unions were smaller and only represented about 10 per cent of the union members. They were more exclusive than their British counterparts and failed to organise the new industrial workers; consequently the unionisation of industrial workers in the 1930s was left to the industrial unions. This, together with managements' attempts to stabilise employee relations, led to the earlier development of more comprehensive internal labour markets which provide career progression through all grades of unskilled and semi-skilled work. In addition internal markets were not confined to unionised firms for some employers had imposed them in an attempt to keep unions out. Thus, although union influence is less extensive this has not meant that internal markets are absent from larger firms.[7]

The scope of collective bargaining is much broader in the USA. The early development of internal markets has meant a greater concern with transfers, lay-offs, promotions and the part played by seniority on such occasions. The absence of extensive state welfare provisions has also produced a greater concern with health and pension insurance. Thus those workers in industries or occupations in which they are supported by unions or have access to internal markets tend to have a wide range of benefits.

Table 4.7 details the distribution of two such benefits,

pension and health plans. It shows the importance of occupation in the provision of such security and the effect of unions, professions and internal markets. It also highlights the plight of a large proportion of workers who lack any of these forms of protection, such as farmworkers, service workers, labourers and sales workers. It illustrates what Freedman (1976) argues is the main worry of American workers, namely security, health and safety hazards on the job, and not being able to pay bills in the event of illness.

Table 4.7: Employees with Employer or Union-Provided Pension Plans or Group Health Plans by Occupation, USA, 1980

	% with pension plans	% with health plans
Professional & technical	63.5	74.8
Managers & administrators	55.2	78.8
Sales workers	28.3	47.7
Clerical & kindred	45.1	61.4
Craft & kindred	55.0	76.1
Operatives	49.3	72.3
Transport operatives	46.0	67.7
Labourers	30.7	46.9
Service workers	23.0	34.0
Farmworkers	5.7	18.1

Source: Statistical Abstract of the United States (1982/83), Table 676.

The third aspect of institutional regulation is the extent of legal regulation of the conditions of labour. In Britain the Health and Safety at Work Act 1974 extended safeguards for workers and the power of workers representatives in the workplace. The Contracts of Employment Act 1963 made written contracts, with certain minimum conditions specified, compulsory; the Employment Protection Act 1975 gave certain categories of workers protection against unfair dismissal and the Redundancy Payments Act 1965 made severance payments obligatory for certain categories of long-service employees. In addition, legislation on equal pay, and race relations, have imposed further regulations on the behaviour of employers in hiring labour. All these were in addition to the earlier regulation of wages in a limited number of industries through the Wages Councils. Although some of the rights given to workers were subsequently amended by the Conservative governments of 1979 and 1983 and some Wages Councils were abolished, the principle of state regulation has not been abandoned.

In the USA the attempts by the federal government to regulate these aspects of labour market behaviour have been far more limited. The Occupational Safety and Health Act 1970 gave the federal government authority to set and enforce safety and health standards for most of the country's workers, although this has been weakened by the action of the Reagan administration. Civil rights legislation has also placed regulations on the behaviour of employers to control discrimination but outside these measures, and minimum wage legislation, there is nothing equivalent to the British Employment Protection, Contracts of Employment or Redundancy Payments Acts that are uniformly enforced throughout the USA. In practice this means that employers have a much greater range of discretion and control over their hiring and firing practices. However, the range of discretion available to the employer does vary from state to state. In some states, notably those in the 'sun belt', 'right to work' legislation has weakened the power of unions to influence the employment contract, giving management still wider powers. In other states, legislation comparable to some of the British Acts have been passed, regulating the behaviour of employers in fields such as employment discrimination, equal pay for jobs of comparable worth, mandatory retirement requirements and aid to workers and communities facing mass lay-offs or plant closures (Nelson, 1984). As we have seen the decentralised form of legal regulation of the labour market is also a characteristic of the state's licensing activities. In so far as licensing is an important means of regulating hiring decisions, the degree of regulation can be seen to vary markedly from one state to another. When compared with Britain it leaves fewer areas of labour market behaviour regulated.

To summarise, these differences in the institutional regulation of the labour market affect the form of market shelters and segments in a number of ways. In Britain the broader union base gives a greater proportion of workers union protection, especially in the field of wages but also, through institutions such as the closed shop, over hiring practices. However, once in a job, internal markets are more fragmented and the possibilities of career mobility based on seniority within the firm are more restricted. For those workers who are not unionised but in full-time work, the legal system provides some form of constraints on employers' hiring and firing practices as well as of working conditions. These are not usually as extensive as those provided by unions but in those areas where the unions are weak, as in the service industries, they are important in providing a uniform base-line which governs the conditions under which labour is hired and fired. This means that the only groups of workers without some form of protection are part-time and casual workers, youths, and others on short-term contracts or recently employed. These are to be found in construction, distribution, catering, cleaning and the leisure industry. However the tendency is for this group to increase in size. This is partly because of the structural changes in the economy we noted earlier. It is also a product of the political action of the governments of 1979 and 1983 as they 'rolled back' the legal regulations which provide security of employment. However, for all workers the existence of a national health service removes the insecurity associated with ill-health. The result is a market that is segmented but in which the difference between groups of full-time workers in the hiring and firing practices, conditions at work and in the possibility of redress against arbitrary management is one of degree rather than kind. The major division between those with protection and those without is between permanent full-time workers and the growing numbrs of short-term and part-time workers.

In the USA the pattern of segmentation is very different. First, the narrow union base, the restricted federal legislation regulating the hiring and firing of workers and the differences between states in their labour legislation and licensing activities, mean that the institutional regulation of the labour market is decentralised. The national market lacks the uniformity exhibited in Britain and is better seen as a mosaic of separate markets in which there are considerable differences between the various states. Secondly, the dividing line between those workers who have regulated conditions of hiring and firing and career prospects and those who do not is drawn at different points in the labour market. The American workers who are protected in this way, either through employer-created internal markets or union negotiated regulations, constitute a much smaller proportion of the labour force than in Britain. Again they tend to be concentrated among manual workers in manufacturing, construction and transport and certain groups of white-collar workers. Unlike the British workers, they tend to have long career ladders, in which seniority is a more important criterion for advancement. Yet, there remain large groups of full-time workers in both the manufacturing and service sectors who do not have this form of protection and for whom the state provides variable (depending upon which state the worker is in) but limited regulation. Thirdly, because protection against ill-health is not universally provided by the state and is largely confined to those occupations to which access is subject to regulation, this tends to amplify the differences between workers in the different segments. It is precisely this combination of factors which gives the idea of a basic duality in the labour market much greater force in American society than in Britain, where protection is more extensive and the differences between workers are less marked. However, the cost of that greater security for those in work in Britain is that those in the more insecure jobs share a greater burden of unemployment and find it more difficult to re-enter work once they are unemployed. The result is that a higher proportion are confined to the ranks of the unemployed. In the USA the evidence suggests that that insecurity is shouldered by a larger section of the labour force, who find it easier to re-enter work but for whom the insecurity of the labour market is a more serious threat than it is in Britain.

Youth Unemployment

Like the problem of long-term unemployment, that of youth unemployment is primarily caused by the failure of society to create sufficient jobs. As the level of unemployment rises, youth unemployment gets progressively worse (see Table 4.8).

However the way in which it manifests itself in the two societies is very different because of differences in the institutional regulation of the labour market and the educational systems. Youth unemployment was a problem in the USA long before it was defined as such Britain. These differences require clarification before we consider the question of the underlying causes.

Table 4.8: Youth and Adult Unemployment

	USA			Great Britain (adjusted to US concepts)		
	All working ages	Under 25	25 and over	All working ages	Under 25	25 and over
1960	5.5	11.2	4.4	1.9	2.4	1.7
1970	4.9	11.0	3.3	3.9	5.9	3.3
1974	5.6	11.8	3.6	3.1	5.2	2.6
1975	8.5	16.1	6.0	4.6	10.9	3.1
1976	7.7	14.7	5.5	6.0	13.7	4.1
1977	7.0	13.6	4.9	6.3	14.3	4.4
1978	6.0	12.2	4.0	6.2	14.3	4.2
1979	5.8	11.7	3.9	5.6	12.2	3.8
1980	7.1	13.9	5.1	7.0	16.1	4.6
1981	7.6	14.9	5.4	10.5	21.4	7.6
1982	9.7	17.8	7.4	11.9	23.7	8.6
1983	9.6	17.2	7.5	—	—	—

Source: Bureau of Labor Statistics, Supplement to Bulletin 2098, (October 1984).

The USA has experienced relatively high rates of youth unemployment throughout the post-war period, whereas in Britain high rates are a more recent phenomenon (see Table 4.8). In the US teenage unemployment rates (16–19-year-olds) were particularly high, rising from 13–15 per cent to 19 per cent in 1976 (Sorrentino, 1981a). This led some authorities to view it as a structural problem especially as it did not appear to respond to the usual Keynesian cure of increasing aggregate demand, that is, teenage unemployment rates remained high even when the general level of unemployment fell. In Britain the situation was very different, for although teenage (16–19-year-olds) and youth (16–24-year-olds) rates were higher than those for adults, the general level of unemployment was so low in the post-war period that youth unemployment did not constitute a separate problem (Casson, 1979). Young people had considerable discretion in choosing jobs on entering the labour market (Carter, 1962; Maizels, 1970). The first signs of a problem occurred in the late 1960s (Department of Employment, 1974). In 1975 youth unemployment rates started to soar (Table 4.8) and by the late 1970s surpassed those found in the USA.

In terms of its share of total unemployment in 1979, youth, while forming only about a quarter of the US labour force, came to account for almost a half of total unemployment. In Britain two-fifths of the unemployed were youths who accounted for only one-fifth of the labour force (Sorrentino, 1981a). Britain, along with some other European societies, started to experience the distinctive problems of youth unemployment.

Youth unemployment in the USA

There are a number of reasons why the US has experienced a long-term structural problem of youth unemployment. First, it has experienced a rapid growth over the last two decades in the youth labour force, both teenagers and young adults. This moderated in the latter part of the 1970s, and in 1979 the teenage labour force decreased in size. Secondly, and perhaps more importantly, the method of collecting statistics in the USA has led to the conflation of two very different types of young unemployed. One group consists of those still engaged in education, the working student, which is very much an American phenomenon. They combine part-time or casual work with their education and because 80 per cent of those 18 and under are still enrolled in educational institutions, this constitutes a sizeable group, which is characterised by considerable movement into and out of work. When their vacation period unemployment and in-school unemployment are combined, these students serve to increase the annual youth unemployment rate. This may help to explain the very high rates experienced by young people in the USA in the 1960s and 1970s (Sorrentino, 1981a).

The other group are the high school drop-outs, who seek full-time work in the secondary labour market. In view of the larger size of this market in the US and the unstable character of the jobs it contains, high rates of unemployment are to be expected (Osterman, 1980), and it is here that the main problem of youth unemployment is located. Thus in a recent study of youth unemployment Freeman and Wise (1982) found that unemployment was largely concentrated among a small group who lacked work for extended periods of time. On the basis of 1976 data they report that over half of male teenage unemployment was among those who were out of work for over six months, a group constituting less than 10 per cent of the youth labour force and 7 per cent of the youth population. This group was drawn disproportionately from the high school drop-outs, those in poverty and the blacks. It was this core group which expanded during the 1979/82 recession (Urban Institute, 1984).

This puts the American problem of youth unemployment in perspective. For, in spite of the high rate of youth unemployment that was officially recorded, most of the unemployed were either in school or had just left, and, hence were either people for whom work was a secondary activity or those who had just started to search for full-time work. Thus a part of the exceptionally high level of youth unemployment in the USA is a function of the way in which unemployment is measured. This is not to deny the financial hardship caused to young people who cannot secure part-time work. However, their problem does mask the more serious concentration of long-term unemployment among disadvantaged youth in general and blacks in particular. A number of studies report that, while whites form a majority of the longer-term unemployed, their position in the labour market has not deteriorated over time as has that of blacks (Adams and Mangum, 1973; Osterman, 1980; Freeman and Wise, 1982; Urban Institute, 1984). Indeed, while the proportion of black youths with jobs has fallen that of white youths with jobs has not. This situation cannot be accounted for merely by the increasing numbers of blacks staying on at school. The position of the black American school-leaver is getting worse. It appears that while most of the white high school drop-outs leave the secondary market on reaching adulthood, many blacks remain confined to it and to prolonged periods of unemployment by the forces of racial discrimination.

Youth unemployment in Great Britain

Problems of measurement also distort the official British figures on youth unemployment, although this problem is not as great as it is in the USA. Some of those who remain in school and college do participate in the labour market (Ashton *et al.,* 1985), but there is a strong convention which regards education as a full-time activity and serves to inhibit part-time work. Moreover, because unemployment is not measured by a census, those who are looking for work while at college are not included. Only those who have left full-time education and registered at the benefit office are counted.[8] In comparison with the American figures, the British figures underestimate the extent of youth unemployment. However, even after allowing for this the British rate of youth unemployment was still very low in the 1960s and early 1970s.

One possible reason for this low rate in Britain is that the size of the British youth labour force declined between 1960 and 1965 when unemployment was low. It rose again in 1975–79 when unemployment increased (Sorrentino, 1981a). However, changes in labour supply are at best only a contributory factor, and their explanatory potential is limited, for, on closer examination, it appears that the growth in the youth labour force peaked in 1979, before the onset of the very high levels of unemployment which characterised the latest recession in Britain. A more important reason was the relatively smaller size of the secondary or 'unregulated' sector of the labour force in Britain. In the 1960s and early 1970s a high proportion of 15 and 16-year-old school-leavers were entering apprenticeships and white-collar occupations where the rates of job movement are lower. The ease with which school-leavers obtained work in that period shows how, even with an extensive system of institutional regulation, the labour market was capable of absorbing the more 'marginal' youth labour, given a sufficiently high level of aggregate demand.

It was not until the late 1970s when the overall rate of unemployment rose dramatically that youth unemployment became a serious political problem. Until 1979 youth unemployment was largely confined to the unqualified school-leavers entering the smaller 'secondary' sector who experienced periodic spells of unemployment (Casson, 1979; Roberts, 1982). At this stage it was seen by the political authorities as a 'problem of the unqualified'. After 1979 the problem became more serious, and by 1982 almost 1 in 4 were unemployed while about half were having to endure spells of unemployment and others were having to trade down their aspirations to avoid it and secure work or stay on in education. However, not all young people were equally affected. Once again unemployment was disproportionately concentrated among certain groups, notably the poor, the unqualified and the ethnic minorities. Government-sponsored programmes provided an alternative to unemployment for many 16-year-olds, but, as high levels of unemployment persisted, the problem of long-term unemployment among the 18–24-year-olds from these groups started to emerge. By January 1984, of the 1.1 million who had been registered unemployed for more than a year, 30 per cent were under 25 years of age.

Causes

The persistence of high levels of youth unemployment has produced a number of explanations, some of which have figured prominently in the public debate about the problem. In Britain, when youth unemployment first started to rise, considerable attention was directed towards demographic changes. It was argued that the problem was caused by greater numbers entering the labour market. In later phases it was argued that high rates of pay were the root of the problem and that young people had priced themselves out of the labour market. In the USA attention focused on the effects of minimum-wage legislation in reducing the jobs available for youth. These factors have been shown to have only a marginal impact on the problem, in that changes in levels of pay and minimum wage legislation can produce small changes in the number of jobs available to youth, but these are usually at the expense of other groups (Raffe, 1983).[9] The fact that many advanced capitalist societies have encountered an increase in the level of youth unemployment in the early 1980s suggests that other factors are at work.

To understand fully the causes of youth unemployment we need to make a distinction between two sets of factors: those which operate in periods of relatively full employment, and those which operate in periods of high unemployment. In the former it is the fact that young people are entering the market for the first time and tend to move from one job to another which creates high levels of unemployment; in periods of high unemployment it is the fall in aggregate demand, combined with changes in the distribution of occupations, which are responsible.

Youth unemployment in periods of full employment

As many young people are new entrants to the labour market they run the risk of unemployment as they search for their first job. The reasons young people change jobs more frequently than adults is partly because of a desire to experiment and avoid boring jobs or poor working conditions, and partly because many of the jobs they enter are associated with high rates of labour turnover and they are forced to leave. In both societies the development of capitalism has been associated with a tendency to reduce progressively the participation of young people in the labour market. Even now the recruitment practices of employers prohibit the employment of young inexperienced workers in many industries and occupations, especially those offering firm-specific training and career ladders. In Britain research has shown how employers exclude young people from a wide range of jobs. Legislation prohibits the employment of young people in jobs involving shift work, dangerous machinery, the sale of alcohol, etc. (Ashton, Maguire and Garland, 1982). These provide powerful barriers to the employment of youths, restricting them to a narrow range of jobs in which employers can utilise cheap, inexperienced and unskilled labour. Thus, young people are over-represented in the lower-skilled, low-paid jobs in the retail trade and manufacturing—those jobs associated with high rates of labour turnover and few opportunities for training.

In the USA Osterman has documented similar processes

which have excluded young people from large parts of the labour market. These include the extension of schooling, youth relief programmes, and union restrictions on apprenticeships, seniority rules and employers' preferences for older workers. Research findings have shown the extensive closure of full-time jobs to young people under the age of 20–21 (Gavett *et al.*, 1970; Diamond and Bedrosian, 1970). Sorrentino (1981a, p.10) also reports recent studies which show 'that two-thirds to four-fifths of US employers are reluctant to hire people under age 21 for regular, full-time jobs.' This means that jobs for youths in the USA are also confined to a limited part of the labour market. Osterman's work suggests that these are almost exclusively in the secondary market.

Given that young people in both societies entering the lower segments are confined to the more low-paid, insecure jobs, it is not surprising that they exhibit a higher rate of turnover than adults. This contributes to higher rates of unemployment because as they leave jobs they are placed at greater risk of unemployment.[10] Because they leave jobs more frequently than adults they are more prone to experience multiple spells of unemployment. Moreoever, because the average duration of youth unemployment tends to be lower than that of adults, there have to be many more of them moving into and out of unemployment if they are to produce a higher overall rate of unemployment. This creates a 'core' group which is particularly likely to experience extended and/or multiple spells of unemployment, and which expands when the overall level of unemployment rises (OECD, 1983, Ch. 6). In the USA this core group is drawn disproportionately from blacks and high school drop-outs, who frequently withdraw from the labour market and are unemployed for an extended period (Freeman and Wise, 1982); in Britain they are found among the educationally disadvantaged (Department of Employment, 1974; Walker, 1982).

The period of rapid job movement is often referred to in the American literature as the moratorium phase which young people undergo before they settle down in permanent jobs in the primary market. In Britain, where the division between primary and secondary markets is not as rigid, this is not the case. Many young people leaving school at 16 enter appren-

ticeships or white-collar jobs which in the USA would be regarded as being in the primary sector of the labour market. It
is only in those jobs in the lower segments of the labour market
where British youth exhibits high rates of job movement
(Roberts *et al.*, 1981). In times of high unemployment such as
those experienced in Britain in 1983/84 this explanation starts
to lose its explanatory power. During such periods, the rate of
job movement slows down and the spells of unemployment
get longer, but as job opportunities become scarcer, then some
young people spend years unemployed while looking for their
first job (Ashton *et al.*, 1985). In these circumstances it is clear
that alternative causes are at work in creating disproportionately high levels of unemployment.

Youth unemployment in periods of high unemployment
In both countries similar explanations have emerged as to what
these causes may be. Freeman and Wise (1982) conclude that

quantitatively, the employment of youths appears to be one of the
most highly sensitive variables in the labour market, rising substantially during boom periods and falling substantially during less active
periods.

A similar 'cyclical' interpretation has been provided by
Makeham (1980) for Britain. He argues that the main
determinant of youth unemployment is the level of aggregate
demand. After analysing long-term movements in the unemployment rates of young people and adults he points to the
fact that for every 1 per cent increase in male unemployment, the corresponding youth rate rose by 1.7 per cent. A
similar case has been made by Raffe (1984), who argues that
almost all of the increase in youth unemployment in Great
Britain between 1970 and 1982 can be explained by a fall in the
general level of employment.

The reason young people are so adversely affected is
precisely because they are new entrants. As employers face a
fall in demand for their products, their first reaction is to cut
recruitment. This is so particularly for the larger employers
who have commitments to their established workforce. They

can then let the process of natural wastage reduce the the numbers of employees. If they have to make redundancies these are often on a last-in, first-out basis. In both instances it is those who are first entering the labour market who are especially at risk. In view of the evidence that has been marshalled on both sides of the Atlantic, which links changes in the level of youth unemployment to changes in the business-cycle, there can be little doubt that such changes in the general demand for labour are an important factor in explaining the emergence of youth unemployment as a problem in both societies. The question that remains is whether such an explanation is sufficient.

As we have seen, cyclical changes are not the only changes taking place in the labour market. There are also changes in the occupational structure and in the institutional regulation of the labour market which affect the employment opportunities of young people. In focusing on these Gordon (1979) offers what may be termed an alternative, structural explanation. She argues that in advanced industrial societies the demand for youth labour is being affected by: (i) the decline of family employment, especially in agriculture, where extensive use was made of youth labour in the past; (ii) the changing skill structure of industrial societies, especially the decline of unskilled jobs in the manufacturing industry which previously recruited untrained labour; and (iii) changes in the institutional regulation of the labour market, with entry to jobs being affected by labour legislation, seniority agreements and collective bargaining which preclude the employment of young people. She also cites factors such as the increasing cost of youth labour caused by collective agreements raising the minimum wage and locational factors such as minority group concentration in inner-city areas. She sees these changes progressively reducing the opportunities for young people.

A similar analysis of the British situation has been made by Ashton and Maguire (1983), who argue that long-term changes in the occupational structure in conjunction with increasing institutional regulation of the labour market are reducing the points at which young people have access to the labour market.[11] They argue that the growth of part-time jobs in the service sector is not creating new jobs for which young people can compete as, in Britain, employers' recruitment practices prohibit young people from employment in most part-time jobs. In addition, many other jobs which previously provided points of entry for school-leavers—for example, clerical and typing jobs in commerce—are currently being threatened by the new information technology. Together these forces of change are reducing the points at which young people can compete for entry into work.

The two arguments are not mutually exclusive. Indeed, the analysis presented throughout this chapter would suggest that both approaches have contributions to make. Clearly, it is a job problem in that both societies have to create jobs to reduce the high rates of youth unemployment as the US started to do in 1984. However, there is also evidence of other long-term changes which are reducing the demand for youth labour and which in the past have been partially offset by the raising of the school-leaving age, the introduction of youth programmes or by a higher proportion of young people staying in full-time education. How these factors combine to create the specific pattern of youth unemployment in each society is determined by the institutional regulation of the labour market in that society; because of this the problems are different in Britain and the USA. In Britain we have witnessed the virtual collapse of the labour market for youth in some parts of the country and the persistent failure throughout the early 1980s of the rate of youth unemployment to fall. In the USA the work of Adams and Mangum and Freeman and Wise among others, has shown the problem of persistent high levels of youth unemployment to be located among black youth and those entering the secondary labour market.

5. The Experience of Unemployment

In this chapter we show how a person's previous experience of work influences the way in which he experiences unemployment. We argue that those from different segments of the labour market experience unemployment in significantly different ways and we examine some of the mechanisms through which this occurs. We conclude with an evaluation of the contributions psychologists have recently made to our understanding of the processes involved.

The Middle-class Work Ethic

The ways in which people experience unemployment are, as one would expect, related to the ways in which people experience work. If you are a doctor for whom work is a central life-interest and you lose your job, the experience is likely to be different from that of an assembly-line worker for whom work is boring, monotonous and physically demanding. Yet in the public discussion of work, and to a certain extent in the academic literature on the psychology of unemployment, there is only one definition of work that tends to come through. We refer to this as the middle-class work ethic because it is the view of work which is portrayed in the media and fits the experience of large sections of the middle class and some of the working class, but not that of the total population.

The middle-class work ethic consists of three main elements: (i) it usually equates work with employment. The two are, of course, separate; housewives work but are not employed. People may be employed by an organisation but they may not necessarily do any work for it. Nevertheless the two tend to be conflated in our everyday usage of the term work. (ii) it justifies the unequal distribution of income on the basis that those who receive the highest rewards contribute the most to society. Such beliefs function to legitimate the allocation of resources

115

through the market mechanism. (iii) it maintains that work involves making a career or following a vocation. This element has its origins in the Protestant ethic, although it is now secularised. However, it still contains the idea that people should achieve self-fulfilment through their work. The modern theory of vocational guidance is predicated on the notion that work should be a means through which individuals develop their potential or, in the language of the theorists, implement their self-concepts (Ginzberg *et al.*, 1951; Super, 1957). Each individual is encouraged to adhere to the appropriate values of hard work, self-discipline and loyalty in order that they may obtain entry to jobs which will enable them to fulfil themselves, whether this is through a successful career leading to a directorship or through achieving recognition from fellow professionals, as an eminent scientist or craftsman.[1]

Challenges to the middle-class work ethic

This set of beliefs is not universally accepted because there are a number of groups for whom it does not always make sense. First, there are those in the lower occupational segments, the semi-skilled and unskilled workers, both male and female. Their work on assembly-lines or in cleaning streets, hospitals and toilets, is vital to the functioning of society but it provides little in the way of personal satisfaction. It is often subject to close and arbitrary supervision, it may involve physically demanding activities in unpleasant circumstances, and provides only limited opportunity for self-fulfilment or personal development. For the vast majority it does not even provide the opportunity for promotion. Perhaps of even greater significance is the level and method of payment. Not only are these the worst-paid jobs, but the form of payment—piecework, payment by results and hourly rates—together with the casual and insecure nature of much of the work, mean that the income it provides is irregular and unpredictable. In these circumstances the values of the middle-class work ethic are irrelevant, for it is impossible for hard work, self-discipline and loyalty to be rewarded in the form of higher incomes or improved status. For these workers the logic of their situation points in a different direction; towards the creation of cultures which celebrate spontaneity, the 'fiddle', and resistance to authority

(Willis, 1977; Bell, 1977). In this situation work is very often seen as oppressive, a stressful set of activities, in which the individual as a member of a work group is in a situation of confrontation with management over the organisation of work. Management attempts to exert control, both through its control of the technology (for example, by increasing the speed of the production line) and through supervision. In response the workers attempt to contain the power of management and enforce their own forms of control (Burawoy 1979; Edwards, 1979; Gordon *et al.*, 1982; Benyon, 1984). In this context they generate alternative definitions of the world of work in which the values of collective action and spontaneity are celebrated. The satisfaction and commitment to work is derived not from the tasks that are performed but the money received at the end of the week (Goldthorp *et al.,* 1968). Such an alternative view of the world of work rarely comes through in the media or the school, it had to be 'discovered' by sociologists (Sabel, 1982).

The second group for whom the middle-class work ethic is not always convincing are housewives. For them, the labour involved in maintaining the household, providing meals, cleaning, washing clothes and bringing up children is unpaid. Rewards have to be sought if possible in the tasks themselves, but research has shown that these are often seen as monotonous, boring, routine and isolating (Oakley, 1974, 1975). Because the work they do as housewives is outside the main allocative mechanism of the market, it is unpaid and hence unrecognised. In working within the household they can make more efficient use of the resources available to the family, but to increase them substantially women have to enter the labour market. For the wives of middle-class males, the middle-class work ethic may make sense in terms of the experience of the husband if not in terms of their own situation. For the wives of the unskilled workers even this does not apply.

The other sizeable groups whose experience is at variance with the middle-class work ethic are members of ethnic minorities. The work experience of many blacks in both societies is confined to unskilled, low-paid manual or service occupations. In addition they face discrimination in any attempt they may make at moving up the occupational hierarchy. In the USA this discrimination has led to the creation of urban ghettos and a distinctive black experience (Schlozman and Verba, 1979). In Britain, this same combination of factors is producing a similar situation, especially among the young who are exhibiting a scepticism of the values embodied in the middle-class work ethic which in some cases amounts to a rejection of the values of white society (Cashmore and Troyna, 1982).

Another challenge to the middle-class work ethic comes from the fact that the labour market is not the only mechanism available for the allocation of resources. State benefits provide an alternative way of distributing them, not on the basis of the 'contribution' of the individual to society but on the basis of personal need. Under this system it is not 'those who work the hardest' who receive the resources, but those whose need is greatest. In this sense it directly challenges the principle of the market as the method of allocating resources. This is particularly evident at the lower end of the labour market among the unskilled and lower paid where adherence to the middle-class work ethic is weakest and where reliance on the system of state benefits is more extensive.

The other major challenge to the middle-class ethic is from socialism, which provides an alternative set of beliefs about the ways in which resources should be allocated. As we mentioned in Chapter 1 there are important differences in this respect between the two societies. In the USA there is a more widespread adherence to individualism, and the belief that the free enterprise system is the most efficient means of organising the economy is also more widely accepted. The result is that the middle-class work ethic, with its stress on the value of hard work and on the rewards obtained from the labour market as reflecting the just worth of a person, is not as fiercely contested as it is in Britain. Here the history of the working class and its unions have been more extensively influenced by socialism. This provides an alternative ideological justification for work and the allocation of rewards. Private enterprise is replaced by communal ownership and rewards are allocated not on the basis of the sale of labour but on the basis of the needs of the individual and his or her family.

Enforcing the middle-class work ethic–cultural institutions
In view of the contested nature of this dominant work ethic, its main tenets have to be constantly asserted and reasserted through the major cultural institutions. Schools play a central role in this process. In many respects their organisation is predicated on the values of competition, self-discipline, hard work and loyalty as a basis for success in the labour market. Although they are not paid an income in return for adopting these values, pupils are promised a worthwhile 'pay-off' in the form of educational qualifications. These are seen to represent an investment that will provide a return in the form of access to lucrative jobs in the labour market. In addition, the schools also provide more immediate rewards for successful compliance in the form of reports, promotions and honours. In this respect there is a high degree of congruence between the values of the middle classes and those transmitted through schooling. Most middle-class and some working-class families see educational qualifications as a means of securing access to the 'better' jobs. They uphold the value of work as a meaningful activity which provides a chance to develop skills, and an area of personal accomplishment. Attitudinal and behavioural characteristics such as self-discipline, sustained effort, respect for authority, which are seen to produce success at work, form a central pivot in the socialisation of children. School is valued because success within it is essential if children are to acquire the same or a better level of material benefits secured by the parents (Ashton and Field, 1976).

In addition to the educational institutions, the media plays an important part in reinforcing the value of hard (paid) work through celebrating the achievements of successful individuals, whether these are pop stars, footballers or businessmen. Local papers record the progress of prominent businessmen, company newsletters publicise internal promotions, the national press celebrate the rags-to-riches stories of successful entrepreneurs and popular TV programmes glamorise the life of business leaders. History books and popular literature also record the biographies of those who have left their imprint in the field of business endeavour. Against the weight of such 'evidence', the everyday experience of those groups which do not adhere strongly to these values has to be very different from that of middle- and upper-class males for them to maintain an alternative set of meanings and values. Such alternative views do receive occasional expression in the media in plays and comedy programmes but, on balance, much less exposure than those which celebrate the middle-class work ethic.

The role of myths

In view of the contested nature of the meaning of work, one of the main functions of myths is to maintain the commitment of the working population to the legitimacy of the system of distributing work and allocating rewards. By degrading or stimatising those out of work, myths serve to reinforce the commitment of those in work to the existing values.[2] In this respect it is possible to distinguish three different types of myths about the unemployed which are prevalent in both societies. The first concerns the so-called 'welfare scroungers' or 'work-shy', those who are seen to enjoy living off state benefits (Golding and Middleton, 1982; Taylor, 1982, p.41). In this respect the press and the public appear to have an insatiable appetite for stories about those who can 'get away' without working and live off the labour of others. The fact that such myths are so persistent when there is so little evidence of widespread abuse of the welfare system suggests that they perform an important function (Sinfield, 1981, pp.116–18). In addition, the fact that the state spends such a disproportionate amount of resources on investigating potential social security frauds as compared with tax evasion, where the returns from successful convictions would be greater, suggests that the political authorities too are vitally concerned. Part of the reason for this concern by the state stems from its activities in the field of welfare, for by giving benefits according to need, the state is directly challenging the principles of the market. In view of this it has to reassert constantly that welfare is only a safety net. Constant prosecution of fraudulent claimants serves to remind those in work, that those without it are not 'getting away' with anything. In this way, those in work are reassured that they are not working hard for nothing and being 'conned' by the system.

A second set of myths concerns the motivation of the unemployed. They are seen as not really wanting to work, as not making an effort to find work. In short, they are unemployed because of their own personality failings. It is argued that there are plenty of jobs advertised if they really wanted one. What this attitude fails to take into account is the fact that during a recession the numbers out of work far outnumber the vacancies available. For example, in one provincial British city in July 1984 there were 1500 jobs in the city's Jobcentre but 25,900 unemployed.[3] If all the unemployed had been aware of and gone after all the vacancies it would still have left 24,400 unemployed. Job adverts in newspapers are public whereas the mass of unemployed are hidden from view at home. The function of this myth is that it justifies the rewards and security of those in work by deflecting blame or guilt about the low level of resources available to those out of work onto the unemployed themselves: it's 'their own fault'.

The third set of myths we refer to as the golden age of suffering. The core of the myth is that in the 1930s people really suffered, and in some instances, they were without food, clothing and shelter. In addition, many were middle-aged males with dependent families. Today, the myth argues, there is no longer any real suffering, state benefits ensure that no one goes hungry, while changes in the composition of the unemployed mean that they consist of females working for 'pin money' and teenagers (Levison, 1980, p.32). Again, this particular myth is evident in both societies. While there is an element of truth in it, it also involves a gross distortion, as do all myths. The contemporary situation is different in important respects from that of the 1930s but, as we shall see later in this chapter, the links between poverty and unemployment have still not been severed.

The Experience of Unemployment

Our task in this section is to show how, when people become unemployed, their experience of work in one particular segment interacts with other factors to produce a distinctive experience of unemployment. Those from professional and managerial occupations tend to encounter similar problems to each other but the nature of these problems is very different from those encountered by workers from the lower segments, from unskilled work. As the transition to unemployment involves more than just the loss of the employed role, there are a number of other factors which are important in influencing the ways in which people experience unemployment. These include a person's status in the labour market, the extent to which their occupational identity is central to their self-image, their financial situation and their identity in the family.

The ways in which these factors affect the experience of unemployment among the various groups is shown in Figure 5.1. While we treat the factors as analytically separate, in reality they are systematically related to each other. One of the main reasons for this is that a person's previous work experience in a particular market segment will have a powerful influence on the extent to which the occupational identity is central to self-image, on the level of financial deprivation they experience on becoming unemployed and on the person's identity in the family. One consequence of this is that they become mutually reinforcing and work in the same direction. This is not always the case, for example we cannot always 'read off' the financial situation from the previous occupation or work experience and for this reason the arrows illustrating the direction of movement sometimes deviate from the horizontal showing points at which people may differ in their experience from that more typical of their group.

Status in the labour market refers to a person's status in the market before experiencing unemployment. It is important because it provides a measure of the person's dependence on market relationships. Full-time workers are, as we have seen, dependent on the sale of their labour to ensure that they continue to receive an income above the poverty line. Part-time employment is important because it is often indicative of the fact that the person is not totally dependent on income from employment as the sole means of support. There are some people who do rely totally on part-time earnings, but in most cases we take the status of part-time workers to be indicative of a different relationship to the market, which in turn affects the way in which unemployment is experienced. Youths first entering the labour market are a separate category because here again their relationship to the market is characterised by

Status in the labour market	Type of work experience	Work identity		Financial situation		Identity within the family
Full and part-time employees, male and female	Professional or white collar	Threatened	→	Secure	→	Not threatened
	Sheltered manual or skilled manual	Some threat	→	Short-term security	→	Threatened by long-term unemployment
	Work without shelters, usually semi-skilled and unskilled	No threat	→	Insecure	→	Threatened by short- and long-term unemployment
School-leavers seeking entry to labour market	None	Threat to realisation of work identity	→	Insecure	→	Access delayed to adult status and dependence on family enhanced
Females seeking part-time work	No recent experience or low-grade, white-collar and service work	No serious threat	→	Variable—threatens their position in family; threatens family if no other source of income	→	Role as household manager not threatened

Figure 5.1: Factors affecting the experience of unemployment

the fact that many are not totally dependent on the market for their support. As they are still part of their family of origin this is often used as a means of providing an alternative source of support if needed. This is not the case if they have left home or their parents are both unemployed, but for many unemployed young people the family does provide a source of material support independently of their relationship to the market.

Type of work experience is perhaps the most important factor is influencing the experience of unemployment because it determines the level of income available to the person and the opportunities for the development of an occupational identity (Becker and Carper, 1956). Of the three main types of occupation depicted in Figure 5.1, not all offer the same opportunity to develop an occupational identity. The greatest opportunities for this arise among the professional, administrative and managerial occupations, which provide a chance to acquire skills, make a career and exercise authority over others. In the middle levels of the occupational hierarchy, the skilled jobs do provide some opportunities to acquire skill and exercise responsibilities and so facilitate the development of an identification with the occupation, although this identity is unlikely to form such a central part of the person's self-image. In the lower segments, the situation is different, the tasks tend to be repetitive, simple, and make few demands on the cognitive skills of the worker. There are few means through which the worker can develop an identification with the occupation. Thus, one consequence of the way in which we organise work is that the centrality of a person's occupational identity to their self-image varies with their previous work experience.

The most important aspect of the financial situation facing the unemployed is loss of income. This is the single most all-pervasive factor influencing the experience of unemployment. In the USA Scholzman and Verba (1976) report that loss of income was one of the main problems facing their sample. Those in receipt of unemployment benefits were more likely to report that they had made cut-backs than the unemployed without such aid. Moreover, those making efforts to generate additional income did not relieve the financial strain of unemployment.

While it is always hazardous to make general comparisons between two societies because of the different circumstances facing individuals and the complexity of the tax and income support systems, the OECD have recently completed such an exercise. The results are illustrated in Figure 5.2, which represents the profile of income loss facing 'typical' families. It plots the income over time available to the unemployed as a percentage of that available to a household whose principal earner was previously on average earnings. It shows the effect of the more extensive system of social security in Britain which provides for a more comprehensive long-term provision. In the USA by contrast the level of income available to the unemployed, while relatively high in the first six months, drops dramatically thereafter. Thus, because of the greater reliance in the USA on the labour market for allocating resources, the loss of income will have a more all-pervasive effect. As a large part of health insurance is provided through employers, cover is lost once a person is unemployed (Sorrentino, 1976). In Britain the impact of unemployment on life-chances is more circumscribed. While it may still produce acute financial problems it will not directly affect access to health care.[4] What the figure does not show is how the income of the unemployed is affected by the level of their previous earnings. Those in the higher income jobs have a greater chance of cushioning their income loss through recourse to savings, while the level of compensation they obtain for losing jobs also tends to be higher. Those at the bottom of the occupational hierarchy are totally dependent on state benefits for their income.

A person's identity within the family can also be affected by unemployment. For males the traditional role has been that of 'breadwinner'—that is, the husband's position in the family as head of the household is a function of his full-time participation in the labour market. By taking away the husband's ability to provide an income for the family his identity within the family can be threatened.

We now turn to an examination of the way in which these five factors interrelate and work in the same direction to produce a similarity in the experience of different groups. First, we take the full-time worker whose experience of work has been in the higher segments. Because such occupations provide

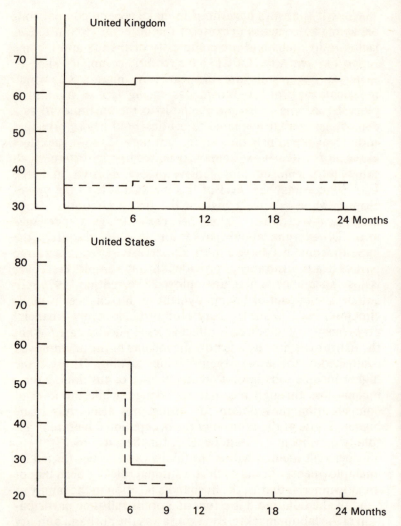

Figure 5.2: The effects of unemployment on income, UK and USA income replacement ratios for households whose principal earner, previously on average earnings, is unemployed; averages over six-monthly periods

Key: ————— Married couple, two children, sole earner unemployed.
      – – – – – Single unemployed person.

Source: OECD, Employment Outlook, 1984, Chart 19, p. 95.

the conditions for the development of an occupational identity we would expect such an identity to form a central part of the self-concept; achievement at work becomes an important part of the person's self-image. In these circumstances unemployment represents a considerable threat to self-identity. Recent evidence suggests that this is indeed the case. Fineman (1983), in a study of unemployment among the middle class in Britain, found over half his sample were considerably threatened by job loss. The job had provided the basis for their pride, confidence, sense of self-worth and security and their non-work roles, family life and social patterns were attuned to it. They felt they had lost something of value and that core elements of themselves were being attacked.

While the middle class may find their identity threatened they are unlikely to experience the same financial problems as those from the lower segments.[5] Their higher incomes in work provide the opportunity of building up financial reserves. Thus, Swinburne (1980) noted that several managers and professional men in her sample had no immediate financial difficulty. More significantly Payne, Warr and Hartley (1983) found that unemployed middle-class men were significantly more likely to have wives with full-time jobs than were men in a comparable working-class sample. As we indicate in Figure 5.1, for those who do not have this form of 'cushion', the financial loss will create emotional stress as it does for those in the lower segments. A number of studies have found such links between financial strain and emotional stress. Estes and Wilensky (1978) reported unemployed professionals with financial strain being significantly more emotionally distressed than those without financial strain; similar relationships were found by Little (1976).

For those who do not face financial problems their identity within the family is unlikely to be threatened, as their control over financial resources will still enable them to maintain or contribute towards the maintenance of the family. The husband's role as head of the household and controller of the family income is not threatened. Only if the family face financial deprivation will the husband's identity within the family be threatened.

Those in full-time work, in the more highly skilled and

sheltered occupations, will also have had an opportunity to develop an identification with the occupation. Because of this the initial experience of unemployment is likely to be similar in some respects to that of the middle class. As both groups share a belief in the middle-class work ethic, the initial reaction is one of shock and a sense of loss but this does not present such a severe threat to the person's identity as it does for the middle class because the occupational identity plays a less central role in their self-image. Thus, a study of a plant closure in the USA by Cobb and Kasl (1977) found that immediately following closure the workers reported strong feelings of work-role deprivation but four to six months later the missing work role was no longer an issue. The more severe threat for these workers comes from the financial problems which stem from their income loss. For those in occupations which have hitherto provided some form of shelter this is likely to translate into financial compensation. In the USA it may take the form of unemployment insurance which the worker may be able to live off until he/she is re-hired. In Britain it is more likely to take the form of redundancy payments which may cushion the immediate financial impact of unemployment. However, unless a job is found within a few months these workers will soon encounter the kind of financial problems which face those from the lower segments. Such payments merely provide a short-term solution to the problem of income loss.

Providing unemployment is only short-term, then the husband's role within the family is not likely to be threatened. However, if the income loss is substantial or the man moves into the ranks of the long-term unemployed then he will be faced with a threat to his identity as 'breadwinner' and head of household.

The third group, full-time workers in the lower segments, face a different set of problems. Jobs such as labourer, cleaner, assembly-line worker do not lead to the development of an identification with the occupation. A number of studies have shown this to be reflected in workers' adopting instrumental attitudes to their work, where they only value the job for the income it provides (Goldthorpe *et al.*, 1968; Blackburn and Mann, 1979). Consequently, when they lose their jobs what is lost which is of central value is money. Moreover, because these jobs are more insecure and labour turnover is higher, they are more at risk of unemployment than the other groups. As unemployment is an integral part of their experience of the labour market they develop ways of adapting to it and hence it is not experienced as shock or threatening when it arrives, it is just part of their taken-for-granted world. For them higher levels of unemployment mean longer spells without work, sometimes stretching into years. Many of these workers, especially those in their forties and fifties with poor health records, know that they are vulnerable to unemployment even in good times (Sinfield, 1981, pp.38–40).

The main problem for these groups is income loss. Given their low incomes from paid employment they will not have had the chance to build up any financial reserves and even if they had, they are likely to have been used up in earlier spells of unemployment. In Britain, because of their short-term attachment to their employers they are less likely to receive redundancy payments. In the USA Schlozman and Verba (1979) found that 58 per cent of the unemployed had been unemployed before. Sinfield argues that in Britain the combination of low pay, previous periods of unemployment and sickness leaves few of those out of work with any resources apart from state benefits. In this respect, a 1980 cohort study found that seven out of ten men still unemployed after a month reported 'no unearned income and no income from a wife's earnings and savings of less than £500' (Sinfield, 1981, p.50). For some this means poverty, as the massive extension of the welfare state which has taken place since the 1930s has still not broken the link between unemployment and poverty (Piachaud, 1981). As late as 1976 Sinfield estimated that the unemployed were 21 times more likely to be in poverty than the employed. Payne, Warr and Hartley (1983) found their working-class sample had substantially greater financial problems than did unemployed middle-class people. The problems they face are the emotional stresses and strains created by living on an inadequate income.

Precisely because work does not provide the basis for development of an occupational identity the worker's identity within the family is likely to play a more central part in his self-conception. In these circumstances the financial problems can pose another serious threat, for even short-term unemployment can reduce their control over resources and threaten their identity as head of the household. Thus, when unemployment occurs, the male ceases to provide and control the income, and his status is undermined in the eyes of the other members of the family, a process which can generate feelings of inadequacy and failure (Fagin and Little, 1984).

Most of the research on unemployment has focused on males, consequently our knowledge of the female's response is limited. There is some evidence which suggests that in Britain at least, for those who are single or the principal wage-earner, the psychological impact of unemployment on the person's occupational identity is the same as for men (Warr, 1983b). However, as yet, there have been few studies which have explicitly explored the manner in which the conflicting ideological pressures to which women are exposed may affect their experience of unemployment (Marshall, 1984; Martin and Wallace, 1984). The situation facing many of those seeking part-time work is discussed below.

Youths
There are important differences between the situation of British and American youth which we discuss in Chapter 4. Here it is sufficient to note that in the USA a much greater proportion of the 16–19-year-olds continue their education than is the case in Britain. However, in both societies school and college-leavers differ significantly from other groups in that they have limited experience of full-time permanent employment. This is not to say that they are a uniform group. As we saw in Chapter 3 their family and school experience generates expectations about the particular segment of the labour market which they expect to enter and the kind of rewards they expect from work. These serve to differentiate school and college-leavers in much the same way as previous work experience differentiates adults, and this affects the ways in which they experience unemployment.

For those from middle-class families, work and success within it is seen as of central significance to the implementation of their self-concept (Ashton and Field, 1976, Ch.5). Although their chances of avoiding unemployment are greater than those of the other groups, those who do experience it are likely to perceive it as a serious threat to the realisation of their identity. Yet for some, a period of unemployment may be preferable to accepting lower status, 'dead-end' jobs, for if they are unemployed but still looking for suitable work they can still see themselves as capable of realising their occupational identity at a later date. If they accept lower-status jobs or fail in the long term to obtain employment then the reality of their situation will start to undermine their self-concept.

For those expecting entry into the middle levels of the labour market, the 'ordinary kids' for whom school has 'paid off' by providing some qualifications and who expect a decent, secure job at the end of the day, if not a career, unemployment will also threaten their identity. Such young people accept many elements of the middle-class work ethic—not least the importance of securing a steady income and avoiding the stigma of unemployment. Because of this they are likely to imbue their job-search behaviour with a sense of urgency and stay in jobs they dislike in order to avoid unemployment (Roberts *et al.*, 1981).

For those seeking entry to semi-skilled or unskilled jobs the main problem unemployment creates is lack of money. Because they do not expect much from work, unemployment does not pose such a threat to their identity. Support for their identity is based less on potential achievements at work and more on achievements within the peer group. The absence of work and the lack of income may cause them to scale down their normal pattern of social relationships and leisure but they are not abandoned. Time on their hands may be a problem, but their previous experience with their peer group of organising their own activities will have taught them ways of handling it, ways of 'doing nothing'. Like the adults in this segment unemployment is no shock, it is just part of the everyday experience of the labour market (Roberts *et al.*, 1981; Roberts, 1984).

The financial consequences of unemployment are often not as severe for young people as they are for adults. Their financial needs are not of the same order as those of prime-age males or females with families to support. For those in education, the income from employment is used to supplement parental or state support for their education. For those seeking full-time employment the income is more important. But even here, providing that their parents are still in employment, the family may provide an alternative source of income and resources (Pahl and Wallace, 1980; Coffield, Borrill and Marshall, 1983). In this case the problem is not likely to create the same level of emotional stress as it does for adults, especially if members of the peer group are in the same situation. In these circumstances membership of the peer group provides support and reassurance, especially among males.

With regard to their identity within the family, the situation facing school-leavers is again different from adults, in that young people are at the point of transition from their family of origin to form their own families. In these circumstances, obtaining paid employment can represent an important status passage to adulthood. It symbolises independence from the family of origin. Unemployment makes the transition to adult status more problematic and tends to delay it, enhancing the dependence of young people on their parents. For males, the impact of this may be mediated by their involvement in peer-group activities which can provide an alternative source of status and prestige. For females the situation is different. One of the main effects of unemployment on young females in Britain is to restrict the scope of their social activities. The problems this creates are more acute for young females than for young males, first because young females rely more on work activities as a means of making new social contacts, and secondly because they tend to be less involved in peer-group activities and hence more easily isolated (Griffin, 1984). In these circumstances females are more likely to be constrained into taking on additional domestic responsibilities within the family.

Females seeking part-time work
Again, this is a group about whom our knowledge is thin but one which also appears to have a distinctive experience of unemployment. As many of those recently in work will have been in relatively unskilled jobs in clerical and personal service occupations they will not have developed a strong identification with the occupation which can be threatened by unem-

ployment. As for their financial situation this is variable. In many low-income families the income from the wife's part-time job is vital in keeping the family above the poverty line. In the 1970s it was estimated that if it were not for working wives there would be a 50 per cent increase in the proportion of families in or near poverty (Sinfield 1981, p.87), and no doubt many of those working wives were part-time workers. However, in addition to stretching the family budget the income from paid employment is often valued for the independence it provides for the housewife within the family. A separate income, 'money of your own', is important even if the amount received is small, because it frees the wife from total dependence on the husband. Thus loss of income can be experienced by women in part-time work in two main ways: it can lower the standard of living of the family as a whole, and enhance the wife's dependence on the husband so long as he is working (Porter, 1982; Sharpe, 1984).

It is in the household division of labour that the main source of women's distinctive experience of work and unemployment is to be found. Within the family, while economically subordinated to the male they are responsible for housework and child-care. The main source of their identity is their role as mother and housewife; participation in the labour market is in many senses conditional upon their also maintaining their role in the household division of labour (Chaney, 1981). This constrains their options in the labour market as the job has to fit in with their family responsibilities. In so far as the main source of their identity lies in their role in the family this will not be threatened by unemployment (Jahoda, 1982, p.54).

Black workers

The reason the distinctive experience of black workers is not included in Figure 5.2, is a presentational one. In many respects they experience a double handicap. Black workers in each of the categories we have identified will experience the same problems and stresses when they become unemployed as white workers (Smith, 1981). In Britain there are strong cultural differences between whites, West Indians and Asians (Rex, 1982). These may be important in mediating the impact of unemployment but notwithstanding these differences, black unemployed unskilled and semi-skilled workers are likely to face similar problems to their white counterparts and different problems to unemployed black professional workers. What they have in common is that they all face the problems of institutionalised racism. This takes a number of forms ranging from violent assaults on the streets to discrimination at the point of entry to work and in promotion. In Britain the Metropolitan Police recorded 1287 incidents of racial attack in 1983 (Hansard, 6 December 1984). Despite legislation in both countries to outlaw the more public forms of discrimination, it continues to exist.

It is difficult to separate out the effects of racism as it is so all-pervasive in its operation. In the USA Schlozman and Verba (1979) reported that the experience of being black induces additional personal strain and dissatisfaction at all occupational levels and leads to a strong sense of collective racial identity. Yet so strong is the belief in individualism, that in spite of that experience only a slightly smaller proportion of blacks adhere to the American dream than whites.

In Britain Roberts reported black unemployment among the Afro-Caribbean school-leavers to be 40 per cent above that for whites even where blacks had left school with superior qualifications and higher aspirations (Roberts *et al.*, 1983). Some obtained entry into the better, more highly skilled jobs but they had to make more frequent applications and wait longer to get them. The majority entered semi-skilled and unskilled jobs. Dex (1979), analysing British data for the 1970s, reports that blacks are more likely to have difficulty in getting jobs, no more likely to leave them when they found them, but to be longer out of work if they lost them. Roberts argues that once they are convinced that it is their colour which excludes them from good jobs, they tend to retreat into their own culture of Rastas and Hustlers. There they can get by in social and economic terms without surrendering their integrity to white culture and its 'trash' jobs. Thus, in Britain, it would appear that the weaker attachment to the values of individualism and the stronger sense of cultural identity in their communities is leading to a more radical rejection of the values of white society, at least among the second generation (Cashmore and Troyna, 1982).

Other factors

While we have focused on five major factors we would emphasise that they are not the only ones. Local unemployment levels, length of unemployment, availability of social support are among those which have also been identified as playing an important role in influencing the experience of unemployment (Sinfield, 1981; Hayes and Nutman, 1981; Warr 1983b). Yet the effect of some of these on the individual's experience is also influenced by previous location in the labour market.

If we take community support as an example, what evidence there is suggests that this is more widely available among those with experience in the lower segments. In cities where unemployment has been high over a number of years the unemployed tend to be geographically concentrated. In Britain this is resulting in the creation of communities from which paid employment is largely absent (Ashton *et al.*, 1985). Such communities can provide a means of support which helps mitigate the more destructive aspects of unemployment. They provide a culture, an assumptive world through which the individual makes sense of his/her predicament. Thus, many working-class whites, particularly those in northern cities, treat unemployment as an inevitable condition of their existence. It is not something they find any pleasure in, but neither is it a threat to their identity. The acute financial deprivation it creates sets rigid parameters to their activities but within those constraints they have succeeded in creating an alternative lifestyle in which paid work plays no part. However, these cultures can only develop in areas of prolonged high unemployment or among groups subject to systematic discrimination because it requires time in a common situation to provide the basis of shared experiences from which shared assumptions can emerge. For those from middle-class occupations these supports are unlikely to be available. This is because fewer of them experience unemployment and those that do are isolated from others. Their stronger adherence to the values of individualism also militates against the emergence of such cultures; for them unemployment is a more lonely experience.

Long-term unemployment

The problems faced by the long-term unemployed are very different from those of the short-term unemployed. As we have seen, those who experience it are largely drawn from the lower segments. In parts of Britain they are often members of the type of communities discussed above. Because paid employment is so scarce in such areas job search becomes counter-productive. As recruitment is often by word-of-mouth, the absence of friends and relatives in paid employment excludes them from the job-information network. In these circumstances paid work and the constraints it imposes on activities recedes from consciousness and a pattern of activity is developed in which work, as paid employment, has no part. In the USA these are the discouraged workers.

The main problems faced by the long-term unemployed in both societies are those of boredom and poverty. Whereas the short-term unemployed will face the problems we outlined above many of these will be resolved by their re-entry into work. The long-term unemployed face all those problems plus, what is for many, the personal humiliation of attempting to obtain other forms of public assistance. This group moves from the category of the 'deserving' to the 'undeserving' poor. For those who have previously been in low-paid, insecure jobs their financial resources will be low or non-existent and part or all of their unemployment benefit entitlement may have been forgone. In such circumstances the family either continue in a state of poverty or rapidly move into one. Once this level of existence is reached, the families encounter the kind of deprivations associated with perpetual debt and the problems of securing sufficient food, clothing and warmth (Townsend, 1979).

As we pointed out in Chapter 4, the problems of the long-term unemployed are more frequently encountered in Britain than the USA simply because they form a larger proportion of the unemployed in Britain. However, those who do enter the ranks of the long-term unemployed in the USA, face more severe financial deprivation than their British counterparts. This is because the wider mesh of the 'safety net' of the American welfare system lets more families through—a safety net which was further weakened by the welfare cuts of the

Reagan administration with its reduction of the food stamp program which resulted in a proliferating number of soup kitchens in Detroit, Pittsburgh and other major cities during the 1982/83 recession. The fact that the long-term unemployed constitute such a high proportion of the unemployed in Britain means that unemployment is much more likely to be a 'cause' of poverty than it is in the USA. However, as the welfare net is more uniformly spread across the country, and has a narrower mesh it means among other things, that the loss of a job does not curtail access to medical care; for this reason fewer may fall through into abject or extreme poverty.

The Psychology of Unemployment

In view of the high levels of unemployment in Britain, it is not surprising that British psychologists have recently made a substantial contribution to our understanding of the experiential aspects of the problem at both the empirical and theoretical levels. From a sociological perspective, two of their foremost contributions have been to locate the analysis of unemployment in the context of a discussion about the psychological functions of employment, and to further our understanding of the 'career' of the unemployed. Unfortunately, both contributions are limited by the assumptions which have been made about the universality of their statements. What we attempt here is to evaluate these achievements and locate the contributions in the context of the framework outlined above.

The Psychological functions of employment
Two of the foremost psychologists working on the problem of unemployment in Britain are Jahoda and Warr, who have argued that the psychological impact of unemployment cannot be fully understood without first considering the functions of employment.

Warr identifies six main functions[6]:

1. *Money*. A paid job is the most important means of income through which we have access to society's resources. Without that income resources are scarce and financial anxiety is high.

2. *Activity levels.* Employment provides outlets for energy and may permit the development and practice of skills and competences. Without it the scope for the development of skills may be considerably reduced.

3. *Variety.* Work enhances the range of behaviour open to people. It takes people out of their restricted domestic surroundings and permits access to facilities and behaviour not otherwise available. In particular, money from work makes possible activities, visits and holidays not otherwise available. Unemployment considerably restricts the range of activities that are available.

4. *Temporal structure.* Work imposes a habitual time structure on the day. The rhythm of work with its fixed schedules and breaks for meals and rests imposes a structure and goals on the working day. The absence of work creates a major psychological burden, boredom becomes a problem and the unemployed lose their sense of time; they fail to keep appointments as time loses its meaning.

5. *Social contacts.* Paid employment provides the main point of contact with others outside the family. It is our main means of participating in the production process and in this sense provides a basis for shared activities with others and a sense of purpose. Deprived of work, scope for such shared activities shrinks and people become more dependent on their family for emotional relationships and lose the calmer emotional climate of relationships at work.

6. *Personal identity.* Most people value the social position which employment provides. Paid work is often used as a measure of our contribution to society. In addition, for males, the income from it forms one of their main contributions to the maintenance of the household. For some, especially in the higher-status groups, the occupational role plays an important part in the formation of their identity and self-conceptions. In this situation loss of job can create a threat to identity.

Some of these factors such as the importance of money and various aspects of personal identity we have developed in the earlier discussion, but others have only been touched upon. We have only hinted at the importance of work in creating a temporal structure or in sustaining activity levels. These aspects of the problem are often overlooked in sociological analysis. Indeed, our earlier discussion of the meaning of work tended to direct attention away from the fact that all work performs an important function in imposing a structure on the day, splitting it up into discrete periods and determining the points at which activities such as eating can take place and defining other periods as leisure (Jahoda, 1982, pp.22–3). Similarly the importance of work activities as a means of learning and developing skills and competence is often overlooked (Stern and Hilgendorf, 1981). The absence of these constraints and opportunities imposed through paid employment can clearly have important repercussions for the unemployed. As we already know, boredom, which is a term often used, refers to the lack of activities, and is one of the most serious problems which the unemployed say they face (Ashton *et al.*, 1985).

While there are insights such as these to be derived from such a psychological approach it does have certain limitations. At first sight, these six factors appear to be value-free, universal and to operate on the individual in a negative manner independently of each other. On the face of it, money (or the lack of it) is going to affect all the unemployed in the same way, restricting the range and variety of activities they can become involved in. Similarly it appears that the lack of social contacts is going to have a universal impact on the unemployed, together with the loss of a temporal structure and the loss of activities; only in the area of personal identity is unemployment seen to have a differential impact. In fact, as we have shown earlier, the financial impact of unemployment as well as the impact of unemployment on the work identity and identity within the family differs substantially from one group to another, depending on their previous location within the labour market. As for the other factors such as the activity levels and temporal structure these may also have a differential impact. For example, in some routine jobs such as assembly-line work and machining, the repetitive character of the activities can be stressful and against the background of that experience, short-term unemployment can be experienced as a relief (Phillips, 1973; Pahl and Wallace, 1980). Similarly, many housewives who also work full-time, may find little difficulty in imposing a temporal structure on their daily activities if they become unemployed, for this is done through their domestic responsibilities. Those who appear to have the greatest difficulty in imposing a temporal structure are working-class males (Payne, Warr and Hartley, 1983). While it is important to take account of these six factors it is also important to remember that they are not value-free or universal in their impact, neither is their impact on the individual always negative.

The phase model

The phase model has been important in highlighting the fact that many people experience unemployment as trauma or shock and that in coping with it they often go through a series of different phases as they adjust to their new situation. The origin of this model derives from the work done in the early 1930s and in the post-war period. From interviews with the unemployed in Britain and Austria it appeared that the majority experience the psychological effects of unemployment in very similar ways. Moreover research carried out independently in the USA suggested a very similar pattern of experience there.[7]

In summarising much of the earlier work in this field Harrison (1976) represented the phase model diagrammatically as in Figure 5.3. This shows the unemployed worker moving through four phases. Hayes and Nutman (1981) summarise these as follows: the first is a phase of shock and immobilisation when the prospective change in a person's circumstances overwhelms them. On first learning that they are unemployed they cannot believe it. In this case, as with most shocks, morale drops. This is often followed by an attempt to minimise the event, as if it had not happened—for example, by delaying a claim for benefits or by taking a holiday as if nothing had changed. Many see their situation as essentially short-term, expecting to find work in the near future. Morale recovers because the person with a good work record and perhaps 20 years of work before him is optimistic about finding another job.

Once the search for work starts in earnest and the person is faced wth persistent failure to find work, or is constantly

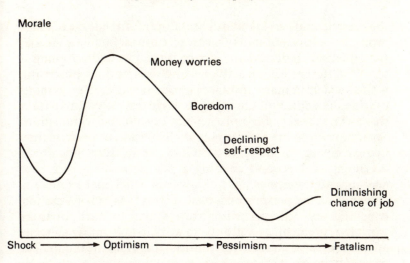

Figure 5.3: The phase model of unemployment

Source: Adapted from Harrison (1976), *Employment Gazette*, vol. 92, p. 339.

turned down at interview, the optimism goes and is replaced by a growing pessimism. At this stage money worries start to surface, boredom becomes a problem as all the odd jobs in the house have been done or the money to fund them has run out, and the person starts to face doubts about his own worth.

As his belief in the reality that work is available is shaken by persistent refusals or failure to locate vacancies, he enters the third phase. This involves a gradual erosion of old assumptions about the world and himself and is often associated with depression, moodiness and withdrawal. When this happens, morale drops and pessimism about the future takes over. He may continue to want to work but questions the belief that jobs are available or open to him. Once he does 'let go' he experiments with new behaviour and attitudes which make better sense of his situation. At this point morale improves slightly as he adapts to his new situation and adopts a new identity.

For Hayes and Nutman, the important point here is that the individual accepts that the achievements of the past can no longer be made criteria for the satisfaction of achievements in the present, and new standards are adopted. In the case of long-term unemployment it may mean accepting a fatalistic view of the situation, reducing the desire for a job and adopting a totally different set of activities and assumptions about the world, which in many instances means seeing it as something outside the control of the individual. Hayes and Nutman treat this as one aspect of a more general psycho-social transition. Such transitions are seen as potentially traumatic because they involve giving up one set of activities and relationships which are highly valued and entering a new situation where new activities and relationships are involved which make different demands on the person concerned. This is the kind of situation which occurs in the transition from school to work, or from work to retirement, as well as from work to unemployment. On an abstract level this general transition provides the theoretical basis for the phase model.

The main tenets of this theory are that in our everyday activities we become accustomed to interacting with a relatively small number of people in a limited range of situations.[8] The circumstances of these everyday interactions shape our ideas and views about the world (what is referred to as our assumptive world). Thus, it is perfectly sensible for a teacher to see work as an area of self-fulfilment and career advancement, as the occupation offers the prospect of incremental increases in income and promotion. As other teachers share the same work situation it is not surprising that they should hold similar ideas. Because each teacher tends to share these assumptions with others in their immediate milieu, they are not usually challenged or questioned. Only when radical changes take place in the people with whom interaction takes place or the circumstances surrounding that interaction do they become aware of them. In this situation people may be forced to change their ideas about the world and themselves—a potentially painful process. This is what is seen to happen when people become unemployed.

The loss of job deprives them of an income, a place of work and the company of workmates. For the teacher his view of himself as a person capable of contributing to society and earning a reasonable income will change. His view of himself as a relatively bright person, capable of making a career and getting on in life will change. His expectations of his future and that of his family will change. They are now likely to have to sell their car and may be forced to move home. The teacher's view of himself as a husband capable of providing for his family may be threatened. If work is not found, the process of 'letting go' or 'giving up' one set of assumptions and associated self-conceptions and acquiring another can involve major traumas. It is this process which gives rise to similarity in the transitional experience.

Evaluation of the phase model

Given the frequency with which different researchers have reported observations in both societies which correspond with the stages of the phase model there can be little doubt that it does represent an important step in our understanding of the psychological impact of unemployment. The main criticism of the model is that it tends to conflate work and paid employment and that it tends to generalise on the basis of the experience of only one group—prime-age males with a high level of involvement in paid employment.

By conflating work and paid employment the model fails to disentangle the effects of a loss of income, and in many cases poverty, from the impact of the loss of work on identity. As we have seen, income from employment is the main way in which resources are allocated in capitalist societies. The loss of income and of control over resources which that implies is one of the major problems facing the unemployed. Yet these problems are of a different order from those which stem from the threat unemployment makes to a person's identity. The model fails to make this clear.

The other major criticism also follows from our earlier discussion of the different ways in which unemployment is experienced by groups located in various parts of the social structure. It portrays as universal the experience of certain middle-class and working-class males, those who adhere to the middle-class work ethic. The experience of female and youth, as well as male unskilled and semi-skilled workers can be very different.

The final criticism we make of this approach is that it tends to conceptualise the human being as a passive agent, just responding to external events rather than actively creating situations. This is an important criticism, for unemployment involves deprivations and costs both to the individual and for the society. Such circumstances do generate behaviour directed at changing the situation of the individual unemployed person and of the position of the unemployed as a group. These are the questions we address in the next chapter.

6. The Social Costs of Unemployment and the Response of the Unemployed

Unemployment hurts. It can affect a person's health and that of his family and is associated with an increasing crime rate. For society it involves increasing costs in the form of lost production increased health care and welfare benefits and social protest. In this chapter we take a brief look at these costs and conclude with an examination of how people have reacted to them.

In the psychological literature and in public discussion, unemployment is often spoken of as though it only affects individuals. It is the individual who experiences shock and despair on learning that he/she is unemployed. It is the individual who suffers depression. Yet to limit our focus in this way is to produce an inadequate and misleading picture of the effects of unemployment and of those who carry the costs. As a closer examination of our discussion of the experience of unemployment would reveal, it affects not individuals *per se* but their relationships. If a person becomes unemployed his/her loss of income affects the rest of the family. If he/she becomes depressed that affects interactions with others. However the precise nature of those effects and their outcome will depend upon the form which such relationships took before unemployment.

To illustrate these points we use two case studies. The first is drawn from the work of Fagin and Little (1984, pp. 168–74) and is of a middle-class design engineer who resigned from his job because he felt that his contribution to the company was not acknowledged. Both he and his wife had been married before and his wife had three children living with them from her previous marriage. His involvement in his previous job caused him to work long and uncertain hours which had created a strain in the marriage.

Initially unemployment came as a relief both for him and his wife. He was pleased to have left his job and his wife saw it as an opportunity for them to develop a more stable relationship.

This 'honeymoon' phase did not last long, and after a month things deteriorated. His inability to get another job quickly affected him.

'I had these fits of absolute blackness. As far as I was concerned, I was a complete failure, with a PhD, a BSc, a qualified architect and land surveyor, and not getting anywhere.'

His moodiness was accentuated and he started drinking heavily. As a result, his behaviour became more erratic and unpredictable, he shouted at the children, who took refuge in their rooms. Rows between husband and wife became more frequent and these also affected the children, who became apprehensive; one of them started to steal from the mother. The health of the husband and children started to deteriorate. In an attempt to solve some of the financial problems his wife obtained a job as a secretary. This created problems for the husband who found it difficult to adjust to the new independence this gave her and the marriage collapsed. The separation produced an improvement in the children's health and outlook.

Under different circumstances the pressures created by unemployment operate in a different direction. From our own research we can cite the case of an unemployed young adult in a working-class family in which only the mother worked. The young person encountered no serious threat to his identity from his unemployment. He organised his time by watching videos, playing with a local music group and occasionally drinking with his mates. Family resources were only at the poverty line. The husband who had been made redundant years ago did not drink but structured his time by playing a more prominent role in the work of the household. In this case the family 'got by' without serious tension emerging in the relationships. The main threat to their well-being stemmed from their relative poverty. The unemployed son supplemented his income from the state with occasional 'fiddle jobs' (for example, casual driving), which were not reported to the social security authorities, producing fraudulent claims. Similarly, his activities with his friends from what was a poor neighbourhood sometimes took him on the wrong side of the law. However, in this area, thefts, especially from employers and those outside the neighbourhood, were not regarded by young people as an illegitimate activity.

These two case studies highlight differences in the internal organisation of the family and how they interact with the financial and emotional problems created by unemployment.[1] However, they are also illustrative of different reactions to unemployment. In the first case, the problems that already existed in the relationship between the husband and wife were exacerbated and tensions increased. The husband's view of himself as a successful engineer and businessman was put in doubt which precipitated depression, sleeplessness and ill-health. This, together with the new role relationships which were welcomed by the wife, proved too much to handle and the family separated.

In the second case, neither the father nor the son had found unemployment as difficult to handle in personal terms. They, like many others in areas of high unemployment, treated it as an inevitable condition of their lives. It was not something they found any pleasure in, but neither was it a threat to their identity. The acute financial deprivation it created set rigid parameters to their activities but within those constraints they had succeeded in creating an alternative life-style in which paid work had no part to play. In this way unemployment pervaded all the relationships in which they were involved.

Because unemployment affects a complex web of existing relationships, it is very difficult to 'prove' that any one factor is a direct consequence of unemployment. In the first of the case studies, the engineer was already prone to spells of moodiness before he became unemployed, but then the emotional stress it generated as a result of the threat it posed to his identity triggered off a state of depression. The health of the children suffered because of a deterioration in the relationship between husband and wife. In poorer families the loss of income can reduce the resources available for adequate food and shelter thereby reducing the child's resistance to infectious diseases, and increasing the chances of fetal and infant health problems. In the USA it may reduce access to medical care because the health care benefits are usually secured through employment (Brenner, 1983, p.1132). In these circumstances, unemployment is not a direct cause in the same way that in billiards or pool one ball strikes another and 'causes' it to move in a given direction. What is in fact happening is that unemployment induces extra strains which increase the probability that certain outcomes, in the forms of ill-health, poverty, and crime will occur.

Monetary Costs

Throughout our discussion we have stressed the diverse effects which the loss of income produces. In Chapter 5 we provided some estimates of the proportion of income loss involved for individuals and families in both societies. Here we are more concerned to show the ways in which that income loss can produce emotional strains and/or a lack of basic material resources which can affect the health of those involved. Apart from these effects there are a number of others which we have occasionally touched on such as the curtailment of leisure activities, holidays and social activities.

Some idea of the dramatic impact of income loss can be obtained from the fact that in 1979 and 1981 in Britain the number of families headed by an unemployed person living below supplementary benefit level more than trebled. In 1981 before long-term unemployment increased so rapidly, 480,000 were living below supplementary benefit level because of unemployment (*Poverty*, No. 56, December 1983). In the USA, 17 per cent of workers with some unemployment in the family in 1982 fell below the federally-designated poverty level but among households maintained solely by a woman, 44 per cent were in poverty, while among workers living alone more than one-third were below the poverty line. As we expect, it is among these groups with low earnings, and especially the blacks and Hispanics, that unemployment spells poverty (Flaim, 1984). It highlights the point we made earlier about the unequal distribution of unemployment. Despite the rhetoric, the direct financial costs of unemployment are borne by a small proportion of the society who suffer a loss of resources. Meanwhile the standard of living of those in work continues to increase as it did in the 1930s.

There are other costs to society but these are not borne directly by the individual or the family. The state has to increase its welfare payments. In 1978/79, when unemployment was 1.5 million in Britain, the government paid out £657 million in unemployment benefits, while in the USA the cost of regular and extended benefits in 1980 was $14 billion (Hughes and Perlman, 1984, p.212). In addition the state loses revenue from the direct and indirect taxes the unemployed would have paid, had they remained in employment. The cost to the state in Britain of benefit payments and lost tax revenues together was calculated for 1980 to represent £3500 for each additional unemployed person in the private sector. (In the public sector the loss would be less as the state makes a saving on their pay, superannuation, etc.) In the USA the Congressional Budget Office estimated that for every 1 per cent increase in the unemployment rate the federal budget deficit increased by about $25 billion. Finally there are the costs of lost production. These are difficult to quantify, but Hughes and Perlman (1984, p.217) estimate that at 1982 levels of unemployment, the equivalent of a whole year's gross domestic product would be lost in less than a decade in both Britain and the USA.

Health Costs

As we saw in the first case study cited above (p. 145), changes in mental and physical health act as a kind of barometer with regard to the effects of stress and physical deprivation on individual and family life. In reality both aspects of health are interrelated; we treat them separately here purely as a matter of convenience. The relationship between ill-health and unemployment has been examined at two main levels. Studies at the macro level have sought to establish a relationship between changes in the rate of unemployment and pathological indices, showing how changes in the level of unemployment affect community health. Studies at the micro individual level have sought to show how changes in the individual's circumstances are related to changes in health.

Physical health

Brenner has attempted to relate changes in the rate of unemployment to changes in a number of pathological indices (Brenner, 1977; Brenner and Mooney, 1983). He claims that a 1 per cent increase in unemployment in the USA over a six-year period was associated with a 2 per cent increase in deaths. In reviewing the evidence from his own work and that of others in a number of countries, but especially the USA and UK, Brenner argues that there is a time-lag between the onset of unemployment and the increase in the incidence of cardiovascular disease, cirrhosis of the liver, infant mortality and total all-cause mortality (Brenner and Mooney, 1983) which affect the unemployed and their families.

One of the problems with this technique is that one is forced to relate changes in the unemployment rate to mortality rates for the community as a whole and not just for the unemployed members of the community. The result is that there can be no certainty about the direction of causality. Work by Eyer (1977, 1977b) has suggested that the time-lag involved between stress and onset of ill-health is not as great as that maintained by Brenner, who sees the rise in mortality associated with the business-cycle as caused by the stress of economic success on the employed, for example, by the increased hours of work, family break-up, etc. Gravelle, Hutchinson and Stern (1981) see unemployment as one factor among many to be taken into account when examining the causes of ill-health in a section of the population. What this and other work in the area (Colledge, 1982; Watkins, 1984) suggests is that there is a link between mortality rates and the business-cycle and that unemployment is a contributory factor.

At the level of individual experience, a number of different studies have pointed to the adverse consequences of unemployment on health. Perhaps the best known is that of Kasl in the USA[2]. This was a longitudinal study in which it was possible to observe the effects of unemployment on the health of the same individuals (Kasl, 1979; Kasl, Gore and Cobb, 1975). They found the blood pressure of workers rose when they were informed of their plant closure. The blood pressure of those who found work quickly began to fall while for those who experienced longer periods of unemployment, it tended to remain high. In terms of their general health, those who found the experience of unemployment more severe indicated a higher level of days when they complained of illness and higher levels of days of disability. In Britain, Colledge and Bartholomew (1980), when they questioned a random sample of long-term unemployed, found that poor health in their respondents increased with age and lower status in their last job, and that those with longer periods of unemployment were more likely to be in fair or poor health. In this case, it may be that poor health causes unemployment, rather than vice versa, but studies which have controlled for this possibility have still found that rates of ill-health among the long-term unemployed were higher than for the general population (Watkins, 1984). At this level the evidence that unemployment and ill-health are related is firmer.

Mental health
Studies of the psychological well-being and mental health of the unemployed point in the same direction, namely that in a significant number of cases there is a relationship between the experience of unemployment and a deterioration of mental health. At the macro level Brenner and Mooney (1983, p. 1129) cite a number of studies showing a relationship between unemployment and the rate of admission to mental hospitals, again with a time-lag of between six months and five years between an increase in unemployment and an increase in the admission rate.

At the level of individual experience, the work of Catalano and Dooley (1977) in the USA points to a link between unemployment, stress and the self-reporting of mental disorders, although a second investigation failed to replicate the result (Catalano *et al.*, 1981). Buss, Redburn and Waldron (1983) in their study of the psychological impact of a plant closing on mental health scores, found that the unemployed showed more stress symptoms than those who had found new jobs, were retired or had been continuously employed. However, these effects were only mild, a finding the authors attributed to the fact that 94 per cent of the sample found new jobs or were eligible for early retirement.

In Britain, an extensive programme of work on the psychological effects of unemployment carried out by Warr has produced harder evidence. Summarising their results Warr states

the results are clear in respect of psychological health. Experiences of strain, anxiety, depression and hopelessness are likely to increase because of unemployment and the level of aspiration, sense of autonomy and positive involvement in the world are all likely to be negatively affected. (Warr, 1983b).

In view of these studies we can be more certain of the direction of causality in the case of psychological stress. In addition, we are now in a position to specify more precisely which groups are at risk. Their findings show that while young men do suffer negative psychological effects from unemployment (Stafford, Jackson and Banks, 1980; Banks and Jackson, 1982) they do not suffer such high levels of distress as middle-aged men with their greater family and financial responsibilities.

Finally, there is the effect of unemployment on suicide and attempted suicide. This is more of a contentious area. At the macro level studies found a direct relationship with no time-lag between unemployment and suicide rates, although others have contested this (Hayes and Nutman, 1981, p.77; Brenner and Mooney, 1983, p.1129). In Britain, Platt's study of parasuicide (non-fatal deliberate self-harm) among males in Edinburgh led him to conclude that the findings were consistent with the view that unemployment increases the parasuicide rate (Platt and Kreitman, 1984). In addition he found that the relationship between parasuicide and duration of unemployment fits the phase model; a high rate associated with the initial shock, an improvement during the optimistic phase and a worsening during the later stages of pessimism and fatalism. In reviewing the literature on suicide and unemployment Platt (1984) states that the evidence of an association between the two is overwhelming but that the nature of the association is problematic.

While there can be little doubt about the existence of a relationship between ill-health and unemployment we would argue that the effect it has on health will vary from one group to another as we outlined in the previous chapter. For the middle-class males who find themselves unemployed the shock is greatest. It is not surprising, then, that Platt and Kreitman (1984) noted that the middle class have the highest risk of all groups of suicide when they become unemployed. For those in the lower segments of the labour market, the situation is likely to be very different. Some of the emotional stress and insecurity which the middle class encounter on becoming unemployed, and which surround the threat of closure for those in 'safe' working-class jobs[3], are part of the everyday experience of work for workers in the lowest segments whose uncertain and irregular income can be just as debilitating as unemployment (Ferman and Aitken 1967; Cobb and Kasl, 1977; Buss and Redburn, 1983). In addition, because they are in low-paid jobs, many workers and their families are already living on the poverty line even when in work. This means in addition to the emotional stress generated by the insecurity of their jobs, their lack of resources is likely to act directly on their physical well-being. When these workers enter spells of unemployment as they frequently do, it is not so much new problems that they face as an intensification of existing ones. It is at this point that the effects of unemployment and poverty become compounded. It suggests that for them it is not the absence of work as an activity which is so important in creating health problems as the absence of the adequate financial and other material resources[4]. The coexistence of low-paid, insecure employment and spells of unemployment in the experience of these workers means that it is virtually impossible to separate the effects of the two elements. However, the consequence in terms of higher rates of mortality is well established (Black Report, 1980).

In concluding this discussion of unemployment and health it should be noted that because ill-health is a very personal experience, its effects tend to be confined to the individual and his/her close friends and relatives. In this sense, the costs of unemployment are borne privately in the home, away from the glare of publicity and political controversy. Yet despite this, it is important to bear in mind that there are other 'public' costs in the form of extra demand for medical resources from the health-care system.

Crime

As was the case with health, there has been some controversy over the nature of the relationship between unemployment and crime, and clearly unemployment is not the only factor involved. However in Britain, Junankar (1984) in a macro-level study found a positive relation between youth unemployment and crime. In general he found unemployment more significant in explaining the number of persons found guilty or cautioned compared with the number of persons sentenced for indictable offences.

In her survey of the literature, Hakim (1982) concludes that higher levels of unemployment can be expected to contribute towards higher levels of crime and delinquency, and produce an increase in the prison population. She identifies three processes through which this occurs: (i) unemployment increases recidivist crime; (ii) parental and youth unemployment increases juvenile delinquency; and (iii) unemployment increases re-conviction, the rate of imprisonment and the size of the prison population. More specifically, it tends to be associated with property crimes such as burglary and theft (Hakim, 1982, p.450). In view of the higher rate of unemployment among the lower socioeconomic groups, it is not surprising that there is also a link between class and crime (Braithwaite, 1981). Surveying American economic literature, Freeman (1982) came to the conclusion that there is a connection between unemployment and crime, but no clearly-defined, quantifiable linkage. Among his main conclusions were the following:

1. There is a cyclical pattern to the crime rate with crime rising over the cycle with unemployment.
2. There is evidence that criminals tend to have poorer work records than non-criminals; but only limited evidence that once a person embarks on crime, moderate changes in these market opportunities will cause him to choose legitimate earning channels.
3. Cities and states have widely different crime rates loosely linked to labour-market conditions.

As with health, the question of causality is complex. In the case of juvenile crime this peaks before young people enter the labour market but nevertheless the crime rate among youths rises in relation to increases in the level of youth unemployment. In addition, attempts to isolate causes face the same problems we identified earlier. At the individual level, if criminal actions are undertaken, as was the case with the youth cited in the second case study cited above, this does not necessarily result in a criminal statistic unless the person is caught by the police and convicted by the courts. Thus the size of the police force and their attitudes to potential offenders, as well as the attitudes of the judiciary are just a few of the other factors to be considered. It is in this complex web of relationships that unemployment enters as one of the factors.

For the community, the costs of unemployment in the form of increased criminal activity and delinquent activity are far more evident, because they impinge more directly on those who are not unemployed. Increases in burglaries and theft place householders at greater risk, while delinquency and vandalism become more widespread. As a result, increases in the crime rate arouse far more concern in terms of demands for increased law and order and government action than does the increase in private suffering and public expenditure associated with ill-health.

The Response of the Unemployed

So far we have documented a considerable body of evidence which specifies the costs of unemployment and the way in which most of them are carried by the unemployed. As we stated at the start of the chapter, unemployment hurts. Because many of the unemployed are known to suffer from their situation it is appropriate to ask what their response is, and how they react to their situation.

In public discussions it is often assumed that one of the political costs of mass unemployment is a threat to the social fabric, a threat which sooner or later will manifest itself as civil unrest. In fact, in neither the 1930s nor the 1980s have such forms of mass action emerged.[5] In view of this the more appropriate question to ask is why there has been relatively little in the form of a collective response from the unemployed. First, let us consider the main forms of collective action which have emerged in recent years.

Riots

Widespread youth unemployment in Britain in the early 1980s did contribute towards the riots which took place in a number of cities in 1980 and 1981. In these riots the young unemployed fought the police, destroyed property and created something of a 'moral panic' among the media and ruling groups (Mungham, 1982). This is what a number of people predicted, given that young people were left with time on their hands and were congregating in large numbers in the centres of urban areas—exactly the kind of conditions one might expect to generate social protest. However, the riots were a distinctly British phenomenon. Black Americans had rioted in a number of cities in the late 1960s and early 1970s, but these did not recur when their unemployment rates rose even higher in the 1980s. Closer examination of the British riots revealed that although they involved both black and white youths, the racial element was of central importance in some areas. The riots were in a large part directed at the police, for one of the triggers was not just a sense of material deprivation and frustration—although these were present—but a sense of moral outrage by young blacks of West Indian descent about their treatment by the police and their entrapment in the system they call 'Babylon' (Cashmore and Troyna, 1982).

The distinctive feature of riots as a form of social protest is that they are sporadic, and while they can bring political and media attention to a particular problem they cannot provide a basis for the sustained pressure necessary to implement a programme of change. In this respect the most effective forms of collective action have come from those in work.

We have already discussed some evidence which suggests that, at the individual level, some of the most traumatic emotional reactions occur when the threat of unemployment is announced. One collective response to this has been the factory sit-in, another has been moves to form cooperatives by redundant workers to take over the running of the business (OECD, 1983). Perhaps the most dramatic response has been the year long British miners' strike of 1984/85 which was called to fight the threat of redundancy. The reasons for these collective responses are not hard to find. The existence of the threat of redundancy while the workers are still employed means that not only is the link between the action of employers and their future life-chances clear, especially in times or regions of high unemployment, but their collective presence at one location and/or membership of a trade union organisation makes the organisation of collective action easier (Weber, 1948). The reason why such action should be more widespread in Britain than the USA is no doubt related to the more widespread union membership in Britain, and its stronger tradition of collectivism and the greater geographical concentration of labour.

In both societies there have been few signs of the unemployed attempting to change their situation through political action. Why is this? What are the cultural conditions which inhibit the unemployed from organising and attempting to alleviate their position? There have been two main attempts to help further our understanding of this problem. Runciman (1966), in his analysis of the 1930s depression argued that the unemployed in Britain did not express great resentment at their position because of their restricted reference group. When evaluating their position in society, their point of reference was not 'the rich' but other working-class groups who were little better off than themselves. The principle that the employed working class should support the unemployed working class was broadly accepted by the members of that class. He concludes that

where poverty is due to unemployment or dependent children, rather than to inadequate wages, the comparative reference groups most likely to suggest themselves are other people who are in work, or who have fewer children, rather than those who are relatively better paid. (Runciman, 1966, p.73)

For him, it was the first and second world wars which brought about a change of reference group and gave greater intensity to feelings of relative deprivation and an upsurge of expectations. However, these were counteracted by the effects of the

Depression in the 1930s and, after the second world war, by gains in the standard of living of the working class.

A more recent attempt to answer a similar question within the American context has been made by Schlozman and Verba (1979). They hypothesised that the jobless would perceive their objective deprivation subjectively and would consider government action relevant to the alleviation of their problems. They would then develop a sense of group consciousness and set of policy preferences in readiness to mobilise political pressure aimed at securing favourable treatment from the government. What they found was very different.

Some of their results have already been discussed—for example, their survey showed that joblessness produces strain. When compared with those in employment the jobless are much less satisfied with their income and accomplishments in life. Although they made strenuous efforts to cope on their own with their predicament their efforts did not significantly reduce the economic or psychological strain of joblessness.

If unemployment hurt, as it did, what were the political implications? To explore these, they looked at the image of society held by the jobless. What they found was a widespread commitment to the American dream of individual opportunity for success and a low level of class-consciousness. This aspect of their investigation revealed little connection between the personal economic situation of the sample and their ideology. In spite of experiencing personal strain the unemployed were not markedly more cynical about the reality of the American dream or more class-conscious. Even their own experience of downward mobility was not related to their social ideology. They did not feel guilty about their plight, but neither did they deny responsibility. They took it upon themselves to alter their circumstances by looking for work and rationalising family finances. At the same time they thought that the government had a responsibility to create jobs and help those in need. When it came to specific policies, the unemployed did support moderate policies directly relevant to the alleviation of the economic problems, more so than those in work. However, when it came to more radical or drastic measures, the jobless were no different to those in work. In part, this reflects the stronger American attachment to the values of individualism.

In that context, race rather than class is the more important factor. Thus, they found that whereas race-consciousness engenders political activity among blacks, class-consciousness did not engender it among the unemployed. Their voting behaviour was a result of long-term, partisan commitments and not related to their unemployment.

The authors conclude that the effects of unemployment are severe but narrowly focused, manifest in ways proximate to joblessness itself. Political action in the form of voting was determined by prior political beliefs and only loosely related to their present life circumstances. In short, there was little evidence of any political mobilisation among the unemployed. While this research took place in 1976 and most of the sample were short-term unemployed, the voting pattern of the British unemployed in the 1983 General Election suggests a similar response. At that election a substantial proportion of the unemployed voted for the Conservative Party and not the Labour Party which traditionally has claimed to champion the cause of the unemployed and which gave employment measures a higher priority in its election manifesto. Here too voting behaviour was only loosely related to personal circumstances.

What both these investigations imply is that the unemployed have a restricted frame of reference when evaluating their situation. The deprivations they endure lead them to compare themselves with other groups or people in the same situation. While they may see the government as having some responsibility for improving job prospects and the lot of the unemployed, the experience of unemployment does not appear to have led to the adoption of radical political views. However, such findings represent only part of the answer to our question, for there are other reasons why the unemployed have not engaged in sustained collective action aimed at improving their position or changing the social order.

The first of these is that the unemployed are at any one point in time composed of a number of different groups: school-leavers, older workers, middle-aged males with family responsibilities, single and married females, blacks and whites. In addition, those entering the ranks of the unemployed come from different social backgrounds. In terms of their previous experience they are not a uniform group. While the unskilled and semi-skilled tend to be disproportionately represented, in times of high unemployment, the unskilled are joined by skilled workers and white-collar workers. Each of these groups brings to their situation a different set of prior experiences and perhaps more importantly, material resources. In many families the existence of more than one job-holder cushions the financial impact (Flaim, 1984). For a manager or professional to become unemployed may mean moving to a smaller house, but it is very doubtful that he/she would sell a house in a prestigious suburb and move nextdoor to an unemployed labourer in the poorest part of town if the spouse remains in work. Given these and other financial and status differences it would require a very long period of shared experience before 'the unemployed' identify as members of the same group.

In addition to differences in their origins, those who become unemployed at any one point in time are not all destined for the same fate. In this respect, at least three main categories can be distinguished: (i) those entering short-term unemployment and who later return to paid employment; (ii) those who enter into long-term unemployment; and (iii) those who after being unemployed leave the labour market. While any one individual cannot be certain that he/she will avoid becoming part of the long-term unemployed, the high level of movement into and out of the condition of unemployment militates against the development of a collective consciousness. This will be especially applicable in America where, given the shorter average duration of unemployment, the majority can realistically expect to move into work in the not-too-distant future. In Britain, the longer average duration of unemployment and its geographical concentration among a more limited number of communities is creating a more collective awareness in the form of a culture of unemployment, but such communities are sometimes internally divided (Seabrook, 1982).

Finally, from the point of view of most of the unemployed, their situation is one from which they hope to escape rather than improve through collective action (Roberts, 1984; Ashton *et al.*, 1985). As we have seen, this is particularly evident in the USA with its stronger ethos of individualism. Even in Britain with its tradition of collectivism, evidence from the long-term unemployed (White, 1983) suggest that their main aim is to return to work. For them the solution is seen to lie in individual action; that is, to get a job and get out of their present situation rather than improve it by collective or political action.

Conclusion

In terms of the costs of unemployment, what does all this mean? It means that most of the direct cost of long-term unemployment is carried by individuals and their families through financial deprivation, poverty and ill-health. The other economic costs are met by the state. For those in work, their standard of living is maintained or improved, the costs they meet are more marginal and specific such as thefts and the occasional destruction of personal and public property through vandalism.

At a societal level it appears from the experience of Britain and the USA that societies can operate with relatively high levels of unemployment without serious social protest, at least in the short run. In the long run the situation may be very different. High levels of unemployment concentrate the subsequent deprivation among certain groups. Such groups have shown remarkable resilience in coping with the personal suffering occasioned by the poverty, insecurity, frustrations and depression frequently associated with long-term unemployment. What evidence there is suggests that rarely do the unemployed see these costs as the 'fault' of the political or economic system. However, when the personal suffering has other moral grievances superimposed upon it the situation can change dramatically. In the USA this has been occasioned by the superimposition of racial discrimination on the poverty which stemmed from the labour market position of the blacks. In Britain the riots of 1980 and 1981 point to the explosive potential of racial discrimination when combined with unemployment. In Northern Ireland the superimposition of religious discrimination on the deprivations engendered by poverty and unemployment has fuelled the violence of civil war. The longer high levels of unemployment are maintained the greater the risk that they will have other 'moral' injustices superimposed upon them. These represent the political cost of unemployment.

7. The State and Unemployment

In discussing the role of the state in creating labour market shelters we made a distinction between the allocative and productive functions of the state (Offe, 1984). This distinction is also important in discussing the state's activities in the field of social policy, as opposed to economic policy and job generation, because the pressures which operate in the two areas are very different. The rules through which the allocative functions operate apply equally to all those affected so that, for example, all those with income above a certain level are obliged to pay tax. In other circumstances the rules may apply to a specific category of people, for example, all those in Britain who contribute to the national insurance system are eligible for benefit payments when they become unemployed. Because of this they can be administered through bureaucratic procedures which are used to determine, in advance, the individual's obligations to pay and their right to benefit. Such rules are imposed by political parties operating through the legislature and represent the outcome of the kind of political struggles we discussed in Chapter 1. In both societies the welfare benefits that are available represent the result of pressure from the public. Moreover, the form such benefits take is conditioned by the political institutions and the administrative arrangements through which resources are allocated, and for this reason the provision is different in each society. In this chapter we examine these differences and the reasons for them.

In the field of the state's productive functions, in the administration of nationalised industries, in the provision of subsidies to firms and the provision of training, the decision-making process is less subject to influence from representative political institutions. Policy is more frequently the outcome of bargains and deals struck between politicians, civil servants and the major interest groups such as large companies, financial institutions, the professions and, to a lesser extent, trade unions. Thus, in Britain, the Youth Training Scheme was set up not after a prolonged political campaign by any of the parties, but in response to the immediate problem of youth unemployment. In this context bureaucratic means of operating are inflexible and inoperative. If government strategies are to work, decisions have to be made quickly and take account of the relative power of the various interest groups involved. For this reason they cannot easily be legislated for in advance and made in accordance with rigid rules. All this means that in the state's productive functions big business and the financial institutions are far more influential in determining government policy and strategy than they are in determining how resources are distributed through the welfare system. Only the latter is at present particularly responsive to public pressure (Cawson, 1982).

Through their productive functions the British and American states have reacted in two ways to the problem of unemployment. First, they have used manpower policy, especially various forms of training measures, as an ameliorative measure to stimulate the economy with the aim of improving the workings of the labour market and thereby placing more people in employment. In conjunction with this, further measures have been introduced to reallocate existing work, either by encouraging employers to locate new investment in depressed areas or by encouraging groups not to enter the labour market or to leave it early. In the second half of the chapter we look at these measures in more detail.

Alleviating the Consequences of Unemployment

Welfare measures

While the state has attempted to relieve the social and financial consequences of unemployment for the individual, the ways in which this has been accomplished reflect the differences in the institutional structure of the state, the relative power of capital and labour, and the dominant values outlined in Chapter 1. As we pointed out there, the labour market plays a far more important role in allocating resources in the USA. In Britain the state provision of unemployment benefits, pensions and social security provides a comprehensive and uniformly administered system. Heidenheimer (1981) estimated that as early as 1947 at least 60 per cent of the UK labour force were covered by the four main social security schemes of accident, old age, sickness and unemployment insurance. This creates a 'safety net' which is more successful than the US system in bringing incomes of the unemployed to nationally-defined poverty levels. In the USA the coverage is fragmentary, the delivery decentralised and the benefits variable. As Sinfield noted (1976) 'there is no "safety net" for the great majority of the unemployed in need of assistance'.

Like the attempts to take medical care out of the market, the attempts to introduce measures of income maintenance for the unemployed and the poor came later in the USA. In this respect it has often been claimed that the United States has been a laggard in the development of welfare programmes (Wilensky, 1975). This is certainly borne out by comparison of the dates at which the major welfare programmes were introduced. Industrial accident insurance was introduced into Britain at the end of the nineteenth century and in the USA in 1930 (Kudrie and Marmor, 1981, p.81). Sickness insurance in Britain came in 1911 and still has not been introduced in the USA[1]; neither have family allowances. Pension insurance came in Britain in 1908, but not until 1935 in the USA; and, finally, unemployment benefit came in 1911 in Britain but again not until 1935 in the USA. Only in the field of public education was provision made earlier in the USA than in Britain (Heidenheimer, 1981).

The reasons for the earlier introduction of the pension and unemployment benefit schemes in Britain were linked to the earlier development of working-class organisations and the fear of socialism on the part of the ruling class. It was this, together with aristocratic concern for the welfare of the poor, which led the Liberal government of 1905 to introduce both schemes 'to avoid the violence to existing institutions that socialists demanded' (Bruce, 1968, p.191). In the USA it took the traumatic experience of the Great Depression to persuade Roosevelt to introduce similar measures through the Social Security Act. In both societies these initial measures were partial. The difference between the two has been that in Britain the stronger emphasis on collectivisim, the greater political power of working-class organisations, together with their cooperation in the war effort led to the implementation of more comprehensive coverage. In the USA the Social Security Act 1935 provided the basic institutional framework within which provision has since developed. With regard to unemployment benefit, Kudrie and Marmor (1981, p.96) note that, with a few exceptions such as the federally-financed temporary extension of benefits during periods of high unemployment, and the introduction of a temporary special unemployment assistance programme for unemployed workers not enrolled in the system, the initial format has remained basically unchanged. They note that 'the most salient feature about the US experience is that, with the exception of the food stamp programme, every measure is an amendment to the original Social Security Act.' In the USA there has been no substantial push from below as occurred with the British labour movement to institute the revised, more comprehensive system of welfare that emerged after the second world war.

The form of provision in both societies is also conditioned by differences in the institutional structures of the state through which they are provided and in the dominant values of the society. The more highly centralised British state facilitated the growth of a uniform national system. In the USA the federal government remained for a long time constitutionally and politically inhibited from launching direct initiatives. As a result, the states retain more options on whether or not they utilise federal programmes. In 1961 federally-aided assistance for families with dependent children where the father was unemployed was introduced, but in 1976 only 28 states had opted to provide it. All states provide some help for female-headed families but for all others in 1976, such as single men and women, couples with no children and male-headed families with dependent children, in nearly half the states, reliance had to be placed on state- or locally-funded assistance. In 20 states in 1969 this meant nothing at all for anyone regarded as 'employable'. When schemes did emerge they tended to be a mixture of federal and state initiatives and often involved joint funding. Although unemployment benefit was the result of a federal initiative, it is the states which run the schemes, usually through employers, with the federal government playing a coordinating role. The 1935 Old Age Assistance programme which also originated in the Social Security Act, involved joint action by the federal and state governments, with federal finance accounting for two-thirds of the cost and the state the remaining one-third. The level of benefits also varies substantially from one state to the next. Sinfield (1976) observed that the industrial states tend to have more liberal provisions of unemployment benefit, while the southern states, together with many in the mid-west, have more restrictive provision, although there are marked exceptions. Heidenheimer (1981, p.286) estimates that overall benefit levels have varied by factors of 4 to 1 among states and localities. In the absence of either a strong labour movement to provide the pressure for uniform schemes, or a strong federal administration to organise them, it is difficult to see how the US could have implemented the kind of centralised schemes of welfare that emerged in Britain and Europe.

In the administration of unemployment benefits the other significant difference between the two societies lay in the fact that the US system was financed by employers. The concern of the legislators and others who argued for such a system was to help employers create a responsible social order. It was envisaged that they could dominate market forces and so the scheme provided incentives to employers not to lay off workers (Nelson, 1969). The result of such a system is a reluctance by employers to pay heavier taxes to expand the programme and a tendency for the American employer to distinguish those unemployed as his own financial responsibility from the rest of the unemployed. It focused attention on the needs of the employers as opposed to those of the unemployed (Sinfield, 1976). However, since the early 1970s the system has depended less and less on state employer taxes to pay for benefits as the initiation of non-regular benefit programmes in 1970 and 1974 signalled the beginning of a significant federal role (Padilla, 1981).

In Britain the concern was to strengthen the social order by incoporating the working poor as citizens into the political community; not by acting through the employers (Marshall, 1950). As a result the system was centrally administered in a uniform manner throughout the country, and emphasis was

placed on ensuring that those who benefited had a stake in the
system by contributing to it. It was designed to provide support
for those who became unemployed through no fault of their
own, and although limited initially to a few industries was
always seen as part of a larger programme.

Compared with the US system of unemployment benefits in
which payments are linked to previous income, the British
system provides for a uniform flat-rate payment to those who
qualify. When this payment ceases, or if it is not considered
sufficient to bring the family up to the national poverty level, it
is supplemented by a means-tested supplementary benefit.

However, in spite of its more comprehensive coverage there
are still large groups in Britain who do not qualify for
unemployment benefit. These include young people entering
the labour market, women who have not paid the full insurance
contribution and those who have been unemployed so long
they have exhausted their benefit. In 1980 this meant that only
45 per cent of the registered unemployed received unemployment benefit (Sinfield, 1981a). Moreover, since 1975 this group
has been growing as many of the workers in part-time jobs no
longer contribute to the national insurance scheme. In 1984
these constituted 2.7 million workers or 13 per cent of the
labour force.

Outside the system of public income maintenance, there are
other forms of income available to the unemployed in both
societies. In Britain this takes the form of a state-organised
system of redundancy payments; in the USA, privately organised insurance. In Britain, workers with a certain minimum
period of service are entitled to redundancy payments when
they are made redundant. The level of compensation specified
in law is not very high, but for those in professional,
managerial and administrative occupations (the higher segments with more secure shelters) employers tend to be more
generous in the compensation they offer. Similarly, manual
workers with more secure shelters tend to be offered awards
well above the legal minimum. For those in the lower segments,
where labour turnover is more rapid and jobs are more casual
and low-paid, redundancy payments, calculated on the basis of
previous earnings, are much lower, assuming that the worker
has sufficient length of service to warrant an award at all. This

means that for many workers especially the young and women in casual and part-time jobs, there are no redundancy payments. Even among those who do receive them, the average level of award is not sufficient to provide the basis for an alternative source of income.

In America private unemployment insurance schemes tend to be a product of labour market shelters. These are set up under collective agreements and have been introduced on a large scale since 1955 (OECD, 1979). They offer benefits which, when combined with the general scheme, ensure an income equivalent to about 70–80 per cent of the former net wage. These are generally paid for 52 weeks and are sometimes supplemented by allowances for dependants, and in certain cases by severance pay, moving allowances and health insurance premiums for laid-off workers. Again it is the lower-paid workers who are least likely to have access to these provisions.

In spite of these considerable differences between the systems of income maintenance their implementation involves confronting similar problems in both societies. As we noted earlier, the introduction of a system of income allocation independent of that provided through the labour market, creates a potential threat to the main means of distributing resources in society. In this instance the threat is perceived in terms of the danger such a system poses to the 'incentive to work'. This is the case especially for those at the bottom of the occupational hierarchy in the low-paid, insecure jobs. In fact there is little hard evidence to suggest that the level of income provided by such benefits has any appreciable impact on the overall level of motivation to work.

An OECD survey of research on the effects of unemployment benefit on the level of unemployment found that in a number of countries, including Britain and the USA, there was a statistically significant association between the two but this involved no more than an extra week or two on-the-job search. In other words, it helped give workers some degree of choice in labour markets so they might not necessarily have to accept the first job offered (OECD, 1983). In spite of this those in powerful positions, such as employers, politicians and newspaper owners, continue to see it as a threat. Moreover, the idea that income should be earned is one that is widely held throughout both British and American society (Wilensky, 1975, p. 37).

In view of this it is not surprising that there has been substantial and sustained pressure on those designing and implementing the schemes to ensure that the provision of benefits does not 'undermine' the incentive to work (Kudrie and Marmor, 1981, p.97; Sinfield, 1981). The result in both societies has been to generate and sustain a distinction between benefits that are earned and hence deserved, and those that are provided without reference to paid employment and are 'undeserved'. In Britain a conscious effort was made to ensure that unemployment benefit, when it was first implemented, would not 'encourage malingering' (Bruce, 1968, p.199). Other measures used in both countries performed the same function; for example, the limited period of time for which it was awarded—one year maximum in Britain, and up to 39 weeks in the USA, depending on the state (OECD, 1979). In addition both insist that unemployment must be involuntary, that recipients regularly attend the labour exchanges, and that they do not refuse jobs considered suitable. If the worker leaves without 'good cause' or is dismissed for misconduct sanctions are imposed. In both societies the administration of the schemes is separate from that of other forms of income maintenance. In this way unemployment pay is seen to be given to those who have worked. They are separated from other forms of claimant for social security.

In Britain this has served to differentiate the unemployed from those claiming supplementary benefit where the use of the means test has helped perpetuate the link with the 1834 Poor Law. As the allowances are paid on the basis of 'need', this has to be assessed by the official taking into account the claimants' resources. Although the levels of provision are laid down in the Social Security Act 1980 and its regulations, help may be reduced, limited in duration, refused or stopped even if the official criteria of need are met, but other conditions are not (Sinfield, 1981, p.111). It is this subjection of the client to a detailed scrutiny of his/her circumstances which helps ensure that supplementary benefit remains a means of last resort for many. In the USA the provision of assistance for those without means of support can be even more intimidating and harrowing. In the early 1960s in Newburgh, New York, welfare recipients were faced with a choice between police interrogation and fingerprinting, or the loss of benefits (Wilensky, 1975, p.33).

Transfer payments

In addition to alleviating the financial consequences of unemployment for the individual, the state's allocative functions have also been used to 'solve' the problem of unemployment in a number of ways. In Britain regional policy has encouraged firms to expand or relocate in the depressed regions through investment subsidies, tax concessions and more directly through planning controls. In addition, subsidies have been made available to encourage workers to move to where the jobs are. Both measures do not, of course, increase the number of jobs, but rather relocate either existing jobs or workers. Amidst the failure of these and other measures to bring about a lasting reduction in the level of unemployment there is a tendency for commentators and politicians to resort to policies which involve either reallocating work or reducing the labour supply. This involves either redistributing existing work so that the unemployed have a share of what is available or reducing the numbers that are looking for work.

Reallocating work or restructuring working-time, can be done in a number of different ways (OECD, 1983). Perhaps the most popular proposal has come usually from union interests and involves reducing the working week (Jenkins and Sherman, 1979). In the EEC 51 per cent of the working population expressed a willingness to trade pay increases against more leisure (OECD, 1983, p.9). In fact unions are usually reluctant to trade pay against working hours; they want both, which means that this option is resisted by employers. Other options which follow this theme are proposals for longer holidays, sabbaticals, job-sharing and early retirement. Longer holidays had in fact already made a substantial impact in lowering the annual hours worked in Europe, even before the present recession. The idea of extending sabbaticals—already a feature of university teachers' conditions—to other groups within the working population is one that is often mentioned, but apart from some manual workers in the USA, it has not formed part of the normal agenda of the collective-bargaining process and has not received governmental support in either society. It is certainly a potentially important way of restructuring working-time over the employee's lifespan in the labour market. The only schemes that have received official backing in Britain have been job-sharing and early retirement. These are attractive to government because they can use funds that would otherwise go to pay the unemployed. In this context, however, job-sharing also involves income-sharing and for this reason has not proved very popular. Of all these measures early retirement has proved the most widespread. This is partly because companies have used it as a means of cutting back on their labour force. By offering financial inducements to older workers the more disruptive process of declaring redundancies has been avoided.

There are two main ways of reducing the supply of labour, one is to lower the age of retirement—a method that would be costly to the state because of the need to meet pension payments; the other is to reduce the numbers entering the labour market. As we have seen this has been one of the ways of combating the problem of youth unemployment. In the past, the progressive raising of the school-leaving age has helped solve the problem, but it is now clear that there are limits to the effectiveness of this course of action. The problem of high school drop-outs which the Americans have experienced for some considerable time indicates the resistence to this policy offered by those destined to enter the lower segments of the labour market. In both societies this has been partially overcome by offering them work-based training programmes instead of conventional education.

All these measures are what may be termed the conventional response. There are however a number of more radical suggestions which involve breaking the link between work and paid employment (Pym, 1975). As we noted earlier these two are often seen as synonymous, but if the link were broken, for example, by paying everyone a minimum wage, a number of new possibilities would emerge. The supply of labour would be reduced, as many would prefer to take more leisure. A range of activities such as housework, DIY repairs, long periods of study, etc. would become more popular as involvement in them would not necessarily result in loss of income. While offering a number of 'new' solutions these suggestions are in many ways as radical a solution as that offered by a socialist revolution which could guarantee work for all, as it does in Eastern Europe. However, because the labour market is the main means of allocating resources, any attempt to disrupt that by providing an income to all, irrespective of their function in the labour market, would threaten a number of powerful vested interests. The threat it poses to the 'incentive to work' would mobilise business while the uncoupling of income and occupational position from social status which it also implies, would threaten the ideologies through which a large part of the middle stratum in both societies justify their privileged positions. Of course, this does not mean that either of these solutions is impossible, only that they are improbable given the prevailing circumstances of British and American society.

Manpower Policies

Manpower policies, by which we mean training programmes, labour subsidies, job-creation, counselling and advice services, like welfare policies, reflect the major differences in the values and institutional structures of the two societies. In the USA manpower policy is targeted at specific groups, its delivery is decentralised and job-creation[2] has traditionally played a central role. In Britain manpower policy is far more comprehensive in its coverage of the labour force, its delivery is centralised and job-creation has played a less important part.

In both societies, manpower policies were introduced at the same time as welfare measures. They were a response to the acute social problems associated with high rates of unemployment, although in Britain they have also been influenced by the pressures of international competition. Since the turn of the century there has been a keen awareness in Britain of the need to keep pace with the country's main economic competitors. As the state has increasingly come to play a larger part in carrying the costs of industrial training in countries such as Germany, this has increased the pressure in Britain for similar action to prevent the country falling further behind[3]. With the USA being less dependent on international trade these pressures are less evident.

As was the case with welfare measures, the state's involvement in manpower policies occurred earlier in Britain than in the USA. Initially it was fear of the dangers from within which led Churchill and the Liberal government of 1905 to introduce a system of nationwide labour exchanges (Bruce, 1968, p.194). They were intended not only to police the system of national insurance but also to facilitate a more immediate and direct contact between job vacancies and the unemployed. During the first world war the state was extensively involved in mobilising manpower, but at the end of the war its activities were reduced (Burgess, 1980). However, it soon became involved in further attempts to modify the operation of the labour market as a result of the rising problem of unemployment. Grants for public work were introduced but these were wound up in 1931/32 (Stevenson and Cook, 1979, p.63). Juvenile unemployment centres, later renamed junior instruction centres, were set up to combat the problem of juvenile unemployment by preventing the 'demoralisation of youth and maintaining their employability' (Rees and Rees, 1982, p.18). Subsidies were also introduced to facilitate the movement of workers from the depressed areas to those parts of the country where more jobs were available.

After the second world war, a new impetus was given to manpower policy by the fears about Britain's continued economic decline. In an attempt to intervene more actively in the operation of the labour market and produce a more highly qualified and adaptable labour force industrial training boards were set up under the Industrial Training Act 1964 (Lindley, 1980, 1983). These were aimed at improving the quality and quantity of training in each of the industries for which they were responsible. (Many of them were subsequently wound up in the early 1980s.) However, the most important innovation in this period was the Manpower Services Commission, introduced in 1973 (Hill, 1981). This is a semi-autonomous government agency with responsibility for coordinating and developing manpower policy. It developed its activities in three main areas; it upgraded the old labour exchanges into more effective agents of job placement at all levels of the labour market; it developed training initiatives through its own skill centres and through funding training courses in colleges; and it provided programmes for youth. The result has been the first steps towards the development of a comprehensive training programme.

In the USA it was the internal tensions and problems created by the 1930s Depression which led to the development of the federal manpower policy with the introduction of the 'New Deal'. Given the size of the country and the decentralised character of the labour market, there was no attempt to impose a uniform system of regulation through an employment service. The main thrust of the programme was job-creation. Since that time the USA has had many job-creation programmes, often as part of larger programmes (Jerrett, 1980). The Manpower Development and Training Act 1962 introduced the large-scale training of unemployed workers and those without qualifications wishing to acquire a skill. This was replaced by the Comprehensive Employment and Training Act 1973 which provided the framework for manpower policy throughout the later part of the 1970s. In addition to providing funds for job-creation, it could fund various forms of training through training allowances, subsidies to firms training their own labour, as well as through its own programmes. Apart from training it could also provide guidance, counselling and placement services. The scale of this intervention was reduced by the Job Training Partnership Act 1982. It continued to fund the major training activities developed under CETA, including on-the-job training, classroom training and counselling, but placed severe restrictions on the payment of training allowances and other forms of income maintenance (Smith, 1983).

In addition to these activities the federal government has also provided subsidies to employers who take on certain categories of disadvantaged workers. For example, employers who took on workers who were previously receiving public assistance were eligible for a tax credit under the work incentive programme. This has been continued in the Targeted Jobs Tax Credit begun in 1978.

Differences in the values of British and American society are evident in the nature of the programmes implemented. In the USA the importance of individualism and self-reliance is manifest in a number of ways. Much greater emphasis is placed on the education system as a means of preparation for work, young people stay in it longer and more obtain vocational qualifications. Thus, in 1981, 73 per cent of the 16–24-year-olds participated in education in the USA compared with between 32 and 40 per cent in Britain, while 78 per cent of the civilian labour force had a recognised qualification compared with 50 per cent in Great Britain (King, 1983; *Competence and Competition*, 1984). Employers in the USA play a more central role in the provision of training, spending at least 3 per cent of annual turnover compared with less than 0.5 per cent in Britain.[4] In addition the individual is also expected to undertake training in his/her own time in the USA.

This emphasis on self-reliance is also apparent in the centrality of job-creation measures as a response to unemployment. In the 1970s Operation Mainstream provided public employment at the local level in rural areas to family heads near retirement age, Public Service Careers for disadvantaged workers, and Neighborhood Youth Corps for young people. The Comprehensive Employment and Training Act 1974 provided for the creation of temporary public employment in areas of high unemployment. This tradition of public service job-creation was curtailed by the Reagan administration's Job Training Partnership Act which replaced CETA, continuing its training activities but dropping the provision for public sector employment (Smith, 1983). However, such was the strength of this traditional American measure for dealing with unemployment, that the President was obliged to reintroduce job-creation measures in 1983. This reliance on job-creation may also be a consequence of the fragmentary welfare provision, for in a society where such welfare is not widely available the only alternative to hunger and destitution is to provide the means whereby self-reliance can be maintained—that is, through employment of one form or another.

The other way in which these values are manifest in manpower policies is through their targeting on specific groups. This was the case with many of the job-creation measures cited above. With regard to training, the assumption was that companies and individuals would meet their own training needs, so that government programmes were only targeted on groups at risk. They provided training for those groups who were especially at risk, and whose employment prospects did not improve in line with the improvement in the overall level of employment in the 1960s, namely the unskilled, youths and ethnic minorities. This was epitomised in the JTP, the aims of which were

to prepare youth and unskilled adults for entry into the labour force and to afford job training to those economically disadvantaged individuals and other individuals facing serious barriers to employment who are in special need of such training to obtain productive employment.[5]

The task of ensuring an adequate level of skill for those in employment was left to private enterprise. The state programmes were directed primarily at the casualties of the system.

The greater emphasis on collective provision of training and labour market services in Britain gives a greater role to the state. The training boards were set up by the state to organise training in each industry and were financed by a levy on all employers with the aim of placing pressure on them to improve the quality and quantity of training they provided. Unlike the situation in the USA, employers could not be trusted to provide adequate training. Following the dismantling of some of these boards the main impetus now lies with the MSC. This body incorporates representatives from both sides of industry and represents a form of corporatist solution. It provides state-financed resources which are used in conjunction with those of employers to develop and improve training provision. The emphasis on the collective provision of welfare has meant there has been less pressure in Britain to utilise direct job-creation measures as a means of dealing with high levels of unemployment. Community service schemes and job-creation measures were reintroduced by the government in the 1970s; but they play only a relatively small part in the measures adopted by the Conservative government to combat the mass unemployment of the 1980s (Markall, 1982). One of the unintended consequences of a comprehensive system of welfare is that it reduces the pressure on government to create jobs, as the casualties are provided for in other ways.

The other point of contrast which reflects differences in values is the scope of the programmes. In Britain both the employment and training services aim to be more comprehensive in their coverage than their American counterparts. The MSC now aims to develop a comprehensive national system of training through its new training initiative. As part of this the recent Youth Training Scheme seeks to include both the employed and unemployed in what is seen as a step towards a uniform national system of training. Thus, while in practice some of its programmes are directed at specific groups these programmes are usually seen as part of a broader, more comprehensive strategy.

The other factor which has played an important part in differentiating the British and American approaches to training and manpower policy has been the institutional structure of the state. In the USA the federal government initiatives of the 1960s created stronger central control over the job-creation and training programmes it funded. In this respect they broke with earlier traditions. However, the power of the states eventually eroded this approach and, when CETA was introduced in 1973, the planning and administration of the scheme was de-centralised to the states. More recently the Reagan administration has pushed that process further with the JTP. The result is the more traditional decentralised American approach. In Britain the more centralised approach to manpower services was epitomised in the establishment of the MSC as a semi-autonomous body with its own resources. This has enabled central government, acting through that agency, to introduce major changes in the approach to vocational training and the training of youths. Because it is a national institution this encourages greater uniformity in provision throughout the society and creates a further impetus towards the creation of a national, centrally administered system of training, which would bring Britain more in line with some of its European competitors.

These differences in the way in which the state utilises manpower policy to tackle the problem of unemployment and the effects of national values and institutional arrangements in shaping such response, can be illustrated by reference to the state's response to the problem of youth unemployment. In view of the greater importance attached to educational provision in the USA (Janowitz, 1976), it is not surprising that concern was first expressed about the high rates of unemployment among high school drop-outs and disadvantaged youths in the deprived inner-city and rural areas (Cohen and Nixon, 1981). The result was the early establishment of a variety of schemes (*Giving Youth a Better Chance*, 1979). The cure for the problem was seen as further training and work experience. Programmes were developed, such as Job Corps, Neighborhood Youth Corps and the Youth Incentive Entitlement—which aimed to prevent young people from dropping out, or to provide training for those who had already done so (Sherraden, 1980). The significance of the youth problem was reflected in the fact that in 1976 20 per cent of all training and 30 per cent of job-creation funds went to youth. To quote Trow (1979) 'The American programs are designed for young people from poor homes who are not going to college' (although he proceeds to criticise many of the programmes for their failure to reach what he terms the deprived). Given the continuance of high levels of unemployment among the disadvantaged groups and especially among blacks, it is not surprising that many of the programmes from CETA have been retained under the less well-funded JTP.[6] The focus still remains on the same groups within the labour market.

The British response to the problem of youth unemployment when it emerged in the 1970s was initially very similar. A number of schemes providing for job-creation and training were introduced, such as Community Industry and the Work Experience Programme. However, whereas the problem of youth unemployment in the USA was seen as a structural problem because of its persistence at times of relatively full employment, the British problem was perceived as essentially temporary and being 'cured' by cyclical changes in the economy. As a result, a number of temporary schemes were initiated, all aimed at improving the attitudes to work, job-related skills and acceptance of work discipline among those young workers who were most at risk.

In 1978 these temporary schemes were incorporated into the Youth Opportunities Programme administered by the MSC, the main element of which was work experience on employers' premises.[7] The programme was aimed initially at the unskilled, unqualified school-leaver but as unemployment rates soared in the early 1980s many well-qualified school-leavers were obliged to enter the programme. With youth unemployment rates approaching 50 per cent it became difficult to maintain that it was the personal characteristics of the unemployed that were at fault: the problem of youth unemployment was starting to look as though it had other causes which required a different solution. In the meantime, the MSC was attempting to develop a more general strategy to improve the skills of the British labour force to meet the challenge of Britain's industrial competitors. While the MSC has been obliged to take on and administer an unemployment measure, its main concern was to improve the skill level of the labour force. To do this it sought to develop a training scheme for all young people. However, the harsh political reality was that the government would only provide funds for measures to combat unemployment. The result was a compromise—the YOP was replaced by the Youth Training Scheme. The objective was to form a bridge between school and work for all school-leavers in the form of a one-year training scheme. Although the scheme does include a number of apprenticeships it has not yet succeeded in incorporating most of those who go straight into jobs. Thus, unlike the USA which continues to fund targeted programmes, what started as a temporary measure in Britain directed at the same group of unqualified school-leavers, became transformed as a result of higher levels of unemployment and a powerful centralised state agency into a more coherent strategy for improving the training of all young people entering the labour market. The significance of the British youth unemployment problem is reflected in the fact that approximately one half of the MSC budget in 1984 was devoted to youth measures.

Precisely because the policies on manpower issues are a product of the values and institutional structures of the respective societies, they play an important part in the reproduction of existing relationships. In the USA the programmes are utilised by 'disadvantaged' youth who are integrated into the mainstream of American society but who lack the necessary financial resources. Yet they are not utilised by 'deprived' youth, who are the source of much of the national anxiety about youth and for whom many of the programmes were designed (Trow, 1979). In Britain the more comprehensive YTS is starting to replicate existing class divisions, as middle-class youth continue in higher education and the YTS becomes a measure utilised by working-class youth. In this sense the scheme is restructuring the entry of working-class youth into work (Roberts, 1984) and reshaping the links between education and the labour market (Finn, 1982; Markall and Gregory, 1982). However, because the British scheme is more comprehensive and centralised it is potentially a more important mechanism of social change.

These examples also show the limitations on the use of manpower policy as a means of 'solving' the problem of unemployment. In both societies youth unemployment continues at high levels. Such policies can, however, limit the financial, social and psychological consequences of unemployment. This is how they are currently being used. At present they ease the problem of youth unemployment by taking young people off the labour market and providing training or work experience. One effect of this is to encourage the substitution of one group of workers for another. Thus, if the problem of unemployment is eased by subsidising the labour of young people on a government-financed scheme, it is often at the expense of adults (Raffe, 1983). Such subsidies only bring a marginal change in the overall demand for labour (OECD, 1982; Smith, 1984). The combined effect of a number of schemes can play a part in reducing the overall level of unemployment but so far they have never amounted to a cure.[8]

8. Strategies for Creating Jobs

If solutions based on manpower policy have not been very effective in reducing high levels of unemployment, what are the alternatives? What insights can a sociological analysis of the problem contribute towards its solution? These are the questions we wish to address in this final chapter of the book.

We have argued that the problem of unemployment is not caused by the personal failure of individuals to equip themselves with the qualities sought by employers or by their insistence on maximising their income. The fundamental problems lie in the processes of change which have increased the rate at which existing jobs are destroyed or made obsolete and the failure to sustain or increase the rate at which new jobs are generated. In the 1930s this problem was resolved by governments adopting what came to be know as Keynesian policies, that is, by public investment and demand management, which was later intensified as the industrial nations armed in preparation for the second world war. This created an increased demand on the productive capacity of the society together with a reduction in the supply of labour to the economy caused by the demand of the armed forces. These social forces rapidly reduced the level of unemployment. We stress this not to commend it, but as a reminder that this has been one of the functions of war, namely to minimise the internal tensions created by high levels of unemployment while at the same time removing the cause.

A second set of circumstances under which unemployment could be lowered or eradicated would be in the context of a socialist revolution, as happened in Eastern Europe. There the state has taken over the role of allocating resources for production and changed the role of the labour market. Labour is not bought and sold but allocated to various tasks although some aspects of the process of allocation—for example, educational performance—have close similarities to those in the West. This means that unemployment does not exist in the sense in which we have used the term, as the state guarantees a job to its citizens. As we mentioned earlier, such a solution seems improbable in Britain, and more so in the USA, because of the power of capital and the centrality of free enterprise and individualism to the American value system. Such a solution is only likely to be imposed on the USA as a result of war. In Britain the stronger socialist tradition could produce a move in the direction of greater state control over the economy given a change in the balance of power between the parties, although such an event is unlikely to produce the degree of centralised control witnessed in communist societies.

What then are the solutions available within the framework of contemporary capitalism? Earlier we argued that to understand changes in the division of labour we have to approach the problem at two levels, namely the international and the national. At both levels we need to examine the institutional arrangements through which the division of labour is organised. It follows from this that the problem of unemployment requires tackling at both levels. As the comparison of national unemployment rates shows the problem of high levels of unemployment is not confined to Britain and the USA, for most of the European societies are also affected. Part of the problem lies in the changes which have taken place in the pattern of international trade and the institutions through which it is organised. While the conditions which generated the post-war boom remain a matter of debate (Maddison, 1982; Rostow, 1983), there appears little doubt that one of them was the international stability created by the post-war accord and the institutional arrangements set up by the Bretton Woods agreement. Since then new industrial nations have emerged, the OPEC countries have come to play a significant part in determining the terms of trade, and new debtor nations have been created, especially in Latin America. At the same time the increasing division of labour has intensified bonds of inter-dependence at the international level. These represent a very complex set of changes involving a series of institutions responsible for regulating international trade and finance. Yet these institutions were designed to regulate affairs when the USA dominated the western economies and before the changes mentioned above took place. A fresh look should now be taken at them and attempts made to bring them more into line with the existing balance of power between nations in order to facilitate the growth of world trade.

At the national level Table 1.1 illustrated the differences in the way the advanced capitalist societies have been affected by world recession. Some, such as Britain, The Netherlands and Canada, and to a lesser extent the USA, have been badly affected; others, such as Sweden, and Japan, have come through with relatively low rates of unemployment. This suggests that there are factors operating at the national level which are also important in determining the rate at which a society can generate jobs. Our analysis has pointed to a number of factors which may be important. In earlier chapters we examined some of the underlying structural changes affecting contemporary societies: the possibility that some of the main changes currently taking place in large areas of manufacturing and the service sector are producing a quantum shift in the relationship between employment and output, reducing the demand for labour; the possibility that we may soon enter a new upswing in the long waves sparked off by the emergence of new products; the underlying shift from full-time to part-time employment. These are all important issues on which further research is needed and may have a bearing on the problem, but the fact remains that despite such changes some societies have proved much more adept at creating jobs and maintaining full employment than others. The short-term economic policy pursued by governments is another important factor in influencing the level of unemployment. Thus, the Reagan administration was able to create a substantial reduction in the level of unemployment in 1984 through the Keynesian technique of a budget deficit without creating a high level of inflation. However, the rate of unemployment still remained well above that achieved in the world boom conditions of the 1950s and 1960s. In Britain where such techniques of economic management have been rejected, the rate of unemployment continued to rise during the 'recovery' of 1982/1984.

In the long term our analysis points to another set of factors which are of crucial importance in determining the ability of a society to generate sufficient new jobs to keep its members employed. These are the institutional arrangements through which the division of labour is organised within the society. At the risk of over-simplifying the issues, this could be described as the way in which the major institutions of the state, business and labour are linked to each other. In Chapter 1 we discussed how the relationship between the state, business and labour differed between Britain and America. If we now cast the net wider it is possible to distinguish at least three different types of configuration which these institutions form, namely the integrative, the *laissez-faire* and the regulative (McKersie and Sengenberger, 1983).

The *integrative* tends to be found in societies which were late-developers: that is, they were late in entering world markets for manufactured goods. This meant that the resources of the state, as mobilised through its allocative and productive functions together with those of capital and labour, had to be coordinated very effectively to ensure a breakthrough into existing markets. It involved the state agencies working closely with capital and labour to ensure that capital was invested in areas in which the society had (or could create) a competitive advantage in world markets. Such a strategy tends to be linked to a clear policy on international trade which is used to guide the flow of capital internally. It assumes that structural change stemming from the movement of capital from one industry to another will be inevitable but can be managed without particular groups having to shoulder all the costs of adjustment in the form of unemployment.In effect, it means that workers are protected from the worst effects of the dislocation which such a policy involves. It involves the owners of capital accepting certain limitations on their 'right' to invest, and labour accepting that uncompetitive industries should be allowed to decline.

Japan is the obvious example of one country which adopted this strategy to good effect, although elements of it can also be found in Sweden and Germany. In Japan the Ministry of International Trade and Industry, in consultation with industry, promotes a long-term (seven-year) plan which seeks to direct investment into those industries where it is believed that growth will take place and in which the country can compete effectively in international markets. In the 1980s precision engineering, electronics and information technology are the current growth industries. Those industries in which it is believed the country cannot compete effectively are closed down. With the cooperation of the large companies, banks and unions, finance and labour is directed away from those industries (usually labour-intensive, such as textiles) and into the growth areas. Both the allocative and productive functions of the state are mobilised in order to achieve these goals, financial assistance in the form of low-interest loans, subsidies, tax credits and financial aid are made available for research and development in the growth sectors. In those industries which are closed down, grants are made available to finance the retraining of workers for jobs in the growth area. This whole process is facilitated by the large multi-industry characteristics of the major enterprises which provide a guarantee of life-time employment for their workforce (McKersie and Sengenberger, 1983). In cases where this is not possible they may be transferred to other firms. This effectively removes the fear and insecurity created by the threat of unemployment and facilitates the rapid relocation of labour. One consequence of this is that there is a very weak relationship between the fluctuations in the business-cycle and unemployment in Japan.

This strategy has enabled Japan to respond rapidly to changes in world markets while maintaining high levels of employment. In terms of labour-market policy, this means integrating it with a policy towards employment generation which in turn is closely linked to changes in the pattern of world trade. It means coordinating and integrating policies in the field of regional employment policy, training policy and education in relation to the goals of employment creation.

The *laissez-faire* type is exemplified by the USA. The state plays a subordinate role to private industry, and market forces are relied upon to determine the allocation of resources. The productive and allocative functions of the state are kept to a minimum. Where they are used it is primarily in the interests of business, unions are accepted as legitimate but their influence is restricted partly as a consequence of the legal system. Welfare rights are kept to a minimum, manpower policy is targeted only at the casualties of the system, and few restrictions are placed on the powers of capital in the labour market. While structural change in the economy is rapid in such

societies there is little protection for workers from the dislocation created by such changes. In the specific case of the USA,
when American industry was challenged by Japanese exports
the response was not to coordinate the activities of the state,
capital and labour and plan a strategy, but to leave it for
business to respond and to re-establish the pre-eminence of the
USA in those parts of the market where it could compete. The
role of the state is confined to injecting extra demand. Given
the continuing dominance of the American economy and its
relatively high degree of self-sufficiency this strategy has been
effective in generating jobs, but it does involve a relatively high
level of unemployment.

In Britain, the relationship between the state, business and
labour is characterised as *regulative*. As the first society to
undergo capitalist industrialisation for some time it approxi-
mated the *laissez-faire* type as the manufacturers sought to
minimise the role of the state in the market and to suppress
worker organisations. Yet for reasons mentioned earlier this
strategy never achieved the success it had in the USA, the state
remained relatively strong in relation to business which was
subordinated to the needs of the aristocracy and finance
capital. In addition labour was organised extensively and
secured important gains both directly through its influence on
the labour market and indirectly through its periodic control of
the apparatus of the state. The result was that the state, while
remaining in a relatively powerful position *vis-à-vis* industrial
capital, left it relatively free to determine where investment
took place. However, because of the greater relative power of
labour, workers were sheltered from the dislocation created by
economic change. This was done, as we have seen, through an
extensive system of welfare benefits which reduced the insecur-
ities inherent in the labour market. In addition it was achieved
through nationalisation which eased the run-down of industries by spreading it over a longer period of time. Also, the legal
powers of the state were utilised to protect the employment
rights of workers. This particular configuration was characteristic of Britain until the 1970s. It ensured very high levels of
employment throughout the 1950s and 1960s but failed to
sustain them in the late 1970s. Since then, with the advent of the
Conservative administration in 1979 there has been a cons-

cious attempt to change the internal balance of power between capital and labour, to reduce the activities of the state and so return to a *laissez-faire* type of relationship with the relatively high level of unemployment such a strategy implies.

This analysis implies that the *laissez-faire* model is not the only strategy available to Britain and the USA. In view of Britain's greater reliance on world trade it may make sense to move towards an integrative model, in which the industrial base of the society becomes more specialised. Instead of leaving individual companies or entrepreneurs to compete in a broad range of markets against the large Japanese companies with their state support, it would make sense for the state to encourage the growth of selected companies in areas where Britain could develop a competitive advantage, in those industries which are likely to form the basis of the upswing in the next long wave. This would also involve the creation of new institutions which would enhance the value of industrial activity in the society at large and ensure a more cooperative relationship between capital and labour. Many of the major institutions through which capital and labour are organised were formed during a period of intense hostility and conflict between the two groups and this has left its mark on them. At present the organisation of business interests, unions and even the political parties reinforces that distrust and conflict, whereas the experience of other societies shows that this is not the only way of organising the relationship between the three main sources of power. The integrative model suggests that it is possible to moderate the conflicts of interest and to focus the energies of all three groups on the development of the productive forces and the creation of jobs.

In the case of the USA, which is not as dependent on world trade, such a strategy may be of less immediate relevance, and because of its decentralised political structure more difficult to implement. Conventional economic policy has proved important in reducing unemployment levels, but given the maintenance of the existing relationship between capital, labour and the state, unemployment levels are likely to remain relatively high. From the point of view of those who carry the costs of that unemployment the regulative strategy would represent a promising alternative.

All this implies that there are no easy answers but it also shows that political, social and cultural factors influence the ability of society to create jobs and to cater for those who carry the costs of unemployment. Moreover, such institutional factors are not immutable and can be subject to change. The ability of a society to generate jobs and to provide for the unemployed depends in part on the relationships which are forged between the state and capital and labour. It is the task of the sociologist to present to policy-makers and the public the alternative forms of such relationships. That is what we have sought to achieve.

Appendix

A Note on the Problem of Measurement

In the contemporary situation the unemployment statistics have come to play an important part in determining how extensive we see the problem of unemployment to be. Given the controversies which surround the public discussion of the causes of unemployment it is not surprising that there is also debate over what the unemployment statistics measure. In the USA rates are compiled by the Bureau of Labor Statistics from the data supplied through the Current Population Survey, a monthly sample survey conducted by the Bureau of the Census. This method approximates that recommended by the International Labour Organisation, in which a series of questions are asked in the survey to establish whether a person is unemployed. The criteria are that the individual must (i) be without a job and not in full-time education; (ii) be seeking paid employment; and (iii) have taken steps to look for a job within the week preceding the survey. This survey method is generally considered the most reliable way of collecting the information because the survey agency goes directly to the individuals involved (OECD, 1979). Yet it is not without its problems. For example, it excludes 'discouraged' workers. These are often the long-term unemployed who are not looking for work because they believe there are no jobs available in their line of work or in their community. If they have not looked for work in the previous four-week period they are not counted as unemployed. At times of high unemployment and in areas of high unemployment this can lead to an under-estimation of the numbers involved. Another difficulty is the American practice of counting persons seeking part-time work as unemployed, including students. Also, because it is a sample survey, the results are subject to sampling error. This does not constitute a problem for national estimates where the error is small but it does raise a problem in relation to the states and localities, where the sampling error is much greater.

In Britain a totally different method of collecting statistics is involved. The official figures are currently derived from monthly counts of the persons claiming benefit at the local unemployment benefit offices. This is less reliable as a measure for two main reasons. First, it is a product of the unemployment benefit system which was not designed to produce figures for social analysis. Because of this it excludes those who are unemployed but have no incentive to register, such as those married women who are not entitled to benefits. It also includes what is believed to be a smaller percentage who register for benefits because they are entitled to them but who may not be actively looking for work. Secondly, it is subject to administrative and political manipulation. During the period of high unemployment in 1982 an administrative change in the point at which registration takes place, from the Jobcentre or careers office to the unemployment benefit office was estimated to have reduced the unemployed total by between 150,000 and 200,000. In 1983 further changes were made in benefit regulations which reduced the number of older men on the count (LMQ, September 1983). The British government conducts a Labour Force Survey which produces results that are more comparable with the American count and, because it is a survey, these results are considered more reliable.

In view of the political significance attached to the unemployment figures and the difficulty in developing an effective measure of the 'true' extent of unemployment, it is difficult to establish the precise level of unemployment at any one point in time. In Britain, many journalists and the TUC have argued that the official figure of 3 million unemployed in 1983 underestimated the real extent of the problem by about 900,000, half of those being on government training or job-creation schemes. Yet those on some government-sponsored schemes are in receipt of an income in return for their contribution to the national product and in that sense are difficult to distinguish from other government employees on short-term contracts. On the other hand, there are some who argue that the official figures over-estimated the true extent of unemployment because in the British case they included people who were moving between jobs, the short-term unemployed, school-leavers, adult students, faudulent claimants and the so-called unemployables.

The problems with this argument are numerous. First, the definition of the unemployable is contentious and even if accepted, the definition used by employers changes in accordance with the level of demand in the labour market. As for school-leavers and the short-term unemployed, the length of time they spend waiting to acquire work depends on the general level of demand in the economy; in this sense they clearly constitute part of the unemployed. As the official figures in Britain are collected for purposes other than those of providing an accurate count of the unemployed, and as the definition of what constitutes an unemployed person is subject to different interpretations by members of opposed political groupings, then the debate is likely to continue. For a social scientist interested in establishing the proportion of people who would work, if employment were available, the official rates under-estimate the level of unemployment. This had always been the case with the 1948–82 series of counts but has become more acute since the changes made in 1982. If the pre-1982 count had continued the Unemployment Unit estimated that the total numbers unemployed in January 1985 would be 3,728,500 as opposed to the 3,341,000 that appeared in the official count.

The discrepancies in the way in which figures are obtained and compiled make international comparisons of the level of unemployment extremely hazardous. The Bureau of Labor Statistics publishes international comparisons where the British and other data are 'adjusted' to American concepts, and these have been included in Table 2.1. However, when we have no reliable knowledge of what the 'true' rate of unemployment is in either country, such figures have to be treated with caution. This is particularly evident in relation to the 1930s (Garside, 1980). If the adjusted figures presented by Maddison which make allowances for the inadequacies of the earlier figures are a closer approximation to the reality of the situation, then the recession of 1979–83 in Britain has produced a level of unemployment which in January 1985 was officially measured as within 1.4 per cent of that reached at the height of the Great Depression. If however, the official figures are used, the situation in the early 1980s remains far less severe than that encountered in the 1930s. In the USA the reliance on survey data reduces this problem of comparability.

Notes

Chapter 1

1. There is a huge literature addressed to these questions which were also the issues tackled by Marx, Weber and Durkheim, and formed much of the basis of modern sociology, see Giddens (1971). More empirically-based discussion of the issues raised here can be found in Perkins (1969), Hobsbawm (1968) and Thompson (1968). In the USA the work of Moore and Hoselitz (1963) and Smelser (1959) has been important in raising these questions on a more abstract level in the sociological literature. Perhaps the best-known formulation of the problems of labour management is Kerr *et al.* (1962). For a more recent appraisal of these questions, see Kumar (1978).
2. The effect of this transformation of relationships on the ways in which people experienced their world can be best comprehended through the more detailed work of historians on local communities. For South Wales, one of the first major industrial areas, see Jones (1973) and the work of Williams (1966) and Williams (1978). These provide a vivid account of the costs of 'adjustment' which workers faced.
3. For a more detailed discussion of the ways in which changes in the division of labour enhance bonds of interdependence and are inextricably linked to changes in political organisation, see Elias (1978).
4. This account was taken from *The Guardian*, 12 May 1983.
5. In Britain the national health service does not preclude the use of private medicine.
6. In socialist societies, where the state guarantees employment, worker-motivation is more of a social problem.
7. The complex process of change whereby the manufacturing class was later assimilated with the landed aristocracy and commercial interests to form the contemporary business class has been analysed by Scott (1982, Chs. 4, 5, 6). Guttsman documents changes in the social composition of political leaders until the 1960s. It was not until the Thatcher government of 1979 that representatives of the business class dominated the cabinet.
8. The use of troops to put down the Merthyr rising of 1831 generated considerable apprehension in ruling circles. See Williams, (1965) Jones (1966), and the correspondence in the Home Office records, H.O.52/6.
9. The police force was developed partly as an alternative to the use of troops. See *First Report of the Commissioners appointed to inquire as to the best means of establishing an efficient constabulary force in the counties of England and Wales* (1939), British Parliamentary Papers (169), vol. XIX.

10. For a different interpretation of the relationship between capital, labour and the state in Britain, see Edwards (1983).
11. See Dodsworth and Flemming's report on US trade unions (*Financial Times,* 10 April 1984) for a discussion of the recent use of these tactics in the USA.
12. For useful summaries of the development of unions in the USA, see Schneider (1971, Chs.11, 12), Thomson (1981), Mayhew (1983) and Phelps Brown (1983).
13. There is considerable debate about the reason for the failure of the American working class to develop a self-conscious political movement. See for example, Gordon *et al.* (1982, pp. 4–8) and Laslett and Lipset (1974).
14. The distinctive characteristics of individualism in the Amercan belief system and its effects on identity are dealt with in Field and Travisano (1984). For a discussion of the relationship between American individualism and the origins of symbolic interaction, see Rock (1979).
15. These ideas later came to be embodied in the functional theory of stratification, see for example Davis and Moore (1945).
16. The late development of business schools is also a product of the late development of modern forms of business management in Britain.

Chapter 2

1. The term 'élite' is used to designate those who occupy formally-defined positions of authority at the head of a social organisation or institution (Giddens, 1974, p.4). Its usage here does not pre-empt the question of the primacy of either political or economic power, the conceptualisation of which follows that advocated by Elias (1978).
2. Garraty (1978) provides an invaluable account of the history of unemployment which has been extensively used in what follows.
3. For a brief outline of Keynes' ideas, see Eatwell (1982) or Showler (1981); for a more detailed discussion see Keynes (1936).
4. The effects of changing employment levels on managerial authority and worker behaviour is frequently discussed in the *Financial Times*, for example, the issues of 4 January 1984 and 28 January 1985.
5. For a brief account of monetarism, see Eatwell (1982) and Showler (1981). For a more detailed discussion of monetarist theory, see Friedman, *The Optimum Quantity of Money and Other Essays* (1969); for his views on policy, see the *IEA Occasional Papers* (1970; 1975). The term 'monetarism' is, technically speaking, used to refer to the quantity theory of money. In public discussion it is also used to refer more loosely to the application of the quantity theory and neoclassical theory in the present situation. It is the latter usage we are concerned with.
6. For other discussions of the impact of information technology, see Stonier (1983), Bell (1974) and Gershuny and Miles (1983).
7. For a discussion of the development of long-wave theories see Freeman *et al.* (1982, Ch.2) and Maddison (1982, Ch.4).

8. The term 'waves' is used in preference to cycles because of the connotation of fixed periodicity attached to the latter.
9. The precise role of public policy in both the growth phase of the 1950s and 1960s and in the latest recession is a matter of current dispute, see Maddison (1982, Ch.6) and Rostow (1983, Ch.2).

Chapter 3

1. There is a growing debate on the relevance of educational qualifications to job performance (Berg, 1973; Dore, 1976) and on the precise criteria used by management in the selection of workers for less-skilled work (Blackburn and Mann, 1979, pp.102–9; Maguire and Ashton, 1981; Manwaring Wood, 1984).
2. The concept of market shelters is taken from Freedman (1976), who utilised it to explain differences in earnings between occupational groups. Its potential as a sociological concept to explain occupational autonomy has been developed by Freidson (1982).
3. In Britain this approach has been developed by the Cambridge Labour Studies Group, Craig, Rubery, Tarling and Wilkinson (1983), Wilkinson (1981) and Rubery (1984). See also Loveridge and Mok (1979). In the USA the early work of Bluestone (1973) and Piore (1971) has since been developed by Edwards, Reich and Gordon (1975). See Piore (1971), Gordon, Edwards and Reich (1982) and Schervish (1983).
4. This analytic distinction derives from the work of Offe (1984). It has proved particularly useful in the analysis of social policy, see for example Cawson (1982).
5. In the long run, of course, a sustained fall in the wealth of a nation will affect the level of resources the state can devote to consumption.
6. Schervish (1983) includes all state activities in his analysis and does not distinguish between the two functions.
7. For a discussion of the changes which occurred in the development of the labour process in Britain and the USA, see Littler (1982).
8. This technique has been most extensively developed and utilised in Japan. See Dore (1973).
9. There has been some evidence that in the latest recession the managers most vulnerable to unemployment are those whose activities are least central to the production process, such as personnel and training managers.
10. There has been a long history in Britain of mangement's attempts to buy out restrictive practices and impose uniform conditions. For an account of management's strategy at ICI, see Owen (1979, Ch. 5) Flanders (1964).
11. Schervish (1983, p.67) cites studies by Feldstein (1975, 1976) and Medoff (1979), which suggest that between 66 and 88 per cent are re-hired. Clark and Summers (1979) suggest a rate closer to 50 per cent. For a description of how lay-off procedures operate, see Casey and Bruche (1983, pp.65–71).

12. In Britain this movement has been documented by the Oxford Mobility Group (Goldthorpe, 1980) and shows substantial upward mobility for those entering the labour market during the post-war boom. In the USA the relationship with educational attainment was most comprehensively documented by Blau and Duncan (1967). A more recent study which links educational attainment to careers and labour market structure is Spilerman, vol. 83 (1977).
13. There is some controversy over the precise role of educational qualifications for entry to this level of the labour market, see Gray *et al.* (1983).
14. For American evidence see Osterman (1980, pp.25–7) and Lester (1954). For Britain, see Blackburn and Mann (1979, pp.102–8), Manwaring (1984) Manwaring and Wood (1984).
15. There is an extensive literature on the sources of racism and its relation to the class structure. Here we are only concerned with the impact of racism in the structuring of the labour market.

Chapter 4

1. The use of the term 'society' rather than 'economy' is deliberate in order to refer to the political as well as the economic factors responsible for creating jobs. It is a mistake to regard only the economy as capable of generating jobs.
2. Figures based on Bureau of Labor Statistics Statistical Abstract of the United States, 1982/83, 103rd edn and subsequent data released by the Bureau of Labor Statistics.
3. For a recent attempt to tackle this problem, see Gershuny and Miles (1983).
4. Ginzberg (1977) notes that in the USA the 'good' jobs were largely created by government.
5. Sinfield and Showler (1981, p.11) cite a figure of three times the annual rate; Flaim (1984, p.30) cites a figure in excess of twice the annual rate.
6. For a discussion of the discouraged worker effect, see OECD, *Employment Outlook* (1983).
7. For a more detailed discussion of the earlier introduction of 'systematic' management in the USA and its consequences for the internal organisation of the firm, see Littler (1982), Edwards (1979) and Gordon *et al.* (1982).
8. It is possible for those receiving social security benefits to enter education provided their courses are part-time.
9. The most recent and detailed comparative analysis of this problem can be found in OECD (1984, Ch.V, pp.69–86). It concludes that wage relativities do matter, but their importance cannot be quantified.
10. Aspects of this interpretation of high rates of youth unemployment have recently been questioned by Hasan and Broucher (1984) and Clark and Summers (1982).
11. Similar arguments have been made by Casson (1979), Roberts (1983) and Williamson (1983).

Chapter 5

1. The theoretical basis for these beliefs is to be found in the work of Maslow (1954) and Herzberg (1939).
2. The classic discussion of the way in which deviance reinforces the commitment to a society's dominant values is to be found in Durkheim, *The Division of Labour in Society* (1964).
3. *Leicester Mercury*, 2 June 1984.
4. Indirectly there is an effect because of the lower use made of health care facilities by lower-income groups (*Black Report*, 1980). Current research (Ashton *et al.* 1985) suggests that the children of the unemployed do less well at school than the children of the employed and have less chance of entering employment. It points to the emergence of an underclass in Britain.
5. This discussion is based on the work of Warr and his colleagues in the Social and Applied Psychology Unit, Sheffield University (Warr 1983a, 1983b, 1983c).
6. The six points identified here are taken from Warr (1983a), but Jahoda (1982) also makes five similar points.
7. The idea of a series of stages or phases in the reaction of people stems from studies by Eisenberg and Lazarsfeld (1938), Hill (1977) and Powell and Driscoll (1973), while the phase model has been used by Harrison (1976), Hayes and Nutman (1981) and King (1982) to describe these and other findings. Other studies which have either influenced the development of the phase model or are cited in support of it are Jahoda *et al.* (1933), Bakke (1933) and Marsden and Duff (1973); and in the USA, Slote (1969) and Taber, Walsh and Cooke (1979).
8. Hayes and Nutman develop these ideas from the work of Parkes (1971).

Chapter 6

1. Fagin and Little (1984) argue that a great deal depends on the stage reached in the family cycle.
2. For a useful summary of the work by Kasl, see Hayes and Nutman (1981, pp.74–6).
3. Kasl reported that the threat of unemployment can induce stress and similar findings were reported by Buss and Redburn (1983, p.73).
4. It has often been noted (Jahoda, 1982; Warr, 1983) that some jobs are positively harmful to health and these are usually the more unskilled and low paid.
5. In the 1930s the Unemployed Workers' Association was formed by the unemployed in Britain but it never achieved mass support, (Stevenson and Cook, 1979).

Chapter 7

1. Sickness insurance was introduced in 1965 but a person needed to be unemployable for the last six months and expect another year of the same condition (Kudrie and Marmor, 1981).
2. Job-creation is used here to refer to direct job-creation schemes in which public money is used to create jobs. In the public discussion the term is often used to apply to employment or labour subsidies, business start-up schemes, and training programmes; see Hargreaves, *Financial Times*, 1 February 1983.
3. The most recent manifestation of this is the report *Competence and Competition* (1984).
4. Results of a survey by The Industrial Society, London, February 1985, quoted in the *Financial Times*, 4 February 1985.
5. Quoted in Smith (1983, p.65).
6. For critiques of these policies which treat them as primarily cosmetic and failing to address the real problems, see Gaynor and Nixon, (1981) and Trow (1979).
7. There are a number of recent studies of various aspects of the MSC programmes. See Varlaam (ed.) (1984), Fiddy (ed.) (1983), Atkinson and Rees (eds) (1982), and Gleeson (ed.) (1983), Raffe (1984a).
8. In Sweden in 1983 it was estimated that such measures accounted for 3 per cent of employment (Hargreaves, *Financial Times*, 1 February 1983).

Bibliography

Adams, A.V. and Mangum, G.L. (1978) *The Lingering Crisis of Youth Unemployment*, The W.E. UpJohn Institute for Employment Research, Michigan.

Aldcroft, D.H. (1964) 'The Entrepreneur and the British Economy, 1870–1914', *Economic History Review*, 12.

Aldcroft, D.H. (1984) *Full Employment*, Wheatsheaf, Brighton.

Althauser, R.P. and Kalleberg, A.L. (1981) 'Firms, Occupations, and the Structure of Labor Markets: a Conceptual Analysis', in Berg, I. (ed.) (1981).

Anderson, B.E. and Sawhill, I.V. (eds) (1980) *Youth Unemployment and Public Policy,* Prentice-Hall, Englewood Cliffs, N.J.

Anderson, D.S. and Blakers, C. (1983) *Youth, Transition and Social Research*, Australian National University Press, Canberra.

Ashton, D.N. and Field, D. (1976) *Young Workers: The Transition from School to Work,* Hutchinson, London.

Ashton, D.N. and Maguire, M.J. (1980) 'The Functions of Academic and Non-academic Criteria in Employers' Selection Strategies', *British Journal of Guidance and Counselling* 8(2).

Ashton, D.N. and Maguire, M.J. (1980a) 'Young Women in the Labour Market: Stability and Change', in Deem, R. (ed.) (1980) *Schooling for Women's Work,* Routledge & Kegan Paul, London.

Ashton, D.N. and Maguire, M.J. (1983) *The Vanishing Youth Labour Market*, Youthaid, London.

Ashton, D.N. and Maguire, M.J. (1984) 'Dual Labour Market Theory and the Organisation of Local Labour Markets', in Beardsworth, A. (ed.) (1984).

Ashton, D.N., Maguire, M.J. and Garland, V. (1982) *Youth in the Labour Market*, Research Paper No. 34, Department of Employment, London.

Ashton, D.N., Maguire, M.J., Bowden, D., Kennedy, S., Stanley, G. and Woodhead, G. (1985) *Young Adults in the Labour Market,* Research Paper, Department of Employment, London (forthcoming).

Atkinson, P. and Rees, T.L. (eds) (1982) *Youth Unemployment and State Intervention*, Routledge & Kegan Paul, London.

Badie, B. and Birnbaum, P. (1983) *The Sociology of the State*, trans. Arthur Goldhammer, University of Chicago, Chicago/London.

Bain, G.S. (1970) *The Growth of White-Collar Unionism,* Oxford

University Press, Oxford.

Bain, G.S. and Price, R. (1980) *Profiles of Union Growth*, Blackwell, Oxford.

Bain, G.S. and Price, R. (1983) 'Union Growth: Dimensions, Determinants and Destiny', in Bain, G.S. (ed.) (1983) *Industrial Relations in Britain*, Blackwell, London.

Baird, C.E., Gregory, R.G. and Gruen, F.H. (1981) 'Youth Employment, Education and Training', Centre for Economic Policy Research, Australian National University Press, Canberra.

Bakke, E.W. (1933) *The Unemployed Man*, Nisbet, London.

Baldamus, W. (1961) *Efficiency and Effort*, Tavistock Publications, London.

Ballance, R. and Sinclair, S. (1983) *Collapse and Survival*, George Allen & Unwin, London/Allen & Unwin, Winchester, Mass.

Banks, M.H. and Jackson, P.R. (1982) 'Unemployment and Risk of Minor Psychiatric Disorders in Young People: Cross-sectional and Longitudinal Evidence', *Psychological Medicine*, 11, pp.561–80.

Banks, O. (1975) *Sociology of Education*, 2nd edn, Batsford, London.

Baran, P. and Sweezy, P. (1966) *Monopoly Capital: An Essay on the American Economic and Social Order*, Monthly Review Press, New York.

Barrington-Moore, J. (1966) *The Social Origins of Dictatorship and Democracy*, Beacon Press, USA/Allen Lane, London, 1967.

Barron, R.D. and Norris, G.M. (1976) 'Sexual Divisions and the Dual Labour Market', in Barker, D.L. and Allen, S. (eds), *Dependence and Exploitation in Work and Marriage*, Longmans, London.

Beardsworth, A. (ed.) (1984) 'Employers and Recruitment: Explorations in Labour Market Demand', *International Journal of Social Economics*, 11 (7).

Becker, H.S. and Carper, J.W. (1956) 'The Development of Identification with an Occupation', *American Journal of Sociology*, 61, pp.289–98.

Bell, D. (1974) *The Coming of Post-Industrial Society,* Heinemann, London.

Bell, D. (1977) *The Culture Contradictions of Capitalism,* Heinemann, London.

Bendix, R. (1963) *Work and Authority in Industry*, Harper & Row, New York.

Benyon, H. (1984) *Working for Ford*, Penguin, Harmondsworth, 2nd edn.

Berg, I. (1970) *Education and Jobs: The Great Training Robbery*, Praeger, New York/Penguin, Harmondsworth (1973).

Berg, I. (1981) *Sociological Perspectives on Labor Markets*, Academic

Press, London/San Francisco.

Beveridge, W.H. (1909) *Unemployment: A Problem of Industry*, Longman, London.

Black Report (1980) *Inequalities in Health*, Penguin, Harmondsworth.

Blackburn, R.M. and Mann, M. (1979) *The Working Class in the Labour Market*, Macmillan, London/New York.

Blau, P.M. and Duncan, O.D. (1967) *The American Occupational Structure*, Wiley, New York.

Bluestone, B. and Harrison, B. (1980) *Capital and Communities*, The Progressive Alliance, Washington D.C.

Bluestone, B. and Stevenson, M.H. (1981) 'Industrial Transformation and the Evolution of Dual Labor Markets: The Case of Retail Trade in the United States', in Wilkinson, R. (ed.) (1981).

Bluestone, B., Murphy, W.H. and Stevenson, M. (1973) *Low Wages and the Working Poor*, The Institute of Labor and Industrial Relations, Ann Arbor, Michigan.

Booth, C. (1902) *Life and Labour of the People in London*, vol.1, London.

Bosanquet, N. and Doeringer, P.B. (1973) 'Is There a Dual Labour Market in Great Britain?', *Economic Journal*, 83, pp.421–35.

Bowers, N. (1979) 'Young and Marginal: An Overview of Youth Unemployment', *Monthly Labor Review*, October.

Bowles, S. and Gintis, H. (1976) *Schooling in Capitalist America: Education Reform and the Contradictions of Economic Life*, Basic Books, New York.

Braham, P., Rhodes, E. and Pearn, M. (eds) (1981) *Discrimination and Disadvantage in Employment*, Harper & Row, London.

Braithwaite, J. (1981) 'The Myth of Social Class and Criminality Reconsidered', *American Sociological Review*, 46(1), pp.36–57.

Braverman, H. (1974) *Labor and Monopoly Capital*, Monthly Review Press, New York.

Brenner, M.H. (1973) *Mental Illness and the Economy*, Cambridge University Press, Cambridge.

Brenner, M.H. (1977) 'Health Costs and Benefits of Economic Policy', *International Journal of Health Studies*, 7(4).

Brenner, M.H. and Mooney, A. (1983) 'Unemployment and Health', *Social Science and Medicine*, 17(6), pp.1125–38.

Briar, K.H. (1979) *The Effects of Long-Term Unemployment on Workers and their Families*, R & E Research Associates, Inc., San Francisco.

Bruce, M. (1968) *The Coming of the Welfare State*, Batsford, London.

Burawoy, M. (1979) *Manufacturing Consent: Changes in the Labour Process Under Monopoly Capitalism*, The University of Chicago Press, London/Chicago.

Burgess, K. (1980) *The Challenge of Labour*, Croom Helm, London.

Buss, T.F. and Redburn, F.S. with Waldron, J. (1983) *Mass Unemployment: Plant Closings and Community Mental Health*, Sage Studies in Community Mental Health, Beverly Hills, California/London.

Caplovitz, D. (1979) *Making Ends Meet*, Sage Publications, Beverly Hills/London.

Carmichael, C. and Cook, L. (1981) 'Redundancy and Re-employment', *Employment Gazette*, May, pp.241–4.

Carr-Kill, R.A. and Stern, N.H. (1979) *Crime, The Police and Criminal Statistics*, Academic Press, San Francisco/London.

Carter, M.P. (1962) *Home, School and Work*, Pergamon, London.

Cashmore, E. and Troyna, B. (1982) *Black Youth in Crisis*, George Allen & Unwin, London.

Casson, M. (1979) *Youth Unemployment*, Macmillan, London.

Casy, B. and Bruche, G. (1983) *Work or Retirement?*, Gower, Aldershot.

Catalano, R. and Dooley, D.C. (1977) 'Economic Predictions of Depressed Mood and Stressful Life Events in a Metropolitan Community', *Journal of Health and Social Behaviour*, 18, pp. 292–307.

Catalano, R., Dooley, C.D. and Jackson, R. (1981) 'Economic Predicters of Admissions to Mental Health Facilities in a Nonmetropolitan Community', *Journal of Health and Social Behaviour*, 22, pp. 284–97.

Cawson, A. (1982) *Corporatism and Welfare, Social Policy and State Intervention in Britain*, Heinemann, London.

Chandler, A.D. (1962) *Strategy and Structure: Chapters in the History of the Industrial Enterprise*, Cambridge, Mass., MIT Press.

Chandler, A.D. (1976) 'The Development of Modern Management Structure in the US and UK', in Hannah, L. (ed.) *Management Strategy and Business Development*, Macmillan, London.

Chandler, A.D. (1977) *The Visible Hand: The Managerial Revolution in American Business*, Cambridge, Mass.

Chaney, J. (1981) *Social Networks and Job Information: The Situation of Women who Return to Work*, EOC/SSRC Joint Panel on Equal Opportunities, London.

Channon, D.F. (1973) *The Strategy and Structure of British Enterprise*, Boston, Mass.

Clark, G. (1982) 'Recent Developments in Working Patterns', *Employment Gazette*, July.

Clark, K.B. and Summers, L.H. (1979) *Labor Market Dynamics and Unemployment: A Reconsideration*, Brookings Papers on Economic Activity, no. 1, pp. 13–72.

Clark, K.B. and Summers, L.H. (1982) 'The Dynamics of Youth Unemployment', in Freeman, R.B. and Wise, D.A. (eds) (1982).

Cobb, S. and Kasl, S.V. (1977) *Termination: The Consequences of Job Loss,* Report no. 76–1261, OH National Institute for Occupational Safety and Health, Behavioral and Motivation Factors Research, Cincinnati, June.

Cockburn, C. (1982) *Brothers: Male Dominance and Technological Change,* Pluto Press, London.

Coffield, F., Borrill, C. and Marshall, S. (1983) 'How Young People Try to Survive Being Unemployed', *New Society*, 2, June.

Cohen, G. and Nixon, J. (1981) 'Employment Policies for Youth in Britain and the USA', *Journal of Social Policy,* 10(3), pp. 331–51.

Colledge, M. and Bartholomew, R. (1980) *A Study of the Long-Term Unemployed,* Manpower Services Commission, London.

Colledge, M. (1982) 'Economic Cycles and Health: Towards a Sociological Understanding of the Impact of the Recession on Health and Illness', *Social Science & Medicine,* 16, pp. 1919–27.

Competence and Competition: Training and Education in the Federal Republic of Germany, the United States and Japan (1984) National Economic Development Office, London.

Crouch, C. (1978) 'Inflation and the Political Organisation of Economic Interests', in Hirsch, F., Goldthorpe, J.H. (eds).

Davis, K. and Moore, W.E. (1945) 'Some Principles of Social Stratification', *The American Sociological Review,* 10(2), pp. 4242–9.

Department of Employment (1974) *Unqualified, Untrained and Unemployed,* Report of a Working Party set up by the National Youth Employment Council, HMSO, London.

Dex, S. (1979) 'A Note on Discrimination in Employment and its Effects on Black Youths', *Journal of Social Policy,* 8(2), pp. 357–69, July.

Dex, S. (1979a) 'Economists' Theories of the Economics of Discrimination', *Ethnic and Racial Studies,* 2(1).

Dex, S. (1984) 'Women's Occupational Profiles, Evidence from the 1980 Women and Employment Survey', *Employment Gazette,* December, pp. 545–9.

Diamond, D. and Bedrosian, H. (1977) 'Industry Hiring Requirements and Employment of Disadvantaged Groups', New York University School of Commerce.

Doeringer, P.B. and Piore, M.J. (1971) *Internal Labor Markets and Manpower Analysis,* D.C. Heath, Lexington, Mass.

Domhoff, G.W. (1967) *Who Rules America?,* Prentice-Hall, Englewood Cliffs, N.J.

Dore, R. (1973) *British Factory, Japanese Factory*, George Allen & Unwin, London.

Dore, R. (1976) *The Diploma Disease,* George Allen & Unwin, London.

Durkheim, E. (1948) *The Division of Labour in Society,* London.

Eatwell, J. (1982) *Whatever happened to Britain?* Duckworth, London.

Economic Policy Review (1978) no. 4, Dept of Applied Economics, University of Cambridge, Cambridge.

Edwards, P.K. (1983) 'The Political Economy of Industrial Conflict: Britain and the United States', *Economic and Industrial Democracy,* 4, pp. 461–500.

Edwards, R. (1979) *Contested Terrain: the Transformation of the Workplace in the Twentieth Century,* Basic Books, New York.

Edwards, R.C., Reich, M. and Gordon, D.M. (1975) *Labor Market Segmentation,* D.C. Heath, Lexington, Mass.

Eisenberg, P. and Lazarsfeld, P.F. (1938) 'The Psychological Effects of Unemployment', *Psychological Bulletin,* no. 35, pp. 358–90.

Elbaum, B. and Wilkinson, F. (1979) 'Industrial Relations and Uneven Development: A Comparative Study of the American and British Steel Industries', *Cambridge Journal of Economics,* 3.

Elias, N. (1978) *What is Sociology?,* Hutchinson, London.

Employment and Training Report of the President (1978) Government Printing Office, Washington, US.

Estes, R.J. and Wilenskey, H.L. (1978) 'Life-cycle Squeeze and the Morale Curve', *Social Problems,* 25, pp. 277–92.

Eyer, R.J. (1977a) 'Prosperity as a Cause of Death', *International Journal of Health Services',* 7(1) pp. 125–49.

Eyer, J. (1977b) 'Does Unemployment Cause the Death Rate to Peak in each Business Cycle?' *International Journal of Health Services,* 7(4) pp. 625–62.

Fagin, L. and Little, M. (1984) *The Forsaken Families,* Pelican, Harmondsworth.

Feldstein, M.S. (1976) 'Temporary Lay-offs in the Theory of Unemployment', *Journal of Political Economy,* no. 84, pp. 937–58.

Field, D. and Travisano, R. V. (1984) 'Social History and American Preoccupation with Identity', *Free Inquiry in Creative Sociology* 12(1).

Field, F. (1977) *The Conscript Army; A Study of Britain's Unemployed,* Routledge & Kegan Paul, London.

Ferman, L. A. and Aitken, M. (1967) 'Mobility and Situational Factors in the Adjustment of Older Workers to Job Displacement', *Human Organisation,* 26(4).

Fiddy, R. (1983) *In Place of Work–Policy and Provision for the Young Unemployed,* Falmer Press, Brighton.

Fineman, S. (1983) *White-Collar Unemployment: Impact and Stress,* John Wiley, New York/London.

Finn, D. (1982) 'Whose Needs? Schooling and the 'Needs' of Industry', in Atkinson, P. and Rees, J.L.

Flaim, P.O. (1984) 'Unemployment in 1982: The Cost to Workers and their Families', *Monthly Labor Review,* April.

Flanders, A. (1964) *The Fawley Productivity Agreements,* Faber & Faber, London.

Flora, P. and Heidenheimer, A. (1981) *The Development of Welfare States in Europe and America*, Transaction Books, London.

Freedman, M. (1976) *Labor Markets: Segments and Shelters,* Allan-held, Osman, New York.

Freeman, C., Clark, J. and Spete, L. (1982) *Unemployment and Technical Innovation; A Study of Long Waves and Economic Development*, Pinter, London.

Freeman, R.B. (1982) *Crime and the Labor Market*, National Bureau of Economic Research, Working Paper 1031, November.

Freeman, R.B. and Wise, D.A. (1982) *The Youth Labor Market Problem: Its Nature, Causes and Consequences,* Chicago University Press, Chicago/London.

Freidson, E. (1982) 'Occupational Autonomy and Labour Market Shelters', in Stewart, P.L. and Cantor M.G. *Varieties of Work, Sage, London.*

Friedman, A. (1977) *Industry and Labour,* Macmillan, London.

Friedman, M. (1970) 'The Counter-Revolution in Monetary Theory', Occasional Paper no. 33, IEA, London.

Friedman, M. (1969) *The Optimum Quantity of Money and Other Essays*, Aldine, Chicago.

Friedman, M. (1975) 'Unemployment versus Inflation?', Occasional Paper no. 44, IEA, London.

Frobel, F., Heinrichs, J. and Kreye, O. (1979) *The New International Division of Labour,* Cambridge, Cambridge University Press.

Galbraith, J.K. (1967) *The New Industrial State,* Houghton Mifflin, Boston.

Garraty, J.A. (1978) *Unemployment in History, Economic Throught & Public Policy*, Harper, New York.

Garside, W.R. (1980) *The Measurement of Unemployment*, Blackwell, Oxford.

Gavett, T. *et al.* (1970) 'Youth Unemployment and Minimum Wages', Bureau of Labor Statistics.

Gershuny, J.I. and Miles, I.D. (1983) *The New Service Economy*, Pinter, London.

Ginzberg, E. (1977) 'The Job Problem', Scientific American, 237(5), November.

Ginzberg, E. (1979) *Good Jobs, Bad Jobs, No Jobs*, Harvard University Press, Cambridge, Mass.

Ginzberg, E., Ginsburg, S.W., Axelrod, S. and Herma, J.L. (1951) *Occupational Choice: An Approach to a General Theory*, Columbia University Press, Columbia.

Giving Youth a Better Chance, The Carnegie Foundation for the Advancement of Teaching, Jossey-Bass, San Francisco/London.

Gleeson, D. (ed.) (1983) *Youth Training and the Search for Work*, Routledge & Kegan Paul, London.

Golding, P. and Middleton, S. (1982) *Images of Welfare*, Martin Robertson, Oxford.

Goldthorpe, J.H. (1978) 'The Current Inflation: Towards a Sociological Account', in Hirsch, F. and Goldthorpe, J.

Goldthorpe, J.H. (1980) *Social Mobility and Class Structure in Modern Britain*, Clarendon Press, Oxford.

Goldthorpe, J.H., Lockwood, D., Bechhofer, F. and Platt, J. (1968) *The Affluent Worker: Industrial Attitudes and Behaviour*, Cambridge, Cambridge University Press.

Gordon, D.M., Edwards, R. and Reich, M. (1982) *Segmented Work, Divided Workers: The Historical Transformation of Labor in the United States*, Cambridge University Press, New York/London.

Gordon, M.S. and Trow, M. (1979) *Youth Education and Unemployment Problems: An International Perspective*, Carnegie Foundation for the Advancement of Teaching, New York.

Gravelle, H.S.E., Hutchinson, S. and Stern, J. (1981) 'Mortality and Unemployment: A Critique of Brenner's Time Series Analysis', *The Lancet*, 26 September.

Gray, J., McPherson, A.F. and Raffe, D. (1983) *Reconstructions of Secondary Education: Theory, Myth and Practice since the War*, Routledge & Kegan Paul, London.

Greenstone, J.D. (1970) *Labor in American Politics*, Vintage Books, New York.

Griffin, C. (1984) 'Young Women and Work', Paper presented at British Psychological Society Annual Conference, York, April.

Guttsman, W.L. (1968) *The British Political Elite*, MacGibbon & Kee, London, revised edition.

Hakim, C. (1982) 'The Social Consequences of High Unemployment', *Journal of Social Policy* 11(4), pp. 433–67.

Hannah, L. (ed.) (1976) *Management Strategy and Business Development: An Historical and Comparative Study*, Macmillan, London.

Hannah, L. (1983) *The Rise of the Corporate Economy*, Methuen, London/New York, 2nd edn.

Hanson, C., Jackson, S. and Miller, D. (1982) *The Closed Shop: Comparative Study of Public Policy and Trade Union Security in Britain, the USA and West Germany*, Gower, Aldershot.

Harris, J. (1972) *Unemployment and Politics*, Oxford.

Harrison, R. (1976) 'The Demoralising Experience of Prolonged Unemployment', *Department of Employment Gazette*, April.

Hasan, A. and Brouchers, P. (1984) 'Turnover and Job Instability in Youth Labour Markets in Canada, in OECD (1984a).

Hawkins, K. (1984) *Unemployment*, Penguin, Harmondsworth, 2nd edn.

Hayes, J. and Nutman, P. (1981) *Understanding the Unemployed: The Psychological Effects of Unemployment,* Tavistock, London.

Heidenheimer, A.J. (1981) 'Education and Social Security Entitlements in Europe and America', in Flora, P. and A. Heidenheimer (eds).

Henderson, R.A. (1980) 'An Analysis of Closure Amongst Scottish Manufacturing Plants Between 1966 and 1975', *Scottish Journal of Political Economy*, 27(2), June.

Herzberg, F., Mausner, B. and Snyderman, B.B. (1959) *The Motivation to Work*, Wiley, New York.

Hill, J.M. (1977) *The Social and Psychological Impact of Unemployment: A Pilot Study*, Tavistock Institute of Human Relations, London.

Hill, M. (1981) 'Unemployment and Government Manpower Policy', in Showler, B. and Sinfield, A. (eds).

Hill, M.J., Harrison, R.M., Sargeant, A.V. and Talbot, V. (1973) *Men—Out of Work*, Cambridge University Press, Cambridge.

Hirsch, F. and Goldthorpe, J.H. (eds) (1978) *The Political Economy of Inflation*, Martin Robertson, Oxford.

Hobsbawm, E.J. (1968) *Industry and Empire*, Weidenfeld & Nicolson, London.

Hobson, J.A. (1896) *The Problem of the Unemployed*, Methuen, London.

Hughes, J.J. and Perlman, R. (1984) *The Economics of Unemployment: A Comparative Analysis of Britain and the United States*, Harvester Press, Brighton.

Humphrey, J. (1980) 'Labour Use and Labour Control in the Brazilian Automobile Industry', *Capital and Class*, 12.

Hunt, J. and Small, P. (1981) 'Employing Young People: A Study of Employers' Attitudes, Policies and Practices', Scottish Council for Research in Education, Edinburgh.

Huntington, S.P. (1968) 'Political Modernization: America Versus Europe', in Bendix R. (ed.) *State and Society*, Little Brown, Boston, pp. 179–99.

Jahoda, M. (1982) *Employment and Unemployment: A Social-Psychological Analysis*, Cambridge University Press, New York/London.

Jahoda, M., Lazarsfeld, P.F. and Zeisel, H. (1933) *Marienthal: The Sociography of an Unemployed Community* (English trans., 1972),

Tavistock Publications, London.

Janowitz, M. (1976) *Social Control and the Welfare State,* Elsevier, New York.

Jenkins, C. and Sherman, B. (1979) *The Collapse of Work*, Methuen, London.

Jenkins, R. (1984) 'Acceptability, Suitability and the Search for the Habituated Worker: How Ethnic Minorities and Women Lose Out', in Beardsworth, A. (ed.).

Jenkins, R. and Troyna, B. (1983) 'Educational Myths, Labour Market Realities', in Troyna, B. and Smith, D.I. *Racism, School and the Labour Market,* National Youth Bureau, Leicester.

Jerrett, R. (1980) 'Job Creation Programmes in the United States', in McIntosh A. (ed.), *Employment Policy in the United Kingdom and U.S.,* John Martin, London.

Johnson, T.J. (1972) *Professions and Power,* Macmillan, London.

Johnson, T.J. (1983), 'The State and the Professions: peculiarities of the British', in Giddens, A. and Mackenzie, G. (eds) *Social Class and the Division of Labour: Essays in Honour of Ilya Neustadt,* Cambridge University Press, Cambridge.

Jones, B. (1982) *Sleepers, Wake! Technology and the future of work,* Wheatsheaf, Brighton.

Jones, D. (1973) *Before Rebecca*, Allen Lane, London.

Jones, D.J.V. (1966) 'The Merthyr Riots of 1831', *Welsh History Review,* 3, pp. 173–205.

Jordon, B. (1982) *Mass Unemployment and the Future of Britain,* Blackwell, Oxford.

Junankar, P.N. (1984) 'Youth Unemployment and Youth Crime, A Preliminary Analysis', Discussion Paper no. 106, Australian National University, Centre for Economic Policy Research, August.

Kasl, S.V. (1979) 'Changes in Mental Health Status Associated with 'Job Loss and Retirement', in Barret, J. (ed.) *Stress and Mental Disorder*, New York, Raven.

Kasl, S. V., Gore, S. and Cobb, S. (1975) 'The Experience of Losing a Job: Reported Changes in Health Symptoms and Illness Behaviour', *Psychosomatic Medicine,* 37(2), pp. 106–22.

Keil, T., Ford, J., Bryman, A. and Beardsworth, A. (1984) 'Does Occupational Status Matter? The Case of Recruitment', in Beardsworth, A. (ed).

Kerr, C., Dunlop, J.T., Harbison, F.H. and Myers, C.A. (1962) *Industrialism and Industrial Man,* Heinemann, London.

Keynes, J.M. (1936) The *General Theory of Employment, Interest and Money,* Macmillan, London.

King, C. (1983) 'The Social Impacts of Mass Lay-offs', Ann Arbor,

Center for Research on Social Organization, University of Michigan, January.

King, E. (1982) 'Learning and Working: An International Perspective', in Anderson, D.S. and Blakers, C. (eds).

Kreckel, R. (1980) 'Unequal Opportunity Structure and Labour Market Segmentation', *Sociology,* 14(2), pp. 525–49.

Kudrie, R.T. and Marmor, T.R. (1981) 'The Development of Welfare States in North America', in Flora, P. and Heidenheimer, A. (eds).

Labour Studies Group, (1983) 'Economic, Social and Political Factors in the Operation of the Labour Market', Department of Applied Economics, Cambridge, November, mimeo.

Landes, D.S. (1969) *The Unbounded Prometheus,* Cambridge, Cambridge University Press.

Larson, M.S. (1977) *The Rise of Professionalism: A Sociological Analysis,* Berkley, University of California Press.

Laslett, J.H.M. and Lipset, S.M. (eds) (1974) *Failure of a Dream? Essays in the History of American Socialism,* Basic Books, New York.

Lawson, T. (1981) 'Paternalism and Labour Market Segmentation Theory', in Wilkinson, F. (ed.).

Lee, D.J. (1981) 'Skill, Craft and Class: A Theoretical Critique and a Critical Case', *Sociology,* 15(1), pp. 56–78.

Lester, R.A. (1954) *Hiring Practices and Labor Competition,* Industrial Relations Section, Princeton University, Princeton N.J.

Levison, A. (1980) *The Full Employment Alternative,* Coward, McCann & Geoghegan, New York.

Lindley, R.M. (1980) 'Employment Policy in Transition', in Lindley, R.M. (ed.) *Economic Change and Employment Policy,* Macmillan, London.

Lindley, R.M. (1983) 'Active Manpower Policy', in Bain, G.S. (ed.)

Little, C.B. (1976) 'Technical–Professional Unemployment: Middle-class Adaptability to Personal Crisis', *Sociological Quarterly,* 17, pp. 262–74.

Littler, C.R. (1982) *The Development of the Labour Process in Capitalist Societies,* Heinemann, London.

Loveridge, R. and Mok, A.L. (1979) *Theories of Labour Market Segmentation,* Martinus Nijhoff, The Hague.

Maddison, A. (1982) *Phases of Capitalist Development,* Oxford University Press, New York/Oxford.

Maguire, M.J. and Ashton, D.N. (1981) 'Employers' Perception and Use of Educational Qualifications', *Educational Analysis,* 3(2).

Main, G.M. and Raffe, D. (1982) 'The Industrial Destinations of Scottish School-Leavers, 1977–1981', University of Edinburgh, mimeo.

Maizels, E.J. (1970) *Adolescent Needs and the Transition from School to Work*, Athlone Press, London.

Makeham, P. (1980) *Youth Unemployment*, Research Paper no. 10, Department of Employment, London.

Mannheim, K. (1953) 'Conservative Thought', in Kecskemeti, P. (ed.), *Essays on Sociology and Social Psychology*, Oxford University Press, New York.

Manpower Services Commission, *Labour Market Quarterly*, Sheffield, quarterly issues.

Manwaring, T. (1984) 'The Extended Internal Labour Market', *Cambridge Journal of Economics*, 8(2).

Manwaring, T. and Wood, S. (1984) 'Recruitment and Recession', in Beardsworth, A. (ed.).

Markall, G. (1982) 'The Job-Creation Programme: Some Reflections on its Passing', in Atkinson, P. and Rees, T.L. (eds).

Markall, G. and Gregory, D. (1982) 'Who Cares? The MSC Intervention! Full of Easter Promise', in Atkinson, P. and Rees, T.L.

Marsden, D. and Duff, E. (1982) *Workless*, Harmondsworth, Penguin/Croom Helm, London, revd edn.

Marshall, G. (1984) 'On the Sociology of Women's Unemployment, its neglect and significance', *Sociological Review*, 32(2).

Marshall, T.H. (1950) *Citizenship and Social Class*, Cambridge University Press, Cambridge.

Marshall, T.H. (1964) 'Citizenship and Social Class', in *Class Citizenship and Social Development*, Doubleday, Garden City, New York.

Martin, R. and Wallace, J. (1984) *Working Women in Recession*, Oxford University Press, Oxford.

Maslow, A.H. (1954) *Motivation and Personality*, Harper, New York.

Mayhew, K. (1983) *Trade Unions and the Labour Market*, Martin Robertson, Oxford.

Mayhew, R. and Rosewell, B. (1979) 'Labour Market Segmentation in Britain', *Oxford Bulletin of Economics and Statistics*, 41, March.

McIntosh, A. (1980) (ed.) *Employment Policy in the United Kingdom and the US*, John Martin, London.

McKersie, R.B. and Hunter, L.C. (1973) *Pay, Productivity and Collective Bargaining*, Macmillan, London.

McKersie, R.B. and Sengenberger, W. (1983) *Job Losses in Major Industries*, OECD, Paris.

Medoff, J.L. (1979) 'Lay-offs and Alternatives under Trade Unions in US Manufacturing', *American Economic Review*, 69, pp. 380–95.

Mills, C.W. (1956) *The Power Elite*, Oxford University Press, New York.

Moore, G. (1983) *Business-Cycles, Inflation and Forecasting*, National

Bureau of Economic Research Studies in Business Cycles, no. 24, Ballinger, Cambridge, Mass.

Moore, W.E. and Hoselitz, B.F. (1963) *Industrialization and Society*, Monton, Thelfaque in collaboration with UNESCO.

Mungham, G. (1982) 'Workless Youth as a "Moral Panic"', in Atkinson, P. and Rees, T.L. (eds).

National Institute of Social and Economic Research (1984) Report no. 110, London, November.

Nelson, D. (1969) *Unemployment Insurance, The American Experience 1915–1935*, University of Wisconsin Press, Milwaukee/London.

Nelson, R. (1984) 'State and Labor Legislation Enacted in 1983', *Monthly Labor Review*, January.

Norris, G.M. (1978) 'Unemployment, Sub-employment and Personal Characteristics. (a) The Inadequacies of Traditional Approaches to Unemployment, (b) Job Separation and Work Histories: the Alternative Approach', *Sociological Review*, 26.

Oakley, A. (1974) *Housewife*, Allen Lane, London.

Oakley, A. (1975) *The Sociology of Housework*, Martin Robertson, London.

OECD (1977) *Entry into Working Life*, Paris.

OECD (1979) *Measuring Employment and Unemployment*, Paris.

OECD (1979a) *Unemployment Compensation and Related Policy Measures*, Paris.

OECD (1982) *Marginal Employment Subsidies*, Paris.

OECD (1983) *Employment Outlook*, Paris.

OECD (1984) *Employment Outlook*, Paris.

OECD (1984a) *The Nature of Youth Unemployment: An Analysis for Policy-makers*, Paris.

Offe, C. (1984) *Contradictions of the Welfare State*, in Keane, J. (ed.), Hutchinson, London.

Osterman, P. (1980) *Getting Started. The Youth Labor Market*, MIT Press, Cambridge, Mass./London.

Owen, T. (1979) *The Manager and Industrial Relations*, Pergamon, Oxford.

Padilla, A. (1981) 'The Unemployment Insurance System: Its Financial Structure', *Monthly Labor Review*, December.

Pahl, R.E. and Wallace, C. (1980) '17–19 and Unemployed on the Isle of Sheppey', University of Kent, mimeo.

Parker, C.M. (1971) 'Psycho-social Transitions: A Field for Study', *Social Science and Medicine*, 5, pp. 101–15.

Parkin, F. (1974) 'Strategies of Social Closure in Class Formation', in Parkin, F. (ed.), *The Social Analysis of Class Structure*, Tavistock, London.

Parkin, F. (1979) *Marxism and Class Theory: A Bourgeois Critique*,

Columbia University Press, New York.

Payne, R.L., Warr, P.B. and Hartley, J. (1983b) 'Social Class and the Experience of Unemployment', MRC/SSRC SAPU, mimeo 549.

Perkins, H. (1969) *The Origins of Modern English Society*, Routledge & Kegan Paul, London.

Phelps Brown, E.H. (1965) *The Growth of British Industrial Relations*, Macmillan, London.

Phelps Brown, E.H. (1983) *The Origins of Trade Union Power*, The Clarendon Press, Oxford.

Phillips, D. (1979) 'Young and Unemployed in a Northern City', in Wier, D. (ed.), *Men and Work in Modern Britain*, Fontana, London.

Piachaud, D. (1981) 'The Dole', Centre for Labour Economics, LSE Discussion Paper no. 89, May.

Piore, M.J. (1971) 'The Dual Labor Market: Theory and Implications' in Gordon D.M. (ed.) *Problems in Political Economy: An Urban Perspective*, D.C. Heath, Lexington, Mass.

Piore, M.J. (1975) 'Notes for a Theory of Labor Market Stratification', in Edwards, R.C., Reich, M. and Gordon, D.M. (eds).

Piore, M.J. (1979) *Unemployment and Inflation—Institutionalist and Structuralist Views*, M.E. Sharpe, White Plains, N.Y.

Platt, P. (1984) 'Unemployment and Suicidal Behaviour', in Unemployment Health and Social Policy, Nuffield Centre for Health Service Studies, University of Leeds.

Platt, S. and Kreitman, N. (1984) 'Parasuicide and Unemployment in Edinburgh, 1968–1982', Paper presented to ESRC Workshop on Employment and Unemployment, October. In *Psychological Medicine* (forthcoming).

Pollard, S. (1965) *The Genesis of Modern Management,* Penguin, Harmondsworth.

Pollard, S. (1982) *The Wasting of the British Economy,* Croom Helm, Beckenham.

Porter, M. (1982) 'Standing on the Edge: Working-Class Housewives and the World of Work', in West, J. (ed.).

Powell, D.H. and Driscoll, P.J. (1973) 'Middle-class Professionals face Unemployment', *Society*, vol. 10, pp. 18–26.

Price, R. and Bain, G.S. (1983) 'Union Growth in Britain: Retrospect and Prospect', *British Journal of Industrial Relations*, 21(1).

Pym, D. (1975) 'The Demise of Management and the Ritual of Employment', *Human Relations*, 28(8), pp. 675–98.

Raffe, D. (1983) 'Can there be an Effective Youth Unemployment Policy?', in Fiddy, R. (ed.).

Raffe, D. (1984) 'Change and Continuity in the Youth Labour Market: A Critical Review of Structural Explanations of Youth Unemployment', Paper presented to the British Sociological Association's annual conference, Bradford.

Raffe, D. (1984a) 'Youth Unemployment and the MSC: 1977–1983', in McCrone, D. (ed.) *Scottish Government Yearbook 1984*, University of Edinburgh, Edinburgh.

Rajan, A. (1984) *New Technology and Employment in Insurance, Banking and Building Societies*, IMS/Gower, Aldershot.

Ray, G. (1980) 'Innovation in the Long Cycle', *Lloyds Bank Review*, no. 135, pp. 14–28.

Rees, G. and Rees, T.L. (1982) 'Juvenile Unemployment and the State between the Wars', in Atkinson, P. and Rees, T.L. (eds).

Rex, J. (1983) 'West Indian and Asian Youth', in Cashmore, E. and Troyna, B.

Roberts, K. (1984) *School Leavers and their Prospects*, Open University Press, Milton Keynes.

Roberts, K. (1982) 'The Sociology of Youth Unemployment in Britain: Re-structuring of work entry', Paper delivered to workshop on The Management and Mismanagement of Labour, University of Loughborough.

Roberts, K., Duggan, J. and Noble, M. (1981) *Unregistered Youth Unemployment and Outreach Careers Work. Final Report, Part 1. Non-registration*, Research Paper no. 31. Department of Employment, London.

Roberts, K., Duggan, J. and Noble, M. (1982) 'Out-of-School Youth in High-Unemployment Areas: An Empirical Investigation', *British Journal of Guidance and Counselling*, 10(1).

Roberts, K., Noble, M. and Duggan, J. (1983) 'Young, Black and Out of Work', in Troyna, B. and Smith, D.I. (eds).

Rock, P. (1979) *The Making of Symbolic Interactionism*, Oxford University Press, New York.

Rones, P.L. (1984) 'Recent Recessions Swell Ranks of the Long-term Unemployed', *Monthly Labor Review*, April.

Rose, A. (1967) *The Power Structure: Political Process in American Society*, Oxford University Press, New York.

Rose, J. (1982) 'West Indian and Asian Youth', in Cashmore, E. and Troyna, B. (eds).

Rosen, R.J. (1984) 'Regional Variations in Employment and Unemployment during 1970–82', *Monthly Labor Review*, April.

Rostow, W.W. (1983) *The Barbaric Counter-Revolution: Cause and Cures,* University of Texas Press/Macmillan, London.

Rubery, J. (1978) 'Structured Labour Markets, Worker Organisation and Low Pay', *Cambridge Journal of Economics*, 2, pp. 17–36.

Rubery, J., Tarling, R. and Wilkinson, F. (1984) 'Labour Market Segmentation Theory: An Alternative Framework for the Analysis of the Employment System', Paper presented at the British Sociological Association Conference, Bradford.

Runciman, W.G. (1966) *Relative Deprivation and Social Justice*, Routledge & Kegan Paul, London.

Sabel, C.F. (1982) *Work and Politics—The Division of Labour in Industry*, Cambridge University Press, London.

Schervish, P.G. (1983) *The Structural Determinants of Unemployment*, Academic Press, New York/London.

Schlozman, K.L. and Verba, S. (1979) *Injury to Insult, Unemployment, Class and Political Response*, Harvard University Press, London/Cambridge, Mass.

Schneider, E.V. (1971) *Industrial Sociology*, McGraw-Hill, New York/London, 2nd edn.

Schumpeter, J.A. (1939) *Business Cycles: A Theoretical, Historical and Statistical Analysis of the Capitalist Process* (2 vols), McGraw-Hill, New York.

Schumpeter, J.A. (1943) *Capitalism, Socialism and Democracy*, Harper & Row, New York.

Scott, J. (1982) *The Upper Classes*, Macmillan, London.

Seabrook (1982) *Unemployment*, Granada, London/New York.

Sharpe, S. (1984) *Double Identity: The Lives of Working Mothers*, Penguin, Harmondsworth.

Sherraden, M.W. 'Youth Employment and Education: Federal Programs from the New Deal through the 1970s', *Children and Youth Services Review* 2(1).

Showler, B. (1981) 'Political Economy and Unemployment', in Showler, B. and Sinfield, A. (eds).

Showler, B. and Sinfield, A. (eds) (1981) *The Workless State*, Martin Robertson, Oxford.

Sinfield, A. (1976) 'Unemployment and Inequality', Paper presented to Tenth Annual Conference of the Social Administration Association, Exeter.

Sinfield, A. (1981) *What Unemployment Means*, Martin Robertson, Oxford.

Sinfield, A. (1981a) 'Unemployment in an Unequal Society', in Showler, B. and Sinfield, A. (eds).

Sinfield, A. and Showler, B. (1981b) 'Unemployment and the Unemployed', in Showler, B. and Sinfield, A. (eds).

Singelmann, J. (1978) 'The Sectoral Transformation of the Labor Force in Seven Industrialized Countries, 1920–1970', *American Journal of Sociology*, 83(5), pp. 1224–34.

Slote, A. (1969) *Termination: The Closing at Baker Plant*, Bobbs-Merrill, New York.

Smee, C. (1980) 'Unemployment and Poverty: Some Comparisons with Canada and the United States', Paper presented to the SSRC

Research Workshop on Employment and Unemployment, June.

Smelser, N. (1959) *Social Change in the Industrial Revolution*, University of Chicago Press, Chicago.

Smith, D.J. (1981) *Unemployment and Racial Minorities,* Policy Studies Institute, London.

Smith, E.O. (1981) *Trades Unions in the Developed Economies*, Croom Helm, London.

Smith, R.E. (1981) 'Training Schemes, Job Creation Schemes and Employment Subsidies for Youth: the U.S. Experience', in Baird, C.E., Gregory, R.G. and Gruen, F.H. (eds).

Smith, R.E. (1983) 'Youth Employment and Training Programs during the First Two Years of the Reagan Administration', *Newsletter* 2(1), National Clearing House on Transition from School, Australian National University, Canberra, February.

Smith, R.E. (1984) 'How Effective Has the SYETP Job Subsidy Really Been?', Discussion paper no. 104, Centre for Economic Policy Research, Australian National University, Canberra, August.

Sorrentino, C. (1976) 'Unemployment Compensation in Eight Industrial Nations', US Bureau of Labor Statistics, *Monthly Labor Review,* July.

Sorrentino, C. (1981) 'Youth Unemployment: An International Perspective', *Monthly Labor Review,* July.

Sorrentino, C. (1981a) 'Unemployment in International Perspective', in Showler, S. & Sinfield, A. (eds).

Spilerman, S. (1978) 'Careers, Labor Market Structure, and Socio-economic Achievement', *American Journal of Sociology,* 83(3), pp. 551–93.

Stafford, C.M., Jackson, P.R. and Banks, M.H. (1980) 'Employment Work Involvement and Mental Health in Less-qualified Young People', *Journal of Occupational Psychology*, 53, pp. 291–304.

Stanworth, P. and Giddens, A. (1974) *Elites and Power in British Society*, Cambridge University Press, London.

Statistical Abstracts of the United States, (1982) US Department of Commerce, Bureau of the Census, 103rd edn.

Stern, E. and Hilgendorf, L. (1981) *Developing Learning at Work*, Tavistock Institute, London.

Stern, J. (1979) 'Who Bears the Burden of Unemployment?' in Beckerman, W. (ed.) *Slow Growth in Britain*, Oxford University Press, Oxford.

Stern, J. (1982) 'Job Durations of Men Becoming Unemployed', *British Journal of Industrial Relations*, November, pp. 373–6.

Stevenson, J. and Cook, E. (1979) *The Slump. Society and Politics During the Depression*, Quartet Books, London/New York.

Stewart, P.L. and Cantor, M.G. (eds) (1982) *Varieties of Work*, Sage, London.

Stinchcombe, A.L. (1959) 'Bureaucratic and Craft Administration of Production: A Comparative Study', *Administrative Science Quarterly*, 4, pp. 168–87.

Stonier, T. (1983) *The Wealth of Information*, Methuen, London.

Super, D.E. (1957) *The Psychology of Careers*, Harper & Row, New York.

Swinburne, P. (1980) 'The Psychological Impact of Unemployment on Managers and Professional Staff', *Journal of Occupational Psychology*, 54, pp. 47–64.

Taber, T.D., Walsh, J.T. and Cooke, R.A. (1979) 'Developing a community-based Program for Reducing the Impact of Plant Closing', *Journal of Applied Behavioural Science*, 15, pp. 133–55.

Taylor, R. (1982) *Workers and the New Depression*, Macmillan, London.

Thompson, E.P. (1968) *The Making of the English Working Class*, Penguin, Harmondsworth, revd edn.

Thomson, A.W.J. (1981) 'The United States of America', in Smith, E.O. (ed.).

Townsend, P. (1979) *Poverty in the United Kingdom*, Allen Lane, London.

Troyna, B. and Smith, D.I. (1983) *Racism, School and the Labour Market*, National Youth Bureau, Leicester.

Turner, H.A. (1962) *Trade Union Growth Structure and Policy*, George Allen & Unwin, London.

Urban Institute (1984) 'Black Youth Unemployment: A Long-term Problem', *Policy and Research Report*, 14(2), October.

Urquhart, M. (1984) 'The Employment Shift to Services: Where did it come from?', *Monthly Labor Review*, April.

Urry, J. and Wakeford, J. (eds) (1973) *Power in Britain*, Heinemann, London.

Varlaam, C. (ed.) (1984) *Rethinking Transition: Educational Innovation and the Transition to Adult Life*, The Falmer Press, Lewes.

Wainwright, H. (1978) 'Women and the Division of Labour', in Abrams, P. (ed.), *Work, Urbanism and Inequality*, Weidenfeld & Nicolson, London.

Walker, A. (1981) 'The Economic and Social Impact of Unemployment: A Case Study in South Yorkshire', *Political Quarterly*.

Walker, A. (1982) *Unqualified and Underemployed*, Macmillan, London.

Warr, P. (1983a) 'Job Loss, Unemployment and Psychological Well-being', in Van de Vliert, E. and Allen, V. (eds) *Role Transitions*, Plenum Press, New York.

Warr, P. (1983b) 'Work and Unemployment', in Drenth, P.J.D., Thierry, H., Willems, D.J. and de Wolff, C.J. (eds) *Handbook of Work and Organizational Psychology*, Wiley, London.

Warr, P. (1983c) 'Work, Jobs and Unemployment', *Bulletin of the British Psychological Society*, 36, pp. 305–11.

Watkins, S. (1984) 'Unemployment and Physical Health', in *Unemployment, Health and Social Policy*, the Unemployment and Health Study Group, Nuffield Centre for Health Service Studies.

Weber, M. (1948) 'Class, Status and Party', in Gerth, H.H. and Mills, C.W. (eds) *From Max Weber*, Routledge & Kegan Paul, London.

West, J. (ed.) (1982) *Women, Work and the Labour Market*, Routledge & Kegan Paul, London.

Westwood, S. (1984) *All Day Every Day*, Pluto Press, London.

White, M. (1983) *Long-Term Unemployment and Labour Markets*, Policy Studies Institute, London.

Wiener, M.J. (1981) *English Culture and the Decline of the Industrial Spirit, 1850–1980*, Cambridge University Press, Cambridge.

Wilensky, H.L. (1975) *The Welfare State and Equality*, University of California Press, London.

Wilkinson, F. (ed.) (1981) *The Dynamics of Labour Market Segmentation*, Academic Press, London/San Francisco.

Williams, G.A. (1965) 'The Insurrection at Merthyr Tydfil in 1831', *Transactions of the Honourable Society of Cymmrodorion*, pp. 222–43.

Williams, G. (ed.) (1966) *Merthyr Politics: The Making of a Working-class Tradition*, University of Wales, Cardiff.

Williams, G.A. (1978) *The Merthyr Riots*, Croom Helm, London.

Williams, K., Williams, J. and Thomas, D. (1983) *Why are the British Bad at Manufacturing?*, Routledge & Kegan Paul, London.

Williams, R. (1976) *Keywords*, Fontana, London.

Williamson, B. (1983) 'The Peripheralisation of Youth in the Labour Market: Problems, Analyses and Opportunities. Britain and the Federal Republic of Germany', in Ahier, J. and Flude, M. (eds) *Contemporary Education Policy*, Croom Helm, London.

Willis, P. (1977) *Learning to Labour*, Saxon House, Farnborough.

Wood, S. (ed.) (1982) *The Degradation of Work? Skill, Deskilling and the Labour Process*, Hutchinson, London.

Wright, E.O. (1978) 'Race, Class and Income Inequality', *American Journal of Sociology*, 83(6), pp. 1368–97.

Name Index

The following list includes only those authors who are mentioned in the text, but not those referred to in the Notes

Subject Index